Third Edition

Strategies for Inclusion

Physical Education for Everyone

Lauren J. Lieberman, PhD

Cathy Houston-Wilson, PhD

The College at Brockport, State University of New York

HUMAN KINETICS

Library of Congress Cataloging-in-Publication Data

Names: Lieberman, Lauren J., 1965- author. | Houston-Wilson, Cathy, 1962-
author.

Title: Strategies for inclusion : physical education for everyone / Lauren J.
Lieberman, PhD; Cathy Houston-Wilson, PhD.

Description: Third edition. | Champaign, IL : Human Kinetics, 2017. |
Includes bibliographical references and index. | Description based on
print version record and CIP data provided by publisher; resource not
viewed.

Identifiers: LCCN 2017002404 (print) | LCCN 2017027375 (ebook) | ISBN
9781492550525 (e-book) | ISBN 9781492517238 (print)

Subjects: LCSH: Physical education for children with disabilities--United
States. | Physical education for children--United States. | Inclusive
education--United States.

Classification: LCC GV445 (ebook) | LCC GV445 .L54 2017 (print) | DDC
371.9/04486--dc23

LC record available at https://lccn.loc.gov/2017002404

ISBN: 978-1-4925-1723-8 (print)

Copyright © 2018, 2009, 2002 by Lauren J. Lieberman and Cathy Houston-Wilson

All rights reserved. Except for use in a review, the reproduction or utilization of this work in any form or by any electronic, mechanical, or other means, now known or hereafter invented, including xerography, photocopying, and recording, and in any information storage and retrieval system, is forbidden without the written permission of the publisher.

Notice: Permission to reproduce the following material is granted to instructors and agencies who have purchased *Strategies for Inclusion, Third Edition*: pp. 15, 38-43, 47-48, 51-52, 93-95, 97, 99, 101, 103, 126-136, 138-161, 164-176, 178-183, and 200-202. The reproduction of other parts of this book is expressly forbidden by the above copyright notice. Persons or agencies who have not purchased *Strategies for Inclusion, Third Edition*, may not reproduce any material.

The web addresses cited in this text were current as of April 2017, unless otherwise noted.

Acquisitions Editor: Ray Vallese; **Senior Developmental Editor:** Bethany J. Bentley; **Managing Editor:** Derek Campbell; **Copyeditor:** Shannon Foreman; **Indexer:** Michael Ferreira; **Permissions Manager:** Dalene Reeder; **Graphic Designer:** Dawn Sills; **Cover Designer:** Keith Blomberg; **Photographs (cover and interior):** Matt Yeoman; About the Authors photos courtesy of SUNY; **Photo Production Manager:** Jason Allen; **Senior Art Manager:** Kelly Hendren; **Illustrations:** © Human Kinetics; **Printer:** McNaughton & Gunn

We thank The College at Brockport in Brockport, New York, for assistance in providing the location for the photo shoot for this book.

Printed in the United States of America   10 9 8 7 6 5 4 3

The paper in this book is certified under a sustainable forestry program.

Human Kinetics
1607 N. Market St.
Champaign, IL 61820
Website: www.HumanKinetics.com

In the United States, email info@hkusa.com or call 800-747-4457.
In Canada, email info@hkcanada.com.
In the United Kingdom/Europe, email hk@hkeurope.com.

For information about Human Kinetics' coverage in other areas of the world,
please visit our website: **www.HumanKinetics.com**

Tell us what you think!
Human Kinetics would love to hear what we
can do to improve the customer experience.
Use this QR code to take our brief survey.

We would like to dedicate this book to Dr. Joseph P. Winnick, professor emeritus from The College at Brockport, who pioneered the discipline of adapted physical education and served as a mentor to us and countless other individuals. His influence has had a ripple effect on those he taught who have gone on to teach others, and this pattern repeats year after year. We also dedicate this book to all the children and teachers in our lives who have shared their triumphs over the years. These lived experiences have helped us shape our vision for inclusive practice.

Contents

Preface

Since 1975, children with disabilities in the United States have been included in general physical education classes. Unfortunately, the transition from segregated classrooms to supportive, inclusive environments has been a struggle for students with disabilities and those responsible for their education. Teachers of physical education have been forced to navigate the maze of legislation and its accompanying mountains of paperwork and rely on best intentions instead of best information when it comes to integrating students.

The purpose of this book is to empower you with the information and tools necessary for the successful inclusion of children with disabilities in your programs. In this third edition, we again worked diligently to create a resource filled with practical applications and easily implemented planning and assessment strategies that can be used by physical education teachers; coaches; paraeducators; adapted physical educators; special education teachers; recreation directors; therapeutic recreation specialists; parents; and graduate and undergraduate students in physical education, recreation, and special education.

The book is divided into two parts. The first part provides background information on inclusive education and guidelines for successfully including children with disabilities in traditional physical education settings. The second part of the book contains 38 teachable units that include assessment tools for curriculum planning. The units are also included in the accompany web resource at www.HumanKinetics. com/StrategiesForInclusion; they can be printed for use in the classroom, or you can view them on a mobile device.

The first chapter, Inclusion in Physical Education, provides an overview of legislative mandates that directly affect physical education. Armed with this knowledge, you can advocate for receiving the support you need to successfully educate children with disabilities. Various placements are discussed so you can see the options available in educating children with disabilities. Depending on a child's unique needs and the unit of instruction, he or she can move from one placement option to another. This chapter also discusses current research on inclusive physical education and its effectiveness and the roles and responsibilities of general physical educators.

The second chapter, Assessment: The Cornerstone of Effective Instruction, addresses various types of assessments. The chapter highlights the purposes of assessment and the use of assessment data to drive instruction. This chapter also includes sample rubrics and a sample alternative assessment that can be used with children with severe disabilities.

Chapter 3, The Placement Process in Physical Education, reviews the step-by-step process necessary to ensure appropriate placement. The steps covered in this chapter are based on legal requirements. Each step is described clearly, and some sample forms are provided. In addition, suggested forms for school districts to use are provided to ensure the system supports the process. This chapter also provides a validated inclusion rating scale for physical education to help you determine the most inclusive environment possible.

Chapter 4, Individualized Education Plans, thoroughly addresses this necessary component in the education of children with disabilities. Individualized education plans (IEPs) help ensure that children with disabilities are making progress toward intended goals. The chapter provides steps for developing and implementing physical education IEPs and discusses several ways you can ensure that IEP objectives are implemented in general physical education classes.

Chapter 5, Managing Student Behavior, helps you set up your environment to maximize success and minimize disruptions. The chapter discusses using positive behavioral support and functional behavioral assessments to remediate challenging behaviors. The chapter also provides tips to ensure the best behavior possible from your students.

Chapter 6, Universal Design for Learning, highlights a proactive approach to adaptations. First, we discuss the Universal Design for Learning philosophy that drives modifications in general physical education. Then we provide specific guidelines for adaptation. Four major variables—rules, equipment, environment, and instruction—can easily be adjusted to successfully include children of all ability levels. Examples are provided to help you understand your options. The chapter ends with examples of how to infuse Paralympic sports into the curriculum.

Chapter 7, Support Personnel, includes comprehensive guidelines on how to train, work with, and motivate a variety of support staff in general physical education. This invaluable network of individuals includes peer tutors, paraeducators, senior citizens, and college students. Specific training techniques are provided for peer tutors and paraeducators.

Chapter 8, Transition Planning, provides information about preparing students with disabilities for their transition from school to the community. It focuses on using a functional approach to transition planning in community-based settings and discusses the importance of helping students build necessary skills.

The second part of this book introduces specific strategies for inclusion. Here you will learn how to apply the information provided in part I. Part II includes step-by-step guidelines for implementing an inclusive curriculum. Chapter 9 contains 10 basic skills units; chapter 10 has 11 sport skills units; chapter 11 has 12 recreation and leisure units; and chapter 12 has 5 health and fitness units. Potential adaptations and modifications for equipment, rules, environment, and instruction are provided for each unit. The adaptations can be recorded to keep track of what works for each child. In addition, each unit has at least one assessment rubric that breaks down a specific skill.

This book includes three helpful appendixes. Appendix A, Disabilities in Kid Terms, provides definitions of many disabilities in terms that children can easily understand. Appendix B, Special Education Terminology, provides definitions of special education terminology as well as any implications for PE teachers. Appendix C, Brockport Aquatic Skills Checklist, provides an aquatic skills assessment to help you evaluate the swimming abilities of children.

We hope this book will empower you to advocate for yourself and your students with disabilities, and we hope you receive the necessary support to help you lead all children in developing healthy and active lifestyles. It is also our hope that you will instill in all your students the notions that anything is possible and that hopes and goals can be achieved through understanding, cooperation, and creativity.

eBook available at HumanKinetics.com

Acknowledgments

We would like to acknowledge The College at Brockport; our faculty in the department of Kinesiology, Sport Studies and Physical Education; and our students past, present, and future. You are making a difference every day and making the world a more inclusive place. We would also like to acknowledge and thank our families for their continued support and understanding as we worked on the third edition of this book. Their understanding of the time needed to complete this work and pursue our passion is very much appreciated.

We would also like to thank the following picture models for the time they devoted to this project: Kiera Wilson, Luke Wilcox, Skylar Walsh, Brooke Walsh, Makayla Haibach, Maija Young, Jasmine Miller, Nathan Spurr, Riley Spurr, Lily Panning, Hudson Panning, Julia Martin, Van Hart, Christina Too, Matthew Too, and Dr. Danny Too, as well as our cover models Ms. Schecyl Santiago, Grace LaRocca, Skye Sullivan, Kaelynn Wood, and Caleb Burrows.

PART I

Understanding Inclusion

More than 95 percent of children with disabilities in the United States are educated in public schools (National Center for Education Statistics, 2016). This change from segregated placements to more inclusive environments is a result of the Education for All Handicapped Children Act of 1975, which was reauthorized as the Individuals With Disabilities Education Improvement Act of 2004 (IDEIA). The legislation requires that children with disabilities receive physical education and, if necessary, that such education be adapted to meet their unique needs. The law also requires that children with disabilities be educated in the environment in which they will be most successful (the least restrictive environment). In physical education, the most successful environment could be a totally inclusive class, a modified class, a segregated class, or something in-between. The most important thing to remember is that children with disabilities can receive adapted physical education in any environment, because adapted physical education is a *service* rather than a *placement*.

Inclusion, which is the process of educating children with and without disabilities together, has become the norm for most school districts across the United States. Even if a district has not embraced the concept of total inclusion, many children with disabilities are included in general physical education classes. Thus, physical education teachers are faced with the challenge of providing appropriate education to students with a variety of abilities. Unfortunately, many teachers lack the professional preparation to successfully include children with disabilities in physical education (Block, 2016; Lieberman, Houston-Wilson, & Kozub, 2002). They might have the best intentions, but they have limited knowledge about how to adapt the curriculum. Most undergraduate programs offer only one class in adapted physical education, and this is seldom adequate preparation for adapting the whole curriculum for children with disabilities. In addition, most school districts do not offer in-service training to assist teachers and paraeducators in successfully including all children (Davis, Kotecki, Harvey, & Oliver, 2007; Hodge, Lieberman, & Murata, 2012). The challenge faced by physical educators is compounded by the fact that children with disabilities are often behind their typically developing peers in fitness levels (Murphy & Carbone, 2008) and motor skills (Haibach, Wagner, & Lieberman, 2014).

The solution to these problems—and the purpose of the first part of this book—is to educate and empower physical education teachers by introducing the variables that can be adapted to ensure appropriate inclusion in physical education. It is only when teachers are willing to plan and analyze the curricula, instructions, rules, equipment, and environments that children with disabilities will have a chance at full participation in general physical education. Surveys of children with disabilities indicate that these children want to be included. The following lists show how children feel when they are excluded versus when they are included (Falvey, Givner, & Kimm, 1995):

Excluded		Included	
• Angry	• Worthless	• Proud	• Appreciated
• Resentful	• Invisible	• Secure	• Reinforced
• Hurt	• Substandard	• Special	• Loved
• Frustrated	• Unwanted	• Comfortable	• Grateful
• Lonely	• Untrusted	• Recognized	• Normal
• Different	• Unaccepted	• Confident	• Open
• Confused	• Closed	• Happy	• Positive
• Isolated	• Ashamed	• Excited	• Nurtured
• Inferior		• Trusted	• Important
		• Cared about	• Responsible
		• Liked	• Grown-up
		• Accepted	

Inclusion is worth the time and energy it requires, because all students should experience the feelings that result from being included. The strategies presented in this book will help pre-service teachers, teachers, administrators, and support staff in this critical area excel in the art of inclusion.

Inclusion in Physical Education

Chapter Objectives

After reading this chapter, you will

- ▶ know the historical and legislative mandates that affect the education of students with disabilities;
- ▶ understand physical education placement options available to students with disabilities;
- ▶ be familiar with research on the effectiveness of including students with disabilities in physical education;
- ▶ know the roles and responsibilities of general physical education teachers and adapted physical education teachers in the education of students with disabilities; and
- ▶ understand the terminology used in special education to better understand the needs of students with disabilities.

Isabel is a 5-year-old girl with cerebral palsy, a condition that effects the central nervous system and movement. Isabel attended an inclusive preschool where she made great gains, especially in her motor skills. She can now walk slowly without a walker and faster with a walker. At the start of kindergarten, Isabel was assigned a teacher's aide named Ms. Adams.

Preparing for kindergarten was a little scary for Isabel, but once she met Ms. Adams, she was more comfortable. Isabel's mother made sure Ms. Adams and the teachers knew about Isabel's disability—as well as her abilities—during her individualized education plan (IEP) meeting. The IEP team decided that Isabel would be included in the general physical education (GPE) class because her skills are adequate for the intended curriculum and she would benefit from being included with same-age peers.

The GPE teacher, Mrs. Bishop, attended the meeting. She did not have much experience teaching children with physical disabilities, but she was willing to do her best to accommodate Isabel. Mrs. Bishop was assured by the team that she would receive support from an adapted physical education (APE) consultant.

The APE consultant showed Mrs. Bishop how to modify and adapt activities to include Isabel in the GPE class. As the school year progressed, Mrs. Bishop began to think of her own strategies, and she also solicited advice from Isabel and the other students. The children were supportive and were enthusiastic about helping Isabel succeed in physical education. Mrs. Bishop modified some equipment, the pace of some games, and the instructional grouping, and Isabel did well. Mrs. Bishop reflected on the experience and concluded that all good teaching is adapted.

As illustrated in the opening scenario, schools are responsible for planning for the inclusion of students with disabilities. The scenario also demonstrates the need for and value of including physical education (PE) teachers in preliminary discussions. For example, when Mrs. Bishop described her limited experience working with students with physical disabilities, the district provided an APE consultant. Unfortunately, scenarios like this are not the norm. Physical educators often don't know until the first day of school that they will have students with unique needs in their classes; they are often left out of the placement planning for students with disabilities and do not receive students' IEPs. This lack of information and communication is frustrating, but it is important that these teachers continue to work to involve themselves in the process. Only through persistence will they become fully valued members of the team. Similarly, teachers who involve themselves in the planning and implementation process will be more able to secure the necessary resources and supports to make inclusion a successful experience for themselves and for their students with disabilities.

Legislative Mandates: A Historical Perspective

Educating students with disabilities was not always required. In fact, before much attention was paid to the subject, several parent activist groups filed suit on behalf of their children with disabilities who were being denied education. Two specific landmark lawsuits filed in 1972 in the United States (*Pennsylvania Association for Retarded Children v. Commonwealth of Pennsylvania* and *Mills v. Board of Education of the District of Columbia*) set the stage for the passage of several laws that ensured the right to schooling opportunities for all students with disabilities. It was determined that excluding children with disabilities from public education violated the 5th (due process) and the 14th (equal protection under the law) constitutional amendments.

As a result of these watershed lawsuits, two legislative mandates were passed. The first law, Public Law 93-112, is known as the Rehabilitation Act of 1973. One component of the Rehabilitation Act is Section 504, which stipulates that no person with a disability shall be discriminated against or denied opportunity equal to that afforded to nondisabled individuals in any programs or activities that receive federal funding. This stipulation has been especially significant because all public schools receive some form of federal support; as a result, students with disabilities are guaranteed equal protection under the law. This law also stipulates that students with disabilities should be provided with physical education and opportunities in sport-related programs comparable to those available to their nondisabled peers. As a result of

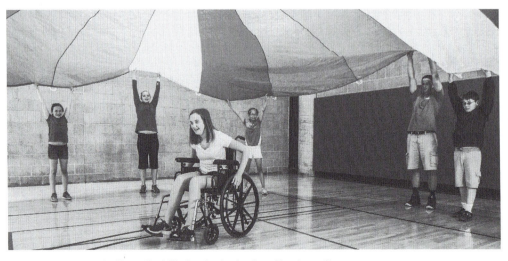

Including a student with a disability in physical education benefits everyone.

this law, some students with disabilities are provided with 504 plans, which identify their unique needs and provide strategies to support and assist these students (e.g., accommodations, modifications) in successfully accessing the curriculum. The other law, Public Law 94-142, is known as the Education for All Handicapped Children Act. It paved the way for full access to education for all students with disabilities. This law has undergone a series of reauthorizations and is currently known as the Individuals with Disabilities Education Improvement Act (IDEIA) of 2004 (Public Law 108-446). All components of the Education for All Handicapped Children Act have been retained, and other mandates have been added over the years. The mandates of IDEIA are summarized here.

First, this legislation guarantees that special education is provided to qualified students. **Special education** is specially designed instruction that meets the unique needs of the learners with disabilities and is provided at no cost to parents. Instruction can take place in various environments such as schools, homes, and hospitals. This law also established that instruction in physical education *must* be provided and, if necessary, it can be adapted for students with disabilities. The law defines physical education as the development of (a) physical and motor fitness; (b) fundamental motor skills and patterns; and (c) skills in aquatics, dance, sports, and individual and group games. Physical education is the only curricular area specifically identified in the law. As a result, physical education is considered a direct service. **Direct services** *must* be provided to all students with disabilities, whereas **related services** are provided to students as needed to allow them to benefit from educational experiences (e.g., occupational therapy, speech therapy, physical therapy). Although physical therapy (the development of gross motor coordination and function) and occupational therapy (the development of fine motor coordination and function) can supplement a PE program, these services cannot take the place of physical education (Silliman-French, Candler, French, & Hamilton, 2007).

The second mandate of IDEIA stipulates that special education services must be provided by qualified personnel. Although federal legislation does not define the term *qualified personnel*, states define it in their regulations governing physical education. New York, for example, defines it as anyone certified to teach physical education. Some states allow classroom teachers to provide adapted physical education, and others, such as California, require APE certification. Regardless of state definitions, however, anyone who provides physical education to students with disabilities should be aware of appropriate adaptations and modifications to ensure successful PE experiences (Winnick, 2017).

The third requirement of the law is that students with disabilities must be provided with **individualized education plans** that identify specific educational needs and determine appropriate resources for addressing those needs. Typically, an IEP team is assembled to determine an appropriate plan when the district is first notified that a student with disabilities will be attending the school. IEP teams usually include parents; general education teachers (including the GPE teacher if the student will be participating in regular physical education); special education teachers; special education providers, including adapted physical educators; a school psychologist; a school district representative; others, at the request of the parents or the school district; and, when appropriate, the child (Winnick, 2017). During IEP deliberations, participants make **placement** decisions, determine modifications, and formulate adaptation strategies; they also finalize goals and objectives based on the standard goals and objectives specific to each curricular area and on the results of student assessments. Chapter 4 provides more information about the IEP process.

For a student to qualify for special education services, the child must have a disability that falls into one of the 14 categories of disability identified in table 1.1.

Currently, any student between the ages of 3 and 21 who meets the criteria for one or more of the specified disabilities must be provided with a free, appropriate public education in the **least restrictive environment (LRE)**. The LRE is the environment in which the child learns best. To the extent possible, students with disabilities should

TABLE 1.1 Categories of Disability

Disability	Definition
Autism	Developmental disability that significantly affects verbal and nonverbal communication and social interaction (generally evident before age 3) and adversely affects a child's educational performance.
Deafblindness	Simultaneous hearing and visual impairments that cause such severe communication and other developmental and educational needs that the child cannot be accommodated in special education programs for children with deafness *or* blindness.
Deafness	Hearing impairment so severe that a child cannot process linguistic information through hearing (with or without amplification), which adversely affects a child's educational performance.
Developmental disorder or delay	From ages 3 through 9 the term (as defined by each state) means a delay in one or more of the following areas: physical development, cognitive development, communication, social or emotional development, or adaptive (behavioral) development.
Emotional disturbance or behavior disorder	Condition exhibiting one or more of the following characteristics over a long period and to a marked degree that adversely affects a child's educational performance: • An inability to learn that cannot be explained by intellectual, sensory, or health factors • An inability to build or maintain satisfactory interpersonal relationships with peers and teachers • Inappropriate types of behavior or feelings under normal circumstances • A general pervasive mood of unhappiness or depression • A tendency to develop physical symptoms or fears associated with personal or school problems
Hearing impairment	Impairment in hearing, whether permanent or fluctuating, that adversely affects a child's educational performance but is not included under the definition of deafness.
Intellectual disability	Significantly less-than-average general intellectual functioning that exists concurrently with deficits in adaptive behavior, is manifested during the developmental period, and adversely affects a child's educational performance.
Multiple disabilities	Simultaneous impairments (e.g., intellectual disability-blindness, intellectual disability-orthopedic impairment) that cause severe educational needs that cannot be accommodated in a special education program for only one of the impairments. Does not include deafblindness.
Orthopedic impairment	A severe orthopedic impairment that adversely affects a child's educational performance. Includes impairments caused by congenital anomaly, disease, and other causes.
Other health impairment	Limited strength, vitality, or alertness that adversely affects a child's educational performance. Can be due to chronic or acute health problems (such as asthma, attention-deficit disorder or attention-deficit/hyperactivity disorder, diabetes, epilepsy, a heart condition, hemophilia, lead poisoning, leukemia, nephritis, rheumatic fever, sickle cell anemia, Tourette syndrome).
Specific learning disability	Disorder in one or more of the basic psychological processes involved in understanding or using language (spoken or written) that may manifest itself in the imperfect ability to listen, think, speak, read, write, spell, or do mathematical calculations. Includes conditions such as perceptual disabilities, brain injury, minimal brain dysfunction, dyslexia, and developmental aphasia. Does not include learning problems that are primarily the result of visual, hearing, or motor disabilities; intellectual disability; emotional disturbance; or environmental, cultural, or economic disadvantages.
Speech or language impairment	Communication disorder such as stuttering, impaired articulation, language impairment, or voice impairment that adversely affects a child's educational performance.
Traumatic brain injury	Acquired injury to the brain caused by an external physical force that results in total or partial functional disability or psychosocial impairment (or both) that adversely affects a child's educational performance.
Visual impairment	Impairment in vision that, even with correction, adversely affects a child's educational performance. Includes both partial sight and blindness.

Based on IDEIA 2004.

be educated with their typically developing peers unless it is not beneficial to do so. Students with disabilities should be removed from the general education class only when the student needs additional one-to-one services, the placement has a negative effect on the other students in the class, the inability to perform physically is deemed significant enough to warrant alternative placements, or the student is not receiving educational benefit from general education placement (Block, 2016). In summary, students with disabilities should be separated from typically developing peers for physical education if there is a probability of harm to students with disabilities or their peers (e.g., disability is exacerbated by involvement in regular physical education, behaviors harm self or others).

The Rehabilitation Act and IDEIA affect how PE services are provided to students with disabilities. The sidebar Physical Education Requirements in IDEIA can be used to support inclusion or placement recommendations when these are being discussed with administrators or colleagues who are not familiar with the laws.

Physical Education Requirements in IDEIA

34 C.F.R.300.39(b)(2). IDEIA defines *physical education* as the development of
- physical and motor skills;
- fundamental motor skills and patterns; and
- skills in aquatics, dance, and individual and group games and sports (including intramural and lifetime sports).

20 U.S.C. 1401(29) Special Education. The term *special education* refers to specially designed instruction that meets the unique needs of a child with a disability. This includes
- instruction conducted in the classroom, in the home, in hospitals and institutions, and in other settings; and
- instruction in physical education.

34 CFR 300.108 Physical Education. The state must ensure that public agencies comply with the following:

a. **General.** Physical education services (specially designed, if necessary) must be made available to every child with a disability who receives a free appropriate public education (FAPE) unless the public agency enrolls children without disabilities and does not provide physical education to children without disabilities in the same grades.

b. **Regular physical education.** Each child with a disability must be afforded the opportunity to participate in the regular physical education program available to nondisabled children unless
   1. the child is enrolled full time in a separate facility; or
   2. the child needs specially designed physical education, as prescribed in the child's IEP.

c. **Special physical education.** If specially designed physical education is prescribed in a child's IEP, the public agency responsible for the education of that child must provide the services directly or arrange for those services to be provided through other public or private programs.

d. **Education in separate facilities.** The public agency responsible for the education of a child with a disability who is enrolled in a separate facility must ensure that the child receives appropriate physical education services in compliance with this section.

See more at www.wrightslaw.com/info/pe.index.htm (Wright & Wright, 2010).

Placement Options in Physical Education

The model of providing services to students with disabilities in the typical environment rather than removing them from the general class is known as **inclusion**. When students with disabilities are provided with specialized instruction in physical education to meet their unique needs, they are receiving *adapted physical education*. Adapted physical education is a *service* rather than a *placement*. While every effort should be made to educate students with disabilities in general physical education by providing the necessary supports to ensure success, there will be instances in which the regular class placement is not in the best interest of the learner and perhaps not in the best interest of his or her peers (i.e., when a student is extremely disruptive or distracting). The law provides for a continuum of placement options for students with disabilities; these options range from a totally inclusive environment to a self-contained environment. Students can move from option to option based on their unique needs within a given curricular area.

The following is an example of a continuum of placement options in physical education. These options provide a basis for making educated decisions about the most appropriate learning environments for students with disabilities in physical education. With the exception of full inclusion with no adaptations or support, specific information regarding the placement must be included in the IEP. In the list, A is most inclusive and E is the least inclusive.

A. Inclusion Options

- Full inclusion with no adaptations or support (no IEP needed)
- Full inclusion with curriculum adaptations and modifications
- Full inclusion with trained peer tutors
- Full inclusion with paraeducators
- Full inclusion with specialists
- Modified physical education (small class) with able-bodied peers

B. Part-Time Self-Contained and Part-Time Integrated Placement Options

- Split placement without additional support
- Split placement with additional support

C. Community-Based Placement Options

- Part-time community-based and part-time school-based placement
- Full-time community-based placement

D. Full-Time Self-Contained Placement Options Within a Regular School District

- Self-contained placement with no additional support
- Reverse integration (typically developing peers attend class with peer with a disability)
- Paraeducator one-to-one support

E. Other Placement Options

- Day school for specific disabilities
- Residential school for specific disabilities
- Home schooling
- Institution
- Hospital

Regardless of the placement option chosen, teachers must understand their unique roles and responsibilities when teaching students with disabilities in their PE classes. See chapter 3 for more information on placement.

Roles and Responsibilities of General Physical Education Teachers

GPE teachers assume multiple roles. They prepare and implement units of instruction and lesson plans in line with state and national standards. They ensure the safety of all participants by minimizing foreseeable risks, checking on the integrity of equipment, and maintaining a safe and secure physical environment. They assess student performance and modify or enhance the curriculum based on students' needs while managing an array of student behaviors to ensure successful and positive learning environments. GPE teachers also engage in public relations to promote their programs. In addition, many GPE teachers coach sports and are involved in other school-related functions.

One of the most important responsibilities of the GPE teacher is engaging in professional development. Keeping current in the field and adhering to best practices in teaching strengthens the profession and assists GPE teachers in accessing information on how to best meet the needs of all their students, especially those with unique PE needs. Professional development training is by far the best way for teachers to gain the knowledge and experience needed to accommodate students with disabilities. Mastering the skills needed to accommodate students with disabilities, such as adapting activities, working with paraeducators and special education teachers, understanding how to read and write IEPs and 504 plans, and collaborating with other professionals who are experts in the motor domain (e.g., physical and occupational therapists) requires a commitment to continued professional development (Choi, French, & Silliman-French, 2013; Grenier, 2011; Silliman-French et al., 2007).

The least restrictive placement for this student is with a peer tutor who provides physical assistance.

School districts are responsible for providing ongoing educational support and training for their employees, and physical educators can request in-service training in adapted physical education. Physical educators can also take advantage of various books and resources geared toward teaching students with disabilities in physical education. In addition, specially trained PE teachers, known as *adapted physical educators*, are available to consult with school districts and, if necessary, provide hands-on assistance. During meetings and deliberations on services that will be provided to the child, the GPE teacher can request professional support—specifically, the support of an APE specialist. APE specialists have extensive training in working with students with disabilities and can greatly assist the GPE teacher in providing the best possible experience to students in need of adapted physical education.

Roles and Responsibilities of Adapted Physical Education Specialists

All APE specialists have training not only in general physical education but also in specific disability populations, communication methodologies, assessment methods, and the legal requirements of educating students with disabilities. An APE specialist typically has a master's degree in adapted physical education or had an undergraduate concentration in the field. Many take the Adapted Physical Education National Standards (APENS) test to become Certified Adapted Physical Education Teachers

(CAPEs) (Obrusnikova & Kelly, 2009; for more information on APENS, see www.apens.org).

APE specialists can work as consultants to school districts as mentioned previously; work as itinerant teachers who service a number of school districts by teaching students in need of adapted physical education; or work as teachers in one school district. All APE specialists can teach general physical education as well. APE specialists are trained in making appropriate curricular adaptations and modifications for particular conditions. They are also well-trained in serving as members of multidisciplinary teams that meet to discuss assessment data, placement, and IEP programming for students with disabilities. They work with parents to determine priorities related to movement and incorporate them into students' programs (Lytle & Hutchinson, 2004). APE specialists are also prepared to provide sport opportunities for students with disabilities, and they help develop movement programs that embed unique sport experiences that encourage lifelong movement (Foley, Tindall, Lieberman, & Kim, 2007). Together, general physical educators and adapted physical educators can work to create the most effective programming for students with disabilities.

Districts hire full-time APE specialists as part of the PE staff, but they also work collaboratively with the special education department. They are assigned their own caseloads, and they provide direct instruction to their students in the LRE. In some cases, students will receive their instruction in small groups, self-contained classes, or inclusive classes in which the GPE teacher and APE specialist work collaboratively as instructors. Recall that adapted physical education is a service, not a placement, and educating the child in the LRE continues to be the goal of special education.

Effectiveness of Inclusion

You might wonder how effective it is to include students with disabilities in general physical education instead of placing them in self-contained environments. Researchers contend that inclusion produces various results (Coates & Vickerman, 2008; Fitzgerald & Stride, 2012; Haegele & Sutherland, 2015; Morley, Bailey, Tan, & Cooke, 2005; Verderber, Rizzo, & Sherrill, 2003). For example, in a study by Goodwin and Watkinson (2000), included students rated their experiences as good days or bad days; on good days they felt a sense of belonging, shared in the benefits of the activity, and mastered tasks, and on bad days their participation was restricted, they felt isolated, or their competence was questioned. These findings mirror those in other research (e.g., Bredahl, 2013; de Schipper, Lieberman, & Moody, 2017).

Some researchers indicate that students' social skills can be improved when they are educated in inclusive environments (Klavina & Block, 2008; Suomi, Collier, & Brown, 2003). Others have found that students with and without disabilities demonstrate favorable attitudes toward peers, coaches, and teachers as a result of inclusion (Obrusnikova, Valkova, & Block, 2003). Furthermore, when games are appropriately modified to create successful experiences for all learners, students without disabilities are more receptive to accommodating students with disabilities (de Schipper et al., 2017; Kalyvas & Reid, 2003; Obrusnikova et al., 2003). Using peer tutors also has positive effects on students with disabilities who are included in general physical education. Planned peer tutoring programs that include training can result in increased physical activity levels (Lieberman, Dunn, van der Mars, & McCubbin, 2000), opportunities to respond (Houston-Wilson, Lieberman, Horton, & Kasser, 1997; Ward & Ayvazo, 2006), academic learning time in physical education (Wiskochil, Lieberman, Houston-Wilson, & Petersen, 2007), socialization (Klavina & Block, 2008), and fitness levels (Halle, Gabler-Halle, & Bembren, 1989).

Having peers stretch together prior to the start of an activity can improve attitudes and understanding.

Inclusion also promotes personal development in students with and without disabilities (Coates, 2012; Fitzgerald & Stride, 2012; Martin & Smith, 2002) by providing opportunities for leadership (Lieberman, Arndt, & Daggett, 2007). For example, when using a sport education model in which each student takes on multiple roles, cohesiveness within the group was strengthened; this means that regardless of ability, the team members worked together to accomplish the goal (Tindall, Foley, & Lieberman, 2016). Finally, research on inclusion suggests that students without disabilities are better able to promote friendships and communication when they have opportunities to interact and engage with students with disabilities (Coates & Vickerman, 2010; Seymour, Reid, & Bloom, 2009).

A poorly administered inclusion program will not yield positive outcomes; for example, students with disabilities might be ridiculed, left out, and made to feel bad if they are on a team that loses a game (Haegele & Sutherland, 2015; James, Kellman, & Lieberman, 2011; Place & Hodge, 2001). This can affect the activity levels of students with disabilities because they fear letting the team down. In addition, poorly administered peer tutoring programs can be harmful to students with disabilities. If students with disabilities are always being assisted, they may lose confidence in themselves and question their own self-worth (Goodwin, 2001); this is often observed when students without disabilities always serve as peer helpers. These students often dominate the decision-making process, thus preventing students with disabilities from making their own decisions. It is imperative that GPE teachers work to ensure successful experiences for all students in their classes and that students with disabilities are warmly embraced and valued (Block & Obrusnikova, 2007; Elliott, 2008). As research has shown, an instructor's competence in including all students grows as he or she gains more experience in working with students with disabilities (Boer, Pijl, Minnaert, & Post, 2014; Hardin, 2005). Furthermore, students tend to follow their teacher's lead, and modeling the behaviors you want your students to demonstrate is one way to encourage a positive experience for all students. This approach, coupled with professional support from an APE specialist and trained paraeducators, helps ensure successful inclusion (Bryan, McCubbin, & van der Mars, 2013).

Summary

This chapter provided information on the legal mandates that currently affect the education of students with disabilities in physical education. It also outlined the many placement options available for students with special needs. Providing quality physical education is best met through collaboration between the general physical education teacher and the adapted physical educator. The roles and responsibilities of these individuals were also presented. A review of the literature on inclusion revealed that properly implemented inclusion practices can yield positive effects, whereas poorly implemented inclusion practices can yield adverse effects.

Assessment:
The Cornerstone
of Effective Instruction

Chapter Objectives

After reading this chapter, you will

- ▶ understand what assessment is;
- ▶ know the role that assessment plays in educating students with disabilities;
- ▶ know the types of assessment, both traditional and authentic, that can be used to assess students with disabilities; and
- ▶ be able to use assessment data for program planning and implementation.

Olivia is a sixth grader who has arthrogryposis, a condition that primarily affects range of motion. Individuals with arthrogryposis typically demonstrate extreme rotation at the shoulder joint, which makes their arms turn inward, and abnormal positioning of the knees and feet. Olivia has many friends. She uses an electric wheelchair to ambulate, but she also has good use of her left leg and uses it as much as possible. Olivia loves swimming, and during the summer she swims independently in her family's outdoor pool. She also swam independently during her swimming unit in elementary school. Unfortunately, her elementary school teacher never documented her ability, and as a result there are no records of Olivia's abilities in swimming or any other unit.

Unaware of this issue, Olivia was excited about middle school physical education because she knew that swimming was offered once a week during the first quarter. She could not wait to show off her skills to Mrs. Bowman, her new PE teacher. On the first day of swim class, however, Mrs. Bowman was reluctant to allow Olivia in the pool. Given Olivia's physical appearance, Mrs. Bowman had a hard time believing she could swim independently, despite explanations by Olivia and her peers. Mrs. Bowman was not going to take any chances and was fearful of possible liability. She allowed Olivia to swim only in the shallow water with a flotation device, and her paraeducator was there to offer assistance if needed. Olivia was crushed and embarrassed. This is one activity she can do independently and do well, and the opportunity was taken away. Olivia's mother contacted Mrs. Bowman right away, and Mrs. Bowman agreed to a private evaluation to assess Olivia's swimming abilities. The whole situation was frustrating, embarrassing, and demeaning to Olivia, and it could have been avoided through appropriate assessment practices.

Assessment is vital to ensure that students receive appropriate educational experiences. Lack of information about students' abilities can compromise PE programs, especially for students with unique needs. Assessments need to accurately reflect what students can and cannot do in relation to the curriculum content. Poor, incomplete, or biased assessments yield weak and inaccurate information, which does little to shape the curriculum in a useful way. Effective assessments—those prepared and administered with clear purposes that are related to curriculum content—are useful in developing appropriate goals and objectives for all students and can help shape and improve student abilities (Kowalski & Lieberman, 2011). Once information is obtained about what students can and cannot do (regardless of unique needs), you can effectively plan programs and implement specific, appropriate activities. Failure to embed assessment in the PE curriculum results in programs that do not address learners' individual needs and thus offer little benefit. Such programs can be targeted for elimination because little value is placed on the subject matter if there is no documented learning. It is important to address the need for more valid and reliable assessments for the students we serve in adapted physical education. Further, those who conduct the assessments need appropriate training (Garrahy, 2015; Haegele & Lieberman, 2016; Kasser & Lytle, 2013).

What sets an effective assessment apart from an ineffective one is how accurately it reflects the capabilities of the students being assessed. An effective assessment is objective and free of guesswork regarding the student's level of performance. To facilitate objective assessment, you can use a variety of methods to obtain data, such as commercial tests and self-made checklists. You can then develop specific activities to help the participants achieve a high level of mastery for any skill.

Before a child with a disability can be assessed, it is extremely important to acquire information about the child. You can record such information on the provided Ability Description Chart. You can ask parents, previous teachers, therapists, or administrators for any information that you do not yet know. Once you have this information, it will be much easier to implement assessments. The web resource that accompanies this book includes a printable version of the Ability Description Chart.

Features of Effective Assessment

Effective assessments produce data that are valid, reliable, and functional. **Valid assessments** measure a specific skill. For example, to assess throwing maturity, the assessment task must yield a throw; however, if you add the variable of accuracy (e.g., hitting a small target on the wall), the throwing assessment becomes invalid because one can demonstrate a mature throw without hitting a specific target. **Reliable assessments** must yield consistent results repeatedly. For example, assessing a student on Monday and then reassessing on Friday should yield the same or similar results. Further, even if two different teachers assessed a student on two different days, a reliable assessment would yield the same or similar results. Finally, **functional assessments** evaluate skills students use on a daily basis. Requiring students to place pegs in a pegboard, for example, is not a functional assessment; rarely is a person asked to place pegs in a pegboard. Assessments that measure fine motor skills should relate to everyday life tasks. Examples of fine motor skills that can be assessed in physical education are tying knots (ropes unit) and zipping up a personal flotation device (swimming unit). Ensuring that tests are valid, reliable, and functional is the cornerstone of appropriate assessment.

An effective assessment is also easy to administer and easy to understand. You must not only understand how to implement the test and interpret the results but also be able to present the information in a way that parents and administrators can understand. Various assessments can produce limited or extensive statistical data.

Ability Description Chart

Student: _____

School: _____

Birth date: _____

Grade: _____

Previous PE teacher: _____

Phone number: _____

Previous APE teacher (if applicable): _____

Phone number: _____

Form completed by: _____

Title of person completing the form: _____

During this semester, this student will receive his or her APE program in the regular PE class. Please fill out the following form as thoroughly as possible.

Disability: _____

Level of current function: _____

Ambulation method(s):

____ Wheelchair (electric/pushes independently)   ____ Crutches

____ Wheelchair (needs assistance)   ____ Walker   ____ Other:_____

Medical concerns:

____ Seizures   ____ Shunt   ____ Eye condition   ____ Ear condition

____ Diabetes   ____ Other: _____

Please elaborate: _____

_____

Communication methods: _____

_____

From Lauren J. Lieberman and Cathy Houston-Wilson, 2018, *Strategies for inclusion* (3rd ed.) (Champaign, IL: Human Kinetics).

The key, regardless of the extent of the data generated, is fully understanding the assessment and clearly articulating its findings.

Using appropriate assessments in physical education is imperative in determining the need for adapted physical education for students with disabilities. Appropriate assessments can (a) determine the unique physical or motor needs of students with disabilities as well as appropriate placements based on those needs; (b) assist in the development of PE goals and objectives; and (c) serve as useful tools in monitoring and evaluating student progress. These major outcomes are highlighted in the following sections.

Determining Unique Needs and Placements

Screening is the first step in determining whether a child has a unique need and is entitled to special education services. Screening involves the professional observation of student actions to determine whether these actions differ considerably from typical behavior. Physical educators are often asked to screen youngsters to determine whether motor delays are evident and whether further testing is warranted. To conduct screening tests, you can develop checklists of PE skill performance and observe students as they perform the listed skills. In order to know what skills are appropriate for each grade level, you can read through the SHAPE America National Standards student learning outcomes (SHAPE America, 2014). For example, if you want to determine if a student can catch a ball, then observe the student's attempt to catch a ball and use a checklist to mark the skills that are present (i.e., arms in ready position—hands are in front of the body and elbows are bent—extend arms to reach for the ball, catch ball with hands). Students who do not demonstrate developmentally appropriate or age-appropriate skill behaviors are identified for further testing.

This identification process is known as a **referral**. Referrals can be made to the **Committee on Special Education (CSE)** by any person who has a vested interest in the child (i.e., parents, teachers, therapists, physicians). Every district must have a CSE (or equivalent) that is made up of the child's teacher; a school psychologist; and a district representative who is qualified to provide, administer, or supervise special education. The CSE convenes to determine whether further testing is warranted; if it is, physical educators or APE specialists can choose from a variety of formal assessments to determine unique needs and eligibility for services. **Formal assessments** are systematic, preplanned methods of testing what students know. Each formal assessment has specific criteria for scoring and interpretation. Once students are deemed eligible for special education, decisions are made about the appropriate environment in which the student will receive services (see chapter 3 for more information on placement).

As mentioned previously, IDEIA requires that all students with special needs receive instruction in the LRE. For example, Olivia, who was introduced earlier, receives general physical education with her peers two times a week and self-contained physical education once a week to further her progress toward her goals and objectives. Because Olivia has limited range of motion and deficits in her physical fitness and motor skills, her goals center on increasing flexibility, muscular strength and endurance, and body coordination. In her GPE classes, she participates in the same units as her peers, and her individual goals are incorporated where possible. In her self-contained PE class, she works predominantly on her individual goals. This is the least restrictive program for Olivia, and she has improved and excelled throughout the year. The lack of assessment data about Olivia at the start of the year created an embarrassing and negative situation. Assessing students to determine their abilities and placement needs sets them up for success from the beginning (Columna, Davis, Lieberman, & Lytle, 2010; Lieberman, Cavanaugh, Haegele, Aiello, & Wilson, 2017).

Determining Program Goals and Objectives

Assessment in adapted physical education also aids in the development of program goals and objectives. Through assessment, you can note individual strengths and weaknesses. Areas of weakness become goals, and the specific activities employed to reach those goals are the objectives. For example, Olivia's goal of developing muscular strength and endurance was incorporated into a soccer unit with her peers. A rubric was developed for the class that included such tasks as dribbling, passing, and shooting. Using various drills, Olivia increased her muscular strength and endurance alongside her classmates. Knowing students' goals and objectives and providing opportunities for their achievement are crucial to student learning.

Monitoring and Evaluating Student Progress

Assessment provides you with a way to monitor student progress. Through ongoing assessment, you can note individual progress and develop new goals as the old ones are achieved.

Monitoring student progress can take many forms. One easy and motivating approach is to create a student progress chart based on the unit of instruction and keep it in the student's portfolio. Olivia's upper-body strength was first evaluated using a lat pulldown machine. With straps tied around her wrists (due to her difficulty with grasp), she could lift 10 pounds (4.5 kilograms) 3 to 5 times for 3 sets. During the rhythm unit, she practiced making circles with streamers tied to her wrists; she could do 10 circles with both arms. After 4 weeks of work on these exercises, Olivia could do 10 to 12 repetitions on the lat pulldown machine and 15 circles with the streamers. Documenting this progress on a chart showed Olivia how much she had improved through training, which motivated her to continue working to develop her strength.

To meet objectives, students must challenge themselves to improve their abilities.

SHAPE America's National Standards for K-12 Physical Education

Standard 1: The physically literate individual demonstrates competency in a variety of motor skills and movement patterns.

Standard 2: The physically literate individual applies knowledge of concepts, principles, strategies, and tactics related to movement and performance.

Standard 3: The physically literate individual demonstrates the knowledge and skills to achieve and maintain health-enhancing levels of physical activity and fitness.

Standard 4: The physically literate individual exhibits responsible personal and social behavior that respects self and others.

Standard 5: The physically literate individual recognizes the value of physical activity for health, enjoyment, challenge, self-expression, and/or social interaction.

Reprinted from SHAPE America, 2014, *National standards & grade-level outcomes for K-12 physical education* (Champaign, IL: Human Kinetics), 12.

Traditional Assessment Techniques

Since the 1950s, assessment in general physical education has traditionally focused on the physical fitness domain. There has been a notable lack of testing instruments in other areas of physical education. In fact, testing in physical education has often been viewed as confusing, time consuming, and unnecessary. To promote accountability in physical education, SHAPE America (2014) established national standards that define what a student should know and be able to do as result of a quality PE program. These standards are detailed in the sidebar SHAPE America's National Standards for K-12 Physical Education.

To maximize the effects of these standards, you must use appropriate assessment methods to ensure that students are meeting the standards. For programs to be held accountable, data need to be available to document student learning; these data can be generated only through assessment.

In the field of adapted physical education, assessment continues to be the cornerstone for effective programming and instruction. A variety of assessment instruments are available to assist professionals in determining whether unique needs exist, identifying areas of strength and weakness, and documenting students' progress and learning. When choosing an assessment tool for students with disabilities, look for qualities such as purpose, technical adequacy (validity and reliability), ecological validity (testing in a natural environment), nondiscriminatory features, ease of administration, cost, and availability. It is also important to consider whether the test is norm or criterion referenced, is curriculum based, or has an instructional link (Zittel, 1994). **Norm-referenced tests** are standardized and compare students who have similar characteristics or traits (age, gender, disability) to one another. **Criterion-referenced tests** compare students to pre-established standards of performance. Some tests are designed primarily for screening, whereas others are used for placement and program decisions. Some tests are considered formal because they must be set up and administered using specific protocols; these tests may require additional time to administer, and in some instances they require training before test administration. Other tests are considered informal because you can gain the necessary information through observation or the use of checklists with no strict protocol. **Informal assessments** can be conducted during class and can be administered by the instructor, a peer tutor, a paraeducator, or support personnel. All tests yield data that can be used in the development of IEPs in physical education.

Answering the following questions can help you choose the most appropriate, efficient test for a particular situation:

- What is the purpose of the assessment (screening, placement, programming, documenting improvement)? Does this test meet your purpose?
- Is this test valid and reliable for the population you are testing?
- Can you implement this test in your current setting?
- Will the test provide qualitative or quantitative data?
- Does the test give criterion-referenced results or normative results?
- Can your district afford this test?
- Are the results understandable to parents and administrators?
- Does the test come with any curriculum suggestions or ideas?

The sidebar Commonly Used Tests in Adapted Physical Education lists appropriate assessments that can be used to measure abilities from birth to 21 years of age.

Commonly Used Tests in Adapted Physical Education

Brockport Aquatic Skills Checklist (Houston-Wilson, 1993)

Ages: any

Tests: pool preparation, pool entry, adjustment to water, floating skills, basic propulsion, swimming strokes, diving skills, water safety, and deepwater skills

Features: checklist for each skill with corresponding levels of assistance needed to complete task

Availability: included in the web resource and appendix C

Bruininks-Oseretsky Test of Motor Proficiency, Second Edition (Bruininks & Bruininks, 2005)

Ages: 4 to 21 years

Tests: fine motor precision and integration, manual dexterity, bilateral coordination, balance, running speed and agility, upper-limb coordination, and strength

Features: gamelike tasks, normative data, and profile analysis to evaluate an individual's strengths and weaknesses

Contact: www.pearsonassessments.com

The Denver II Developmental Screening Test (Frankenburg & Dodds, 1990)

Ages: birth to 6 years

Tests: fine motor, gross motor, social, and language skills

Features: screening test to determine whether a child's development is within the normal range

Contact: www.denverii.com

I CAN Primary Skills K-3 (Wessel & Zittel, 1998)

Ages: 5 to 8 years

Tests: locomotor skills, object control, orientation, play participation, and equipment

Features: instructional link to an early elementary school motor curriculum

Contact: www.proedinc.com

Peabody Developmental Motor Scales, Second Edition (Folio & Fewel, 2000)

Ages: birth to 5 years

Tests: fine and gross motor skills

Features: instructional link to motor activities

Contact: www.theraproducts.com

Smart Start: Preschool Movement Curriculum Designed for Children of All Abilities (Wessel & Zittel, 1995)

Ages: 3 to 6 years

Tests: locomotor skills, object control, orientation, and play skills

Features: instructional link to a preschool motor curriculum

Contact: www.proedinc.com

The Test of Gross Motor Development (TGMD), Third Edition (Ulrich, 2017)

Ages: 3 to 10 years

Tests: locomotor and object control skills

Features: criterion-referenced and normative standards

Contact: www.proedinc.com

Brockport Physical Fitness Test Manual, Second Edition, With Web Resource: A Health-Related Assessment for Youngsters With Disabilities (Winnick & Short, 2014)

Ages: 10 to 17 years

Tests: health-related physical fitness (aerobic capacity, body composition, musculoskeletal function)

Features: criterion-referenced fitness standards for youth with unique needs and computer applications to generate fitness reports

Contact: www.HumanKinetics.com

You must monitor students' progress to determine whether they are meeting standards.

Although these tests can be quite useful in screening and evaluating students, making placement decisions, and developing program goals and objectives, they do have their limitations. For example, some students with severe disabilities may be unable to be tested in traditional ways, and when a test is not conducted in the way in which it was intended, the results are invalid. In addition, some traditional tests are more developmental in nature and, as such, are targeted toward elementary students. Unfortunately, tests for middle and high school students are not readily available, and tests linking assessment to the middle or high school curriculum are almost nonexistent. Authentic assessment was developed based on these limitations.

Authentic Assessment

Researchers have indicated that standardized testing protocols may present challenges in adapted physical education. For example, Block (2016) noted that outcomes from standardized tests have been misused in determining IEP goals and objectives. In addition, some standardized tests do not provide an instructional link to the PE curriculum (Good, 2014), and some items are not functional in relation to PE goals and objectives. For example, although the Bruininks-Oseretsky Test of Motor Proficiency, Second Edition (Bruininks & Bruininks, 2005), is considered a blue-ribbon standardized test for determining the need for special education services (such as adapted physical education), components of this test bear little relation to typical PE curriculum content (e.g., stringing beads [fine motor skill], stopping a falling ruler [reaction time]). Their value should not be minimized, however, because these tasks are used to develop an overall picture of the child's motor proficiency. Although standardized tests are useful, other forms of assessment need to be used to provide content-specific data. Authentic assessment fills this gap.

Authentic assessment is an ongoing feedback system that monitors and records student learning and outcomes under authentic conditions. Authentic assessment is conducted in real-life situations, and it gives students opportunities to demonstrate skills, knowledge, and competencies in age-appropriate, functional activities. It is a performance-based approach to testing, which means that students are evaluated on skills that are directly related to outcomes of the program. The results provide unparalleled information about students' learning and achievement. Many in the teaching field agree that this assessment technique should be infused into the teaching process (Lund & Veal, 2013).

The benefits of authentic assessment include the following:

- Authentic assessment can be used in the current curriculum.
- It is created specifically for the goals and objectives of each unit.
- It can be created in a way that includes every level of ability in the class.
- Students know what is expected ahead of time.
- Students are held accountable for their own learning.
- It is motivating and challenging, and it keeps students interested in learning.

Authentic assessment is a clear, concise, measurable, and motivating way of assessing student learning, improvement, and achievement. Authentic assessment uses tasks that are based on content and situational criteria; as a result, students must rely on higher-level thinking and concept application to complete tasks. In addition, because the assessed skills are directly tied to the curriculum, students are informed in advance and have time to practice the skills. This advance knowledge gives students ownership of the process. They can prepare mentally and physically for testing and thus perform at the highest competency level (Mitchell & Walton-Fisette, 2016). The following sections describe several kinds of authentic assessment.

Rubrics

A **rubric** is a form of assessment used to measure the attainment of skills, knowledge, or performance against a consistent set of criteria. Rubrics are designed to be explicit, observable, and measurable. Scoring relies heavily on the qualitative aspects of a task and generally assigns a numbering system or checklist that yields quantitative data. In some cases, rubrics may be scored based on the levels of physical assistance students with disabilities need to perform the task.

You can develop rubrics for each unit of instruction, and they can easily be individualized based on the learners and the intended objectives. The rubric can cover a wide range of abilities and accommodate heterogeneous classes by including multiple levels of achievement. Rubrics are also useful in developing a progressive curriculum in which students must attain prerequisite levels of a skill before they move on to more advanced forms of the skill. This process can help ensure the safety of the learners. Rubrics allow students to become more independent learners because they are given the rubric at the start of the unit, which allows them to know what is expected. This system enhances motivation in learning because students strive to reach the highest level possible for each given skill set. Rubrics also promote the use of self-assessment and peer assessment, which encourage students to work together to improve performance.

Rubrics should be created with all students in mind. Every rubric should be universally designed and developed with the heterogeneity of the class in mind. For rubrics, universal design is a process whereby consideration is given to all learners before creating a task rather than having to change something that has already been created. (See chapter 6 for a more thorough explanation of universal design.) Students with the highest and the lowest skills should be able to achieve and improve using the class rubric. In order to do this, there must be small variations between rubric levels and a wide range of options for all students. Figures 2.1 and 2.2 are sample rubrics that are universally designed.

Ecological Task Analysis

Another form of authentic assessment that has been used with students with disabilities is **ecological task analysis (ETA)** (Horvat, Block, & Kelly, 2007). ETA provides students with choices for executing skills. You set the parameters or objectives, and students make choices on how best to meet the objectives

Students with disabilities should be included in a GPE class and assessed on their individual skill levels.

FIGURE 2.1

Rubric for Scooters

The rubric for scooters includes options for students who are unable to propel a scooter independently and moves from easy-to-complete tasks to challenging-to-complete tasks.

Instructions: For each applicable task, check when completed or write NA for not applicable.

SLICK RIDER

_____ Student lies on scooter while teacher, paraeducator, or peer pulls or pushes the student across the gym 1 to 3 times.

_____ Student lies on scooter and pulls self across gym with arms, demonstrating control, 1 to 3 times.

HAMMER HOLD

_____ Student sits on scooter and holds a hula hoop or jump rope while teacher, paraeducator, or peer grasps the other end and pulls the student across the gym 1 to 3 times.

_____ Student sits on scooter and pushes self across gym with legs moving backward, demonstrating control, 1 to 3 times.

_____ Student sits on scooter and pushes self across gym with legs moving forward, demonstrating control, 1 to 3 times.

ROADRUNNER

_____ Student sits on scooter and holds a hula hoop or jump rope while teacher, paraeducator, or peer grasps the other end of the hoop and pulls the student around five cones 1 to 3 times.

_____ Student sits on scooter and pushes self around five cones with legs moving backward, demonstrating control, 1 to 3 times.

_____ Student sits on scooter and pushes self around five cones with legs moving forward, demonstrating control, 1 to 3 times.

SPEEDSTER

_____ Student lies on scooter while teacher, paraeducator, or peer pulls or pushes the scooter around five cones 1 to 3 times.

_____ Student lies on scooter and pulls self around five cones with arms, demonstrating control, 1 to 3 times.

FIGURE 2.2

Rubric/Task Analysis of Foul Shooting

The rubric/task analysis breaks the skill of foul shooting into sequential steps needed to perform a foul shot. Each level is given a WNBA basketball team name to motivate students to attain the highest level possible.

Instructions: For each applicable task, check when completed and move continuously through the levels.

MINNESOTA LYNX

1. _____ Knees bent
2. _____ Hands on the ball

CONNECTICUT SUN

1. _____ Knees bent
2. _____ Hands on the ball
3. _____ Eyes on the basket

SAN ANTONIO STARS

1. _____ Knees bent
2. _____ Hands on the ball
3. _____ Eyes on the basket
4. _____ Body extended upward (e.g., knees straightened, hips straightened, standing on toes)

NEW YORK LIBERTY

1. _____ Knees bent
2. _____ Hands on the ball
3. _____ Eyes on the basket
4. _____ Body extended upward
5. _____ Correct hand position on the ball
   a. _____ Nonshooting hand supporting the ball, which is held in the shooting hand
   b. _____ Shooting hand positioned with the palm up and the fingers pointing back toward the shooter
   c. _____ Wrist flexed forward

ATLANTA DREAM

1. _____ Knees bent
2. _____ Hands on the ball
3. _____ Eyes on the basket
4. _____ Body extended upward
5. _____ Correct hand position on the ball
   a. _____ Nonshooting hand supporting the ball, which is held in the shooting hand
   b. _____ Shooting hand positioned with the palm up and the fingers pointing back toward the shooter
   c. _____ Wrist flexed forward
6. _____ Shooting motion marked by extension of the shooting arm up and forward
7. _____ Follow-through marked by full extension and reaching of the shooting arm toward the basket

based on their abilities. Some choices from which students choose include equipment, distance, time, with or without a partner, and individually or in a group, to name a few. Teachers observe and maintain data about these behaviors, and use the data to continually challenge students within their comfort levels. The following is an example of ETA for striking a ball:

1. Present the task goal: striking or propelling a ball.
2. Provide options such as size, color, and weight of the ball; size and weight of the bat; and use of batting tee, a thrown pitch, or a hanging ball.
3. Document student choices (e.g., red ball off a tee with Wiffle bat).
4. Manipulate task variables to further challenge the student (e.g., to a partner, to a location, or change the striking implement).

This system offers several advantages: You learn what movement forms and equipment are most comfortable for the student, the student starts out with success, and you know that the student is being realistically challenged because you set the task goal. There are no right or wrong choices for equipment or execution of performance; however, the type of equipment made available limits the student's choices (Carson, Bulger, & Townsend, 2007). ETA is used to determine preferences and skill level and is a starting point in deciding how to further challenge the student (Mitchell & Oslin, 2007).

Consider this example that illustrates the concept. Felicia is a middle school student with mild intellectual disability, and her class is participating in a volleyball unit. Felicia is being taught the underhand serve and is given a choice between a beach ball, a volleyball trainer, and a regulation volleyball. She is also given a choice about how far from the net she will be when she serves; tape marks are placed on the floor in 1-foot (0.3-meter) increments from the net to the serving line. She chooses a beach ball and serves from a line located 2 feet (0.6 meters) from the net. Based on these choices, the teacher now knows that Felicia is a beginner. The teacher can further refine Felicia's skills and slowly work toward using smaller and harder balls until Felicia feels comfortable making an underhand serve from the service line with a regulation volleyball.

Portfolios

A **portfolio** is a compilation of a student's best work; as such, it reflects a student's progress toward physical literacy (Kowalski & Lieberman, 2011; Melograno, 2006). Portfolios are also the most promising method of exhibiting and recording student performances. Because they reflect the outcomes of performance in each domain (psychomotor, cognitive, and affective), they provide a broad overview that gives teachers, parents, and learners a genuine picture of achievement. The visual presentation of student performance can be used as a motivational tool, a method of communication with the family, a means for grading, and a vehicle for program promotion. Portfolios can be used to chart progress in all domains over the course of a unit, a semester, a year, or a period of multiple years (Melograno, 2006). Following are examples of items that can be included in a portfolio:

- Journals
- Self-reflections or self-assessments
- Rubrics, checklists, or rating scales
- Peer evaluations
- Fitness, cognitive, or affective tests
- Articles, article critiques, or collages

- Videos
- Skill analyses
- Game statistics
- Special individual and group projects
- Teacher comments
- Interest surveys

Portfolio entries can be made to reflect progress each day, or specific achievements can be added when they occur. Students can be evaluated on portfolio contents in various ways depending on the age of the student and the content and purpose of the portfolio. If the portfolio is used as an evaluation or grading tool, you can give an objective point or percentage value to contents in each domain to produce a composite score. For example, the portfolio can be divided into sections such as psychomotor, cognitive, affective, and physical fitness. Within each section, point values can be attached to each item. Portfolio scores can then be generated based on the portfolio contents.

Alternative Assessment

Although authentic assessment helps fill the gaps left by traditional and standardized forms of assessment, students with severe disabilities may need alternative assessment. This section presents two alternative assessments that can be used with students with severe disabilities. These assessments are intended to provide data that can be used to determine present levels of performance, create goals and objectives for instruction and IEP development, and evaluate progress made by students who cannot complete traditional tasks (even with modifications) and those who need physical assistance to perform tasks. In addition, these assessments allow you to assess all students in your PE classes, provide programmatic assessment data, and encourage inclusion by clearly demonstrating that students with disabilities are part

During assessment, provide physical assistance as needed to students with disabilities.

of the assessment process. They are useful in any state that uses performance-based assessment to help demonstrate competency and proficiency.

The two assessments presented here are the basic skills assessment (BSA) (Kowalski, Houston-Wilson & Daggett, in press), which is used with students who can perform skills independently, and the task analysis assessment (TAA) (Houston-Wilson, 1995), which is used with students who generally need physical assistance to complete tasks. Once students master the components of the TAA, they should use the BSA; in turn, once students are able to master the components of the BSA, they should be assessed using other forms of authentic and traditional assessment described in this chapter. These two approaches are not intended to create a separate-but-equal assessment but rather to provide ideas for achieving equity in assessment within the PE curriculum based on the unique needs of learners.

Basic Skills Assessment

The **basic skills assessment** looks at motor performance, knowledge, and personal and social responsibility. Students are assessed on the acquisition of specified skills at three levels: emerging, basic, and acquired. Figure 2.3 shows a sample BSA for softball.

FIGURE 2.3

Basic Skills Assessment for Softball

Name: _____ Age: _____ Date: _____

Instructions: This test consists of seven items, and each test item includes several tasks. To administer the assessment, observe the student as he or she performs each of the tasks within each test item. Check off each task that the student completes successfully. If you are unsure whether a student can complete a task, require the student to successfully perform the task 3 out of 5 times. After the student has completed the seven test items, total the number of checked boxes in each area (emerging, basic, and acquired). Items not completed should be left blank. These totals will provide information on the student's current level of performance. Those scoring primarily in the emerging level are beginners, those scoring primarily in the basic level are intermediates, and those scoring primarily in the acquired level are advanced performers. Data obtained from this assessment can be used to guide instruction in a sequential and progressive manner.

Check each item when performed appropriately.

TEST ITEM 1—THROWING

Grips the ball	☐ Emerging
Throws a softball in any direction	☐ Emerging
Throws a softball in desired direction	☐ Basic
Throws a softball to designated teammate	☐ Basic
Throws a softball underhand	☐ Acquired
Throws a softball overhand	☐ Acquired

TEST ITEM 2—PITCHING

Attempts to pitch a softball	☐ Emerging
Pitches a softball underhand 20 feet (6.1 meters) into a target area	☐ Basic
Pitches a softball underhand 40 feet (12.2 meters) into a target area	☐ Basic
Pitches a softball underhand with good form and height	☐ Acquired
Pitches a softball into a regulation strike zone from 40 feet	☐ Acquired

TEST ITEM 3—CATCHING/FIELDING

Attempts to catch a softball	☐ Emerging
Attempts to field a softball	☐ Emerging
Correctly fields a rolled softball	☐ Basic
Makes an above-the-waist catch	☐ Basic
Makes a below-the-waist catch	☐ Basic
Catches an underhand throw	☐ Basic
Catches an overhand throw	☐ Basic
Catches a hit softball	☐ Acquired
Fields a hit softball	☐ Acquired
Catches or fields a softball and throws to an appropriate teammate	☐ Acquired
Moves to position with body in front of a hit ball in a game	☐ Acquired
Catches or fields a hit softball cleanly in a game	☐ Acquired

TEST ITEM 4—BATTING

Assumes proper batting stance	☐ Emerging
Attempts to hit a softball off a batting tee	☐ Emerging
Hits a softball off a tee in any direction	☐ Emerging
Hits a softball off a tee in desired direction	☐ Basic
Hits a softball off a tee into fair territory in a game	☐ Basic
Attempts to hit a pitched softball	☐ Basic
Hits a pitched softball	☐ Acquired
Hits a pitched softball into fair territory during a game	☐ Acquired
Hits a pitched softball for a base hit in a game	☐ Acquired

TEST ITEM 5—BASERUNNING

Identifies order of running bases	☐ Emerging
Walks to first base	☐ Emerging
Attempts to run to first base	☐ Emerging
Runs to first base	☐ Emerging
Runs to first base within the base path	☐ Emerging

(continued)

Figure 2.3   *(continued)*

Tags first base and runs beyond it	☐ Basic
Attempts to run to first base after hitting a pitched softball	☐ Basic
Runs safely to first base after hitting a pitched softball	☐ Basic
Rounds first base when there is a chance for additional bases	☐ Acquired
When appropriate, tags up and runs on a caught fly ball	☐ Acquired
Follows base coach's advice while on the bases	☐ Acquired

TEST ITEM 6—KNOWLEDGE OF SOFTBALL

Shows basic understanding of softball (hitting, catching, throwing, running bases)	☐ Emerging
Can describe an out	☐ Basic
Can describe a foul ball, hit, strike, out, fly ball, run, and walk	☐ Basic
Can locate pitcher's mound, batter's box, infield, outfield, and foul lines	☐ Basic
Understands rules and regulations of softball	☐ Acquired
Appropriately adapts to changes in game situations	☐ Acquired
Can assist in keeping score for a softball game	☐ Acquired

TEST ITEM 7—PARTICIPATION, SAFETY, AND SOCIAL RESPONSIBILITY

Attempts to participate in softball game	☐ Emerging
Participates a little; recognizes teammates and opponents	☐ Emerging
Practices softball skills	☐ Emerging
Understands the importance of safety and good sporting behavior while playing softball	☐ Basic
Adapts ability to throw, catch, field, run, and bat	☐ Basic
Participates enthusiastically	☐ Basic
Participates in a slow-pitch softball game	☐ Basic
Exhibits safety and fair play while playing softball	☐ Acquired
Participates regularly on a softball team	☐ Acquired
Exhibits enthusiasm while playing softball	☐ Acquired
Helps teammates with rules and play during a softball game	☐ Acquired

SCORING

_____/17 Number of emerging skills

_____/22 Number of basic skills

_____/22 Number of acquired skills

Task Analysis Assessment

The **task analysis assessment** is designed for students who need physical assistance to accomplish tasks. Each skill is divided into its component tasks, and the level of assistance required for each is given a numerical value: total physical assistance (1), partial physical assistance (2), and no assistance (3). Figure 2.4 is a completed sample TAA for the bench press.

In this example, the learner completed 2 of the 7 components independently, 3 of the components with partial physical assistance, and 2 of the components with total physical assistance. The sum is 14 points, and the highest possible score (if each component is completed independently) is 21 points. By dividing the score achieved by the total possible score, we find that this student can perform the bench press with 66 percent independence. The form also includes a space for a product score; in this example the student completed five bench presses.

FIGURE 2.4

Task Analysis Assessment for Bench Press Skills

LEVELS OF ASSISTANCE

No assistance (NA): The individual can perform the task without assistance (3 points).

Partial physical assistance (PPA): The individual needs some assistance to perform the task (2 points).

Total physical assistance (TPA): The individual needs assistance to perform the entire task (1 point).

Bench press	NA	PPA	TPA
1. Lie on back on bench.	③	2	1
2. Place each foot on proper side of bench with knees bent.	③	2	1
3. Extend arms to reach for bar.	3	②	1
4. Grasp bar with both hands directly above the shoulders.	3	②	1
5. Raise bar to a straight-arm position.	3	②	1
6. Lower bar until it touches chest.	3	2	①
7. Raise bar to a straight-arm position.	3	2	①
Score per column	6	6	2
Total score	14		
Total possible score	21		
Independence score	66%		
Product score (number of bench presses)	5		

Figure 2.5 is an additional example of TAA. In this example, the level of assistance for each item is indicated with a code, but there is no numerical scoring component. Using TAAs helps you determine what students can do independently and what they need assistance with so you can set goals and objectives to improve performance.

PE teachers often think assessments are confusing and vague, and some are not sure when to use which assessment and what each assessment is for. Table 2.1 summarizes the variety of assessments used in adapted physical education.

FIGURE 2.5

Task Analysis Assessment for Softball Skills

LEVELS OF ASSISTANCE

No assistance (NA)

Partial physical assistance (PPA)

Total physical assistance (TPA)

BATTING

_____ Student can grasp bat with dominant hand over nondominant hand.

_____ Student can maintain appropriate stance.

_____ Student can swing bat and make contact with a ball placed on a batting tee.

_____ Student can swing bat and make contact with a pitched ball.

BASERUNNING

_____ Student can run to first base.

_____ Student can run to second base.

_____ Student can run to third base.

_____ Student can run to home plate.

FIELDING

_____ Student can field a ground ball.

_____ Student can field a fly ball.

TABLE 2.1 Assessments Used in Adapted Physical Education

Purpose	Type of assessment	Explanation
Screening and referral	Authentic Norm-referenced Criterion-referenced	A variety of assessments can be used to screen students to identify those who will be referred or may need further testing. Teacher-made authentic assessments are generally used for screening. Norm- and criterion-referenced screening tests can also be used if available.
Eligibility for APE	Norm-referenced Criterion-referenced Authentic	Ideally norm-referenced tests should be used to qualify students for adapted physical education to demonstrate the discrepancy between the identified child and typically developing students. However, criterion-referenced tests can also demonstrate discrepancies in abilities. For students who cannot be assessed using either of these forms of assessment, authentic assessment would be appropriate.
Instruction	Authentic Criterion-referenced Norm-referenced	Authentic assessments are generally used for instruction because they can provide both formative and summative data that can be used to inform the curriculum. These assessments also align with units of instruction being taught in physical education. Criterion-referenced and norm-referenced tests can also be used, especially when assessing fitness.
IEP annual and triennial reviews	Norm-referenced	Ideally norm-referenced assessments should be used when reporting data on the child's IEP. However, as previously stated, criterion-referenced or authentic assessments may need to be used if norm-referenced assessments are inappropriate for the child.

Summary

The assessment options presented in this chapter make it possible to assess a wide range of ability levels for students with and without disabilities. Assessment is a necessary component of ensuring that students with disabilities are provided with appropriate PE experiences, and it helps justify the need for adapted physical education. Assessment data are also used to develop IEP goals and objectives and guide instruction. The next chapter provides detailed information on the process of making placement decisions for those students who qualify for adapted physical education.

The Placement Process in Physical Education

Chapter Objectives

After reading this chapter, you will

▶ understand the importance of placement as it relates to adapted physical education;

▶ know how to screen students to determine which ones have unique needs;

▶ be able to make referrals for further evaluation;

▶ use eligibility requirements to determine the need for adapted physical education;

▶ understand the various placement options and how to determine placement for children with disabilities in the least restrictive environment;

▶ appreciate the need to use correct forms and timelines for each step of this process; and

▶ know how to rate an inclusive setting based on the Lieberman-Brian Inclusive Rating Scale for Physical Education.

Dylan is a ninth grader who has Down syndrome. He participates in a self-contained APE class with five of his peers who have disabilities. During the fitness warm-up, Dylan walks on the treadmill while his peers ride bikes or elliptical machines. After 8 minutes, the students go down to a small gym and engage in a modified softball unit. Dylan's peers have disabilities that include visual impairment and physical disabilities. Mr. Voss, the PE teacher, does his best to keep the students engaged and ensure their success. An APE consultant, Ms. Riveria, came to observe the class. She commended Mr. Voss on his accommodation of the various students in his class, but she also asked him why some of the students were not being included in the general class. Mr. Voss stated that these students were eligible for APE classes as identified on their IEPs. Ms. Riveria explained to Mr. Voss that adapted physical education is a service rather than a placement, and they agreed to work with the special education department to determine more appropriate placements for Dylan and some of his high-functioning peers. She explained that adapted physical education can be held in a self-contained class if necessary but that other options are also available, such as a modified class, an inclusive class, or some combination. Mr. Voss was extremely happy and relieved because this class was hard to teach by himself with so many levels of ability. Dylan was thrilled to learn that he would be included with his peers in the inclusive class, and he loved the next unit: Frisbee! Unfortunately, the placement process and complexities of the LRE are not always easy to navigate, even for the most experienced teachers.

Adapted physical education (APE) is designed to meet the unique needs of children with disabilities in the LRE. This service can be provided in a self-contained class, in a modified class, in an inclusive class, in the community, or through a combination of options. The right environment can help children succeed, and the wrong environment can create negative experiences for everyone.

As explained in chapter 1, IDEIA requires that children with disabilities receive a free, appropriate public education that meets their unique needs within the LRE. The LRE is the environment in which the child's learning is best supported. Although mandates for special education may be well established and understood in the public school system, determining the appropriate setting or placement in which students should receive their adapted physical education is often illegally and unethically determined by teacher availability, schedules, or preferences rather than children's educational needs (Block, 2016).

Physical Education Placement Challenges

PE placement and decisions about APE services should be based on comprehensive assessment data that indicate academic achievement and functional performance levels of students (Columna, Davis, Lieberman, & Lytle, 2010). These data should help the IEP team determine the LREs for students with disabilities.

Not all children with disabilities will qualify for or receive APE services, and not all should be placed in a **self-contained physical education class**. For those who qualify, the IEP team should determine the amount of APE service and the placement (see the Placement Options for Adapted Physical Education sidebar). The IEP team plays a vital role in the placement decision-making process for students with disabilities.

Despite the continuum of APE placement options that are identified, many students with disabilities continue to receive inappropriate services and are often placed in inappropriate environments (Gartner & Kerzner-Lipsky, 2011). All state and local education agencies are required to have guidelines in place for determining eligibility for special education services; however, PE teachers are often unfamiliar with these guidelines because they are not given access or consulted by districts when placement decisions are being made. This chapter will provide an invaluable resource for physical educators regarding the process for determining placement for students who qualify for adapted physical education.

A modified physical education class is one of the many placement options for adapted physical education.

Placement Options
for Adapted Physical Education

A. Inclusion Options

- Full inclusion with no adaptations or support (no IEP needed)
- Full inclusion with curriculum adaptations and modifications
- Full inclusion with trained peer tutors
- Full inclusion with paraeducators
- Full inclusion with specialists
- Modified physical education (small class) with able-bodied peers

B. Part-Time Self-Contained and Part-Time Integrated Placement Options

- Split placement without additional support
- Split placement with additional support

C. Community-Based Placement Options

- Part-time community-based and part-time school-based placement
- Full-time community-based placement

D. Full-Time Self-Contained Placement Options Within a Regular School District

- Self-contained placement with no additional support
- Reverse integration (typically developing peers attend class with peer with a disability)
- Paraeducator one-to-one support

E. Other Placement Options

- Day school for specific disabilities
- Residential school for specific disabilities
- Home schooling
- Institution
- Hospital

Modified from Block 2016; Dunn and Leitschuh 2014; Roth, Zittel, Pyfer, and Auxter 2016; Winnick and Porretta 2017.

Understanding and establishing district policy to determine eligibility and placement for PE and APE services demonstrates a commitment to ensuring quality services for students with disabilities. In addition, the establishment of a district-wide decision model that follows federal and state guidelines for determining the types of PE services and placement decisions helps resolve inconsistencies in selecting services and determining placements within the LRE for each student.

Qualification for APE services varies from state to state. In New York, for example, a student with a disability must score below the 15th percentile on a standardized assessment scale to qualify for APE services. In California, each Special Education Local Plan Area (SELPA) has written guidelines for special education programs; some SELPAs suggest cutoff scores for standardized tests (such as 1.5 or 2 standard deviations below the mean) that indicate qualification for special education services. Many states, including Illinois and Texas, have entry and exit criteria for APE services. In every state, however, the final placement decisions rest with IEP teams. Federal law (IDEIA, 2004) provides a general overview of physical education and what is required for students with disabilities as follows:

a. **General.** Physical education services, specially designed if necessary, must be made available to every child with a disability receiving a free and appropriate public education, unless the public agency enrolls children without disabilities and does not provide physical education to children without disabilities in the same grades.

b. **General physical education.** Each child with a disability must be afforded the opportunity to participate in the general physical education program available to nondisabled children, unless

   1. The child is enrolled full time in a separate facility; or
   2. The child needs specially designed physical education, as prescribed in the child's IEP.

c. **Special physical education (adapted).** If specially designed physical education is prescribed in a child's IEP, the public agency responsible for the education of that child must provide the services directly or make arrangements for those services to be provided through other public or private programs.

d. **Education in separate facilities.** The public agency responsible for the education of a child with a disability who is enrolled in a separate facility must ensure that the child receives appropriate physical education services in compliance with this section (Sec. 300.108 Physical education).

Federal law guarantees the opportunity for students to participate in physical education regardless of physical, cognitive, or emotional abilities. Finding the LRE for each learner is a federal mandate and a best practice. The environment is considered to be least restrictive when it matches individual abilities with appropriate services that allow students to be as independent as possible. There are many school districts, however, that have only two placement options: general physical education and separate physical education. Districts are often unaware or unwilling to provide placement options. You should advocate for appropriate placement for the students you are serving. In instances in which students cannot be accommodated by their school district, alternative placement options must be provided with all costs incurred by the district.

Although the idea of placing a student in the environment that is most conducive to learning may sound like an easy task, there are many challenges that teachers have identified that can affect quality decision-making, such as lack of adequate training, PE class sizes, lack of administrative support, few APE teachers in the district or county, high caseloads for APE specialists, lack of experience working with students with disabilities, and teachers' attitudes (de Schipper, Lieberman, & Moody, 2017; Haegele & Sutherland, 2015; Hersman & Hodge, 2010; Hodge & Akuffo, 2007; Hodge et al., 2009; Lieberman, Houston-Wilson, & Kozub, 2002; Obrusnikova, 2008; Özer et al., 2013; Perkins, Columna, Lieberman, & Bailey, 2013). These factors also result in assessment methods that produce inaccurate results of a student's present level of performance. Accurate assessment information is critical when determining the appropriate placement within the LRE for physical education and when determining whether a student qualifies for APE services. (See chapter 2 for more information on assessment.)

Special Education Process

The following is a systematic approach for determining eligibility and placement for students with disabilities in physical education. This systematic process, also known as the *special education process*, serves as a useful guide as you make recommendations for PE services and placements for students with disabilities.

Step 1: Conduct an Informal Screening

Students are first screened to determine whether unique needs exist. The PE teacher generally conducts screening, and the information obtained is used to identify students that may benefit from adapted physical education. This step allows you to observe all students in your PE classes. No individual student may be singled out for screening; it must be based on processes that occur for all students. For example, many kindergarten and elementary programs conduct annual PE screenings (sometimes referred to as *PE round ups*) that give the PE teacher an opportunity to screen all students on selected motor items that are important for success in the GPE curriculum. You might also observe physical and motor skills in other settings, such as in classrooms or the playground, to get an overall view of a student's abilities. Parental permission is not needed to conduct informal screenings. If any concerns are noted in motor performance, physical activity levels, behavior, or cognition, for example, the student is referred to the CSE for further evaluation. See the Adapted Physical Education Screening and Referral Form.

Step 2: Refer for Formal Assessment

If screening indicates concerns that cannot be remediated in the current setting, the student is referred for formal assessment. For students who are receiving special education services but are not receiving adapted physical education, formal assessments occur during the annual or triannual review period or whenever they are requested. The referral is the process whereby a teacher or someone who works closely with the student or has a special interest in the child (e.g., parent, other educational professional) suspects a disability and initiates a request for additional testing. The GPE teacher might notice difficulties and consult with the APE teacher, if available, and other teachers to confirm concerns prior to submitting a referral for evaluation.

Step 3: Seek Parental Permission

This step requires that parents or guardians grant permission before formal evaluation is conducted. Parents have the right to refuse assessment for their child. Before any formal evaluation can take place, the district must send written notification to parents (in their native language) requesting permission for assessment and explaining the importance of conducting the assessment.

Step 4: Formally Assess

The assessment should be conducted by a highly qualified APE teacher. However, because not all districts have APE teachers, general physical educators may be responsible for conducting the formal assessment. The assessment results are used to determine eligibility for services, and the methods used should be based on standardized tests whenever possible. Authentic and alternative assessments are recommended when standardized tests are not available or are not appropriate. The assessments results are analyzed to determine whether the student with a disability qualifies for APE services. Once the formal assessment is complete then the eligibility form is completed. See the Eligibility Criteria for Adapted Physical Education form.

Adapted Physical Education Screening and Referral Form

Student: _____ Grade: _____

School: _____ Physical education teacher: _____

This form should be completed by the student's current physical educator. The adapted physical educator or the person who determined the need for evaluation should complete an additional copy.

INITIAL INFORMATION

1. In order of importance, list the specific reasons you believe this student may require adapted physical education.

   _____

   _____

2. Is the student safe in the PE environment?   Yes_____   No_____

   If not, what are the safety concerns? _____

   _____

3. Is the student successful in general physical education?   Yes_____   No_____

   If not, please explain the difficulties the student is having:_____

   _____

4. What modifications or strategies have been used to increase success for this student?

   _____

   _____

5. Does the student have any medical concerns (e.g., seizures, medical restrictions)?

   _____

Use the following guidelines to screen student performance based on the SHAPE America standards listed below. If the skill is not applicable, check the NA box.

4 Above grade level	3 At grade level	2 Approaching grade level	1 Below grade level
Fluid movement	Uses skill in combination with other skills	More frequent successes	Attempts are choppy and uncoordinated
Uses skills in a variety of situations	Consistent performance	Simple movements become more refined	Occasional success
Effortless performance			

SHAPE America Standard 1: The physically literate individual demonstrates competency in a variety of motor skills and movement patterns.

Skill	4	3	2	1	NA	Comments
LOCOMOTOR SKILLS						
Stand on one foot						
Walk						
Run						
Jump						
Hop						
Slide						
Gallop						
Skip						
OBJECT CONTROL						
Bounce						
Dribble						
Catch						
Throw underhand						
Throw overhand						
Kick stationary ball						
Kick moving ball						
Strike stationary ball						
Strike moving ball						

SHAPE America Standard 2: The physically literate individual applies knowledge of concepts, principles, strategies, and tactics related to movement and performance.

Skill	4	3	2	1	NA	Comments
Understands directions						
Identifies a variety of body parts						
Understands movement concepts						
Applies motor skills to activities						
Uses strategy in game play						
Self-assesses performance						
Corrects movements with verbal feedback						

(continued)

SHAPE America Standard 3: The physically literate individual demonstrates the knowledge and skills to achieve and maintain health-enhancing levels of physical activity and fitness.

Skill	4	3	2	1	NA	Comments
PACER						
Curl-up						
Push-up						
Sit-and-reach (right side)						
Sit-and-reach (left side)						
Trunk lift						
Shoulder stretch (right side)						
Shoulder stretch (left side)						

SHAPE America Standard 4: The physically literate individual exhibits responsible personal and social behavior that respects self and others.

Skill	4	3	2	1	NA	Comments
Listens/follows directions						
Establishes peer relations						
Respects self-space						
Understands sportsmanship						
Is on task						
Enjoys physical activity						
Follows safety rules						
Respects equipment						
Transitions between activities						
Participates independently						

SHAPE America Standard 5: The physically literate individual recognizes the value of physical activity for health, enjoyment, challenge, self-expression, and social interaction.

Skill	4	3	2	1	NA	Comments
Is physically active during recess						
Participates in organized activities outside of school						
Can maintain a physical activity log						
Understands the benefits of a healthy lifestyle						
Willingly tries new skills						
Attempts to refine skills						
Expresses how physical activity makes them feel						
Identifies preferred physical activities						
Enjoys being active with others						

SUMMARY OF PERFORMANCE

Areas above grade level
Areas at grade level
Areas approaching grade level
Areas below grade level

Form completed by: _____

Date: _____

Students consistently performing below grade level should be referred for further evaluation.

From Lauren J. Lieberman and Cathy Houston-Wilson, 2018, *Strategies for inclusion* (3rd ed.) (Champaign, IL: Human Kinetics). SHAPE America standards are from SHAPE America 2014.

Eligibility Criteria
for Adapted Physical Education

Student: _____ Disability: _____

Age: _____ Grade: _____ Previous placement: _____

Team members present: _____

_____

Variables considered before determining placement:

ASSESSMENT DATA

	Met standard	Did not meet standard	N/A
TEST OF GROSS MOTOR DEVELOPMENT (TGMD)—PERFORMING AT GRADE LEVEL			
Locomotor skills			
Object control			
FITNESSGRAM—MEETS THE HEALTHY FITNESS ZONE			
PACER (20 meters)			
Curl-up			
Push-up			
Backsaver sit-and-reach (right side)			
Backsaver sit-and-reach (left side)			
Trunk lift			
Shoulder stretch (right side)			
Shoulder stretch (left side)			
BROCKPORT PHYSICAL FITNESS TEST			
PACER (15 meters)			
Modified curl-up			
Isometric push-up			
Backsaver sit-and-reach (right side)			
Backsaver sit-and-reach (left side)			
Trunk lift			
Shoulder stretch (right side)			
Shoulder stretch (left side)			
Other items (list)			

OTHER ASSESSMENTS (LIST)			

AUTHENTIC AND ALTERNATIVE ASSESSMENTS (LIST)			

ABILITY TO MEET SHAPE NATIONAL STANDARDS FOR PHYSICAL EDUCATION			
Standard 1: Demonstrates competency in a variety of motor skills and movement patterns			
Standard 2: Applies knowledge of concepts, principles, strategies, and tactics related to movement and performance			
Standard 3: Demonstrates the knowledge and skills to achieve and maintain health-enhancing levels of physical activity and fitness			
Standard 4: Exhibits responsible personal and social behavior that respects self and others			
Standard 5: Recognizes the value of physical activity for health, enjoyment, challenge, self-expression, and social interaction			

ELIGIBILITY

Student does not meet the criteria for adapted physical education.	
Student meets the criteria for adapted physical education.	

From Lauren J. Lieberman and Cathy Houston-Wilson, 2018, *Strategies for inclusion* (3rd ed.) (Champaign, IL: Human Kinetics).

Step 5: Determine Eligibility

The assessor reviews the compiled data and creates a written report that is submitted to the parents and the IEP team. This report should include (a) specific information about the student, the evaluator, and the reason for the assessment; (b) a description of the formal and informal assessments used; (c) any behavioral observations (e.g., problems following rules, paying attention); (d) information about the validity and reliability of the tests used; (e) raw data from the assessments; (f) the present level of academic achievement and functional performance, including areas of strength and need; and (g) a summary of the results and recommendations. The following are recommended criteria for determining eligibility for APE services:

- The student scores below the 15th percentile on an assessment.
- The student scores 1 to 2 standard deviations below the mean.
- The student demonstrates a developmental delay of 2 or more years.
- The student fails to meet criterion-referenced standards.
- The student fails to meet at least 70 percent of competency-based standards.

In addition, information regarding cognitive and self-help skills and input from the family are important considerations for the IEP team to review prior to making eligibility decisions.

If assessment results indicate that the student does not qualify for APE services, the data and decision criteria used to make the determination of ineligibility *must* be provided to parents and the IEP team members. Once this is done, the assessment report should be placed in the student's cumulative education file following the IEP meeting. These files should accompany the child if he or she were to move to another school district. All services received in one district should be continued to be offered in the new school district until the school can conduct its own evaluation if necessary.

For students deemed eligible for adapted physical education based on the criteria above, the IEP team must discuss and determine appropriate placement.

Step 6: Determine Placement

As previously discussed, students eligible for adapted physical education must receive the service in the LRE. When deciding on the LRE placement, the following should be considered: safety issues, parental concerns, behavior, cognitive skills, social skills, sensory function, and any other concerns deemed necessary by the IEP team.

Additional anecdotal information collected by the IEP team is critical in determining sound placement decisions. It is important to review the strengths and weaknesses of students in multiple settings so they can benefit from appropriate placements. For example, a student with average motor skills who has autism may have challenges with environmental sensory overload in a noisy gym filled with other students, but he may perform relatively well in a one-on-one or small-group situation in an environment with reduced stimuli. In another example, a student who uses a wheelchair may score low on a fitness test, but due to great motor and social skills can participate in an inclusive class with some easy modifications.

As previously mentioned, adapted physical education is a service rather than a placement; therefore, it is possible for a student to be eligible for adapted physical education in an inclusive class. If it has been determined that the student would benefit from an inclusive environment, consider the following questions (adapted from Block, 2016):

- What assistance do the teacher and student need for this experience to be successful?
- What are the student's sensory needs?

- What is the cognitive function of the student, and what supports will be necessary?
- Will the student and the rest of the students be safe?
- What are the parental preferences?
- What are the student's previous experiences?
- What does the student like to do?

These and other questions can guide the IEP team toward a meaningful decision that is in the best interests of everyone. These questions help determine the best placement options based on the needs of the student with a disability. One placement option that should be considered and has been shown to be effective is modified physical education. A **modified physical education class** is characterized as a small inclusive class of 10 to 20 children with and without disabilities. This placement has also been referred to as *unified physical education* and *buddy or peer physical education*. Although some school districts have been using this option it is generally not universally considered. Modified physical education falls in the category of inclusion as noted in this chapter because children with and without disabilities are taught together but with a smaller number of students. All students in this placement are working on the same curriculum as their same-age peers. There are numerous benefits to using modified physical education, which are outlined in table 3.1.

Lieberman et al. (2017) provide a process for setting up a modified physical education class to accommodate students with disabilities as follows:

1. The children can be preselected by the physical education teachers and the classroom teachers. This preselection can be determined by attendance, patience, disposition, skill level, compassion, and desire.

2. The children can be given the option of the modified class and self-select to be in that setting for one class a week or every PE class.

3. The modified class can be a smaller part of a large class in the same gym or a different gym.

4. The participants can rotate or be permanent depending on the situation.

TABLE 3.1 Benefits of Modified Physical Education

Student needs	Benefit of modified PE for the students and the teacher
Children who may have a hard time in large groups due to noise or distractions	There are fewer children so there are fewer distractions and reduced noise.
Children with visual impairments who need a quieter environment in order to access what is happening in the environment	There is less noise due to a smaller number of students. In addition because these children are carefully selected they are sensitive to the needs of the students in the class.
Children with emotional distress who need a calmer environment	It can be calmer and less stressful.
Children who experience a developmental delay and who need added practice	The participants will get more turns to practice skill development.
Children who need work on socialization	Because the children will be preselected and provided information about the group, they will know the social and emotional needs of their peers.
Children with learning disabilities	This placement can offer a more multisensory approach to ensure learning of all children.
Children with intellectual disabilities	This placement can offer a more multisensory approach to ensure learning of all children.

"The modified physical education class: An option for the least restrictive environment," L.J. Lieberman, L. Cavanagh, J.A. Haegele, R. Aiello, and W. Wilson, *Journal of Physical Education, Recreation and Dance*, 2017, reprinted by permission of the Society of Health and Physical Educators, (http://www.shapeamerica.org).

5. The participants in the modified class can be part of "advanced PE," and this could be an additional class they attend each week.

6. The modified class could choose each unit related to the interest and desires of the children with and without disabilities.

7. The students with disabilities could invite the modified class and choose friends they feel would be best for this setting.

8. The modified class can be explained and the participants can apply to be in the modified class. This application would have a justification as to why they want to be part of this special group.

9. The paraeducators that are assigned to the children with disabilities would still attend the class just like they would in the inclusive class or in the classroom with the same level of support when necessary.

Schools and districts must provide services and consider placement options based on student needs (refer back to the Placement Options for Adapted Physical Education sidebar). If a school cannot provide the necessary services to meet student needs, the school district is obligated by law to find another school, district, or public or private agency that can accommodate the child's needs at no cost to the parent.

The decision on the most appropriate placement option should *not* be based on teachers' schedules or the sizes of their caseloads. If there are caseload or scheduling challenges, these issues should be resolved with the district administration. If you have a schedule conflict or a larger-than-average student load, perhaps this is an opportunity to justify the need for additional PE or APE teachers. Special education administrators are skilled at resolving and working with such issues. They may have creative solutions that you are unaware of, and you should use them as resources.

Well-developed placement forms ensure that all team members use the same criteria for placement decisions. The Suggested Placement for Adapted Physical Education form can be used to assist the IEP team in determining the best PE placement option for students.

After each member of the multidisciplinary team fills out a copy of the placement form, the scores are averaged to determine the best placement for the student. The IEP team can calculate the average of the numerical scores to determine placement. An average closer to 1 indicates that the student can be included in general physical education, whereas an average closer to 3 indicates that the student may learn better in a self-contained setting. An average near 2 indicates that a modified placement or a combination approach should be considered (e.g., general physical education two times per week and a self-contained class two times per week).

Consider the following examples of how the placement form has been used with students with disabilities:

Abdul, a seventh grader with an intellectual disability, received a 3 for motor skill performance from most team members and a 1 in all other areas. His average is 1.2. His team determined that an inclusive PE placement with an emphasis on motor skills and a trained peer tutor were appropriate for him given his current needs.

Devora, a fourth grader who is blind and has average motor and fitness skills, received an average score of 2.1. Devora takes longer to learn motor skills than her peers. It was recommended that Devora attend inclusive physical education with her peers and with the assistance of a paraeducator twice a week and attend a modified physical education class once a week. While in her self-contained class, she will be taught the motor skills that will be covered in the inclusive class; familiarizing her with these skills will better prepare her for success with her peers.

Suggested Placement
for Adapted Physical Education

Student: _____ Disability: _____

Age: _____ Grade: _____ Previous placement: _____

Rater: _____

Complete the general information and assessment data sections. Using your personal judgment, the assessment data, and your knowledge of the student, score each area as indicated (1, 2, 3).

ASSESSMENT DATA (TO BE COMPLETED BY THE PE DEPARTMENT)

TGMD: met standard/did not meet standard

FitnessGram: met standard/did not meet standard

Brockport Physical Fitness Test: met standard/did not meet standard

National standards in PE: met standard/did not meet standard

Alternative or authentic assessments: met standard/did not meet standard

	Inclusive PE class (with support and modifications) (1)	Combination PE class (inclusive and self-contained PE) or modified placement (2)	Self-contained PE class (3)
Locomotor ability recommendation			
Object control ability recommendation			
Fitness ability recommendation			
Sport skill ability recommendation			
Social skill recommendation			
Behavioral need recommendation			
Sensory need recommendation			
Cognitive need recommendation			
Class size recommendation			
Total score from each column			

(continued)

Suggested Placement for Adapted Physical Education   *(continued)*

Based on your average score on the form and your experience with the student, please identify the placement option that will best meet the student's needs:

_____

_____

_____

_____

_____

From Lauren J. Lieberman and Cathy Houston-Wilson, 2018, *Strategies for inclusion* (3rd ed.) (Champaign, IL: Human Kinetics).

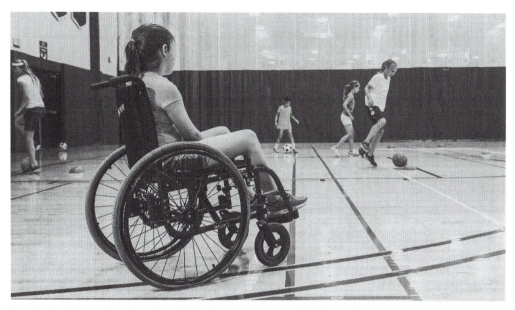

The student shown here is not participating in a soccer dribbling activity because the teacher does not know how to include the student. By providing the student with a bigger ball and perhaps the assistance of a peer tutor, she can easily be included in the activity.

The intent of the placement form is to assist with the process; it is not a substitute for formal assessment. Valid and reliable assessments must be used in making placement decisions. The added use of the placement form can provide clarity on students' strengths and weaknesses and ensure that the most appropriate placement is made based on students' unique needs.

As previously discussed, comfort levels and experience should not factor into the decision-making process. Students are placed in the LRE based on their individual needs. If you lack the knowledge or experience needed to teach physical education to students with disabilities, we suggest that you use specialized consultants (e.g., APE teacher, teacher of the visually impaired, physical therapist, behavioral specialist), enroll in college courses related to adapted physical education, and attend in-service training or workshops to increase knowledge and self-efficacy. It is well-known that the best way to improve self-efficacy in teaching students with disabilities is to teach students with disabilities.

Step 7: Create an IEP

After placement decisions have been made, the team will work toward the completion of the IEP. The IEP identifies the student's present level of performance, annual goals, short-term objectives (when appropriate), and the criteria for evaluation, and it includes a list of all services, resources, time frames, and other pertinent information needed to secure the educational success of the student. Chapter 4 provides an overview of the development of an IEP.

Step 8: Reevaluate

Ongoing evaluation helps ensure that services and placement decisions are meeting students' needs. Collecting data to determine whether students are meeting intended goals and objectives is essential in the special education process. Using **formative assessment**, you can track progress at regular intervals to ensure that students are mastering their goals. Progress should be reported two or three times over the course of the year. Progress reports note whether the student has met an intended goal, the goal is still being worked on, or the goal is inappropriate and must be reconsidered. Further, cumulative assessments will need to be performed triennially for each student who receives special education services.

Establishing clear guidelines and procedures regarding eligibility for APE services and placement decisions will aid the district in having a set protocol. PE and APE teachers should be instrumental in developing the guidelines based on the legal mandates and recommendations outlined herein. It is advised that a team of professionals and parents be convened to write the guidelines and that they be reviewed by the director of special education before they are disseminated. The guidelines might include a review of the special education process; information on how placements will be decided and where referral, eligibility, and placement forms will be housed (i.e., in the school database); potential placement options; potential service providers; contact information for key personnel involved in the process; and any additional information the school district deems pertinent.

Assessing the Placement: The Lieberman-Brian Inclusion Rating Scale for Physical Education

When students with disabilities receive their adapted physical education in an inclusive setting, you must assess whether that placement is meeting the students' needs and whether adjustments need to be made within the setting. The Lieberman-Brian Inclusion Rating Scale for Physical Education (LIRSPE) has been validated to rate the inclusive environment (Lieberman, Brian, & Grenier, in press).

The purpose of this rating scale is to evaluate the *effort* made by teachers to include children with disabilities in a general physical education environment. The LIRSPE measures the actions taken by teachers to ensure students with disabilities are offered physical education opportunities alongside their typically developing peers. However, it should be noted that this instrument does not comprehensively determine whether physical education classes are inclusive because it does not measure a number of complex variables associated with inclusion, such as the nature of interactions between those with disabilities and their peers. High scores on one of these items will not guarantee that a class is inclusive, but the net positive effect of these items demonstrate the effort that teachers take toward inclusion. Any score above a 3 demonstrates that the teacher is attempting to include children with disabilities in classes.

The LIRSPE must be utilized during at least three physical education class periods that include at least one child with a disability. It is recommended that teachers receive the scale at least one day before it is used to prepare. Raters are asked to watch the physical education class in its entirety and circle one number (between 1 and 5 in the score column), providing a rating for each item listed (in the descriptor column) within the LIRSPE.

1 = Poor	Student is not included in class.
2 = Below average	Student is rarely included in class.
3 = Average	Student is sometimes included but not all of the time.
4 = Above average	Student is mostly included in class.
5 = Excellent	Student is fully included all of the time.
*The final score	Total # from each descriptor used above/Total number of descriptors used = Inclusion rating (related to effort the teacher makes to include all children)

The Lieberman-Brian Inclusion Rating Scale for Physical Education (LIRSPE)

Descriptor	Score	Comments
Start of class		
1. When the general physical education teacher welcomes the children into the gymnasium, all of the children in the class are together including the children with disabilities. (Children with disabilities do not walk into the gymnasium late.)	1 2 3 4 5 N/A	
Introduction		
2. Children with disabilities are sitting or standing with their peers and included in the instructions of the introduction.	1 2 3 4 5 N/A	
Warm-up		
3. The class does the warm-up together with children performing at their own pace. (For example, children run as many laps as they can in X mins vs. requiring X laps in X mins.)	1 2 3 4 5 N/A	
Speed of play within the lesson		
4. Speed of play is varied based on present level of performance of all children including children with disabilities so as not to leave anyone behind. (Examples include volleyball [players use a beach ball to slow down the speed of the game], floor hockey [players use a Frisbee instead of a ball or puck], softball [hit ball off a tee], or basketball [eliminating the five-second rule].)	1 2 3 4 5 N/A	
Differentiated instruction		
5. Instruction is provided that allows for all students to succeed and benefit within the general program by accommodating different learning styles. (Audio, visual, kinesthetic, and approaches specific to the needs of the child such as tactile modeling.)	1 2 3 4 5 N/A	
6. The lesson provides a variety of choices to execute skills. (This may be done in stations, within the task, and task-to-task.)	1 2 3 4 5 N/A	
Autonomy supported instruction		
7. Student has opportunities to make some choices driving his or her own learning.	1 2 3 4 5 N/A	
8. Proper accommodations and supports are available for her or his choices. (This may require some pre-teaching so children know what choices are available and may be comfortable for them to use.)	1 2 3 4 5 N/A	
Demonstrations		
9. Use various members of the class including children with disabilities to demonstrate skills to the class. (Only when you know they can demonstrate the skill being taught and that they would enjoy doing so.)	1 2 3 4 5 N/A	
Use of paraeducator		
10. Support staff assists the child in learning as needed.	1 2 3 4 5 N/A	
11. Lesson is provided to the paraeducator before the class and explains their role throughout the lesson.	1 2 3 4 5 N/A	
Peer-partner (when possible)		
12. When using partners, the student with a disability has opportunities to partner with a same-aged peer (if appropriate) and not only the paraeducator when possible.	1 2 3 4 5 N/A	
13. Paraeducator encourages social interactions with peers in the class when possible.	1 2 3 4 5 N/A	
Skill/Activity—partner activity		
14. Teacher plans ahead to organize and manage partners effectively.	1 2 3 4 5 N/A	
15. Teacher ensures that children with disabilities have a partner.	1 2 3 4 5 N/A	

(continued)

Descriptor	Score	Comments
Game/Activity—team sport		
16. Students do not pick teams.	1 2 3 4 5 N/A	
17. Teacher avoids elimination games.	1 2 3 4 5 N/A	
18. Teacher avoids students waiting in line.	1 2 3 4 5 N/A	
19. Teacher distributes as much equipment as possible to maximize opportunities to respond.	1 2 3 4 5 N/A	
20. Teacher maximizes opportunities to respond and engagement time for all students by modifying the organization and rules of the game. (For example, using smaller-sided games like 3v3 instead of 11v11 or allowing two bounces a side for volleyball.)	1 2 3 4 5 N/A	
Equipment		
21. There is a range of equipment to meet the learning needs of all the students in the class. (For example, in a striking unit, the child could use a foam paddle, badminton racket, flat bat, or tennis racket.)	1 2 3 4 5 N/A	
Environment		
22. Noise and distractions are reduced to maximize success.	1 2 3 4 5 N/A	
Assessment		
23. When assessing the class, children with disabilities are assessed alongside their peers and modifications are provided as needed. (For example, a child with a disability may do wall push-ups or curl-ups on a wedge mat, yet he or she is still being assessed along with his or her peers.)	1 2 3 4 5 N/A	
Assessment scores		
24. When children with disabilities are assessed, the scores count at least for their baseline of performance. (For example, when the teacher is collecting scores from the class she will always record the performance of children with disabilities at the same time to ensure inclusion and show that their performance and scores matter. If a child who uses a wheelchair is batting using the TGMD, his or her performance will be recorded and counted to measure present level of performance.)	1 2 3 4 5 N/A	
Skill-related feedback		
25. Feedback on skill performance is given throughout the class to all children when possible.	1 2 3 4 5 N/A	
26. Feedback in regard to skill performance is positive general and/or positive specific feedback with the use of first names. (Children are held to a high standard and not just going through the motions of the performance. The teacher shows that they care about achievement and learning and not just participation.)	1 2 3 4 5 N/A	
Closure		
27. The whole class is together and present when the teacher presents the closure/cool-down of the class.	1 2 3 4 5 N/A	
28. Teacher checks for understanding of all children during closure.	1 2 3 4 5 N/A	
Mean overall score Sum from each item used above / Total number of items used (excluding N/A) = inclusion rating related to effort the teacher makes to include all children. For example, 11 items received a total score of 47 / 11 items (excluding 17 that coded as N/A) = 4.27		

From Lauren J. Lieberman and Cathy Houston-Wilson, 2018, *Strategies for inclusion* (3rd ed.) (Champaign, IL: Human Kinetics).

Please arrive 15 minutes prior to the class start time and remain until all children are dismissed.

Note: It is understood that some of these items may not be within the total control of the physical education teacher. If the physical education teacher makes a good faith effort, for example to get all their children to class on time, but that behavior still does not occur the rater has the option to rate that item as "N/A".

Figure 3.1 provides sample rubrics that can be used to score items on the LIRSPE. These rubrics should help the evaluator understand the variables for LIRSPE items.

Summary

Determining appropriate PE placements for students with disabilities is complex. Once it is determined that a student qualifies for adapted physical education, the next step is to determine how that service will be delivered. Adapted physical education is a *service* and not a placement. The continuum of placement options serves as a guide for determining the LRE for the child. All districts should be able to meet the needs of any placement option. The Suggested Placement for Adapted Physical Education form helps determine appropriate PE placements for students with disabilities. You should be familiar with the special education guidelines for eligibility in your district or state; the district or county special education administrator can assist in accessing such documents. The LIRSPE ensures that inclusive placements are appropriate and meet the students' learning needs. The time, energy, and commitment of team members are worth the effort because students are the ultimate beneficiaries.

FIGURE 3.1

Sample Rubrics

START OF CLASS

1	2	3	4	5
Does not come to class at all but is in school.	Comes to class 10 minutes late and sits on the perimeter.	Comes to class 10 minutes late and is immediately included.	Comes to class 5 minutes late and is immediately included.	Comes to class on time and is immediately included.

WARM-UP

1	2	3	4	5
Class does warm-up and the child with a disability sits out.	Class does warm-up and the child with a disability is peripherally included but not held to the same standard.	Class does warm-up for a certain number of reps; students have to wait for others to finish.	Class does warm-up, but the child with a disability is required to do fewer reps so he or she can finish on time.	Class does timed warm-up; all students start and finish together.

SPEED OF PLAY

1	2	3	4	5
Tennis game is played with no modifications to the serving line, equipment, or rules.	Tennis game is played with modified balls related to the needs of the student, but this seems to be an afterthought.	Tennis game is played with modified balls and rackets if needed.	Tennis game is played with modified balls and rackets if needed, and a variety of places to serve from are clearly defined.	Tennis game is played with modified balls and rackets if needed, and a variety of places to serve from are clearly defined. This is all set up at the beginning of class.

USE OF PARAEDUCATOR

1	2	3	4	5
Child in the class uses a paraeducator, but the paraeducator does not come to PE class at all.	Paraeducator comes sometimes and sits on the side.	Paraeducator helps sometimes but is not sure what to do.	Paraeducator helps when possible and when told what to do.	Paraeducator knows what to do because he or she was trained and given the lesson plans and directions before the class.

GAME, ACTIVITY, OR SPORT

1	2	3	4	5
Teacher plays elimination games; some children sit out when they are eliminated.	Teacher plays elimination games; some children are later tagged back in by peers.	Teacher plays elimination games; some children sit out but can later work their way back in with fitness or motor skills.	Teacher plays elimination games; some children sit out but work their way back in right away with fitness or motor skills.	No elimination games are played.

Individualized Education Plans

Chapter Objectives

After reading this chapter, you will

▶ understand what an IEP is and why it is necessary for students with disabilities;

▶ know the members of the multidisciplinary team and their roles in creating IEPs;

▶ be able to use assessment data to guide the development of an IEP;

▶ know the components of an IEP;

▶ understand the use of goal banks when writing IEPs;

▶ understand the role of physical educators and adapted physical educators in the IEP process; and

▶ know how to incorporate IEP goals and objectives into the GPE curriculum.

Ms. Kelly has been teaching at the same school for the past 14 years, but she has had little contact with students with disabilities because they were previously taught by an APE specialist in self-contained classes. Recently, Ms. Kelly's principal informed her that students with disabilities will now be included in her GPE classes to the extent possible, and the district APE specialist will serve as a consultant to the PE staff. Ms. Kelly will be responsible for teaching students with disabilities and will serve as a member of the multidisciplinary team. In addition, Ms. Kelly will write IEPs based on her students' assessment data. Ms. Kelly feels a little overwhelmed and is unsure of herself, but she knows she needs to do the best job she can for her students. She sought the assistance of her APE consultant, and she is educating herself on the IEP process.

The scenario involving Ms. Kelly may seem familiar; if it doesn't, it may be something you encounter in the future. Because more and more students with disabilities are being included in general education, specifically in PE classes, teachers are being asked to teach *all* children, even if they don't have experience working with students with disabilities. According to Block (2016), many APE specialists are taking on roles as consultants instead of serving as direct care providers. As a result, general physical educators must now give input on physical education for students with disabilities, write IEPs, and serve as members of the IEP multidisciplinary team (Dunn & Leitschuh, 2017; Kowalski, Lieberman, Pucci, & Mulawka, 2005).

As a teacher, you need to understand IEPs to be able to participate in the IEP process. An individualized education plan is a legal document that is developed to ensure high-quality educational programming for students with disabilities. The IEP identifies specific educational needs and determines appropriate resources for addressing those needs for children with disabilities. Students who have one of the 14 disabilities identified in chapter 1 are eligible to receive IEPs (IDEIA, 2004).

The IEP serves as a method of communicating and managing information about a child. The IEP is used to manage data and demonstrate progress in meeting educational benchmarks; identify modifications, supports, and alternatives to traditional education for children in need of such supports; and provide a mechanism whereby services can be agreed upon and written into the plan, thus establishing a commitment by the school to support the child.

One of the services that may be written into the IEP is adapted physical education. Physical education is a required service, so it must be addressed on every IEP. The extent to which physical education is addressed in the IEP will vary depending on the needs of the student. Some students with disabilities can participate in unrestricted general physical education with no modifications. The IEP for a student in this category will indicate general physical education, and the student will follow the general education curriculum. However, a student who has unique needs that require modifications or specially designed physical education will require adapted physical education, and the goals and objectives related to physical education will be developed as part of the IEP. This differs from *related services*, which are provided to students with disabilities to allow them to benefit from their special education services (e.g., not every student with a disability is eligible for speech therapy; only those students who need such a service are eligible). An *adapted* designation on the IEP does not necessarily mean the student receives separate physical education; adapted physical education is a *service* rather than a placement, and the environment in which adapted physical education is provided depends on the needs of the student.

The IEP Process

An important aspect of the IEP process is establishing the multidisciplinary or IEP team. As mentioned in chapter 1, the team consists of

- a representative of the school district who can ensure that all components of the IEP are addressed and that appropriate services are provided;
- a school psychologist who can interpret assessment data;
- teachers (including those for special education and general education as applicable);
- therapists (e.g., physical, occupational, speech; a teacher of the visually impaired; an audiologist);
- physical educators and adapted physical educators;

- other individuals with knowledge or expertise about the child;
- parents or guardians; and
- the child (when appropriate).

The team members meet at least once a year to review student data, determine services needed to support the child, develop appropriate goals and objectives (if applicable), and address any concerns that may arise.

To determine whether a student qualifies for adapted physical education, an assessment must be conducted. Generally, students are assessed in the motor domain, which includes physical fitness. Some students may also be assessed on their cognitive and social-emotional behaviors. Assessments can be standardized or authentic, but they must determine the student's current level of educational performance. Based on the assessment data, eligibility for services and unique needs are determined. If there are motor or other deficits that would compromise the student's ability to participate in the GPE curriculum without restrictions, then adapted physical education is warranted. Individualized goals and objectives (when applicable) are then generated to ensure that the student receives an appropriate education. Once a service or support is identified in the IEP, the school district is held accountable for providing it. Periodic reviews and due process (the right to appeal decisions when disagreements occur) help ensure that an appropriate educational program is provided to the student. The following sections explain the IEP process in greater detail.

The Role of Assessment in IEPs

Questions may arise as to who should assess students' PE abilities. In most cases, the GPE teacher should be able to conduct valid assessments. Some districts employ APE specialists who coordinate adapted physical education throughout the district and conduct the assessments. Other districts might contract out the work to an APE

consultant. Regardless of who conducts the assessment, data generated should determine eligibility for adapted physical education. If assessment results reveal that a student is eligible for services (see the Recommended Eligibility Criteria for Adapted Physical Education sidebar), IEP goals and objectives (when applicable) must be generated.

Various standardized assessments are available to help determine a student's unique motor and fitness needs: the Test of Gross Motor Development 3 (TGMD-3) (Ulrich, 2017), the Bruininks-Oseretsky Test of Motor Proficiency, Second Edition (Bruininks & Bruininks, 2005), and the Brockport Physical Fitness Test (Winnick & Short, 2014). For students who cannot be assessed using standardized tests, authentic assessments are valuable alternatives to determine whether unique needs exist. Regardless of the type of assessment chosen, results provide a means for developing relevant IEP goals and objectives in physical education.

Assessing students' locomotor skills is important for developing IEP goals and objectives.

Recommended Eligibility Criteria for Adapted Physical Education

- The student scores below the 15th percentile on a standardized test.
- The student scores 1 to 2 standard deviations below the mean on a standardized test.
- The student demonstrates a developmental delay of 2 or more years compared to typically developing peers.
- The student fails to meet criterion-referenced standards.
- The student fails to meet at least 70 percent of competency-based standards.

Components of the IEP

If a student is eligible for APE services, the IEP must including the following:

- A statement of the child's educational performance, which is also known as **present level of performance (PLP)**
- Annual goals
- Short-term objectives (when applicable)
- A list of special education and related services that will be provided (see appendix B)
- A list of support services and supplementary aids (as needed)
- A statement describing participation in general physical education
- A schedule of services
- Procedures for evaluation
- A statement describing participation in state- and district-wide assessments (with modifications if necessary)
- A statement describing transition services (if applicable)
- A schedule for parental reporting

These items are described in the following sections.

Present Level of Performance Statement

A PLP statement must be written in objective, observable, and measurable terms and should reflect what the student can accomplish. If a standardized assessment was conducted for the student, the PLP statement should relate to the assessment data. For example, Kiera is an 8-year-old girl with developmental disabilities who was assessed with the TGMD 3 (Ulrich, 2017). Kiera attained scores that placed her in the fifth percentile on both locomotor and object control skills. Using this information, the following PLP statement could be written about Kiera:

> *Kiera scored in the fifth percentile on locomotor skills and the fifth percentile on object control skills as measured with the TGMD 3.*

If the Brockport Physical Fitness Test (Winnick & Short, 2014) was used to assess fitness levels of Zoe, a 15-year-old girl with an intellectual disability, her PLP statement might read as follows:

Zoe completed 8 laps on the 15-meter PACER test as measured with the Brockport Physical Fitness Test.

When standardized tests are not appropriate, authentic assessments may be used to yield PLP statements. Assume you are assessing Julie, a 12-year-old girl with cerebral palsy, on serving the volleyball underhand. Based on task analysis, Julie would need to achieve the following five components: (1) step toward the net with the foot that is opposite the serving arm, (2) put the palm up to hold the ball and make a fist with the serving hand, (3) shift weight forward, (4) contact the ball in front of the body, and (5) follow through. Julie is provided with a lighter trainer ball, and she can step toward the net with the foot opposite her serving arm and contact the ball with her fist. Julie is given five attempts to serve the volleyball trainer underhand from midcourt. She can push the ball off her hand in 2 out of 5 attempts.

You can write PLP statements that use authentic assessment data by using the 3Ps system (Houston-Wilson & Lieberman, 1999). Each P stands for part of the evaluation: *process* describes how the movement is completed, *parameter* is the condition in which the skill is completed, and *product* is the outcome or score of the performance. Each of these terms is explained next.

Process information relates to the form or quality of a movement. Skills can be broken down into component parts through task analysis or the use of checklists. You must use the task analyses for the sport skills that you are teaching to the class and determine which parts a student can accomplish and which parts are lacking (Fronske & Heath, 2015). The parts the student can accomplish are written into the PLP statement, and skill deficiencies are used to formulate annual goals and short-term objectives.

Parameters refer to the conditions under which the skill is performed, such as the type of equipment used, distance at which the skill is executed, environmental arrangement (e.g., indoor, outdoor, group, one-to-one), and levels of assistance (e.g., independent, verbal cue, demonstration, physical assistance). A student's parameters for a skill may change with developmental or motoric gains or increases in independence. Parameters can also be used to formulate annual goals and short-term objectives.

The **product** of a skill relates to the quantitative values produced by the student's performance. Skills are quantified differently depending on the desired outcome, the student's age, and the class goals. Product information answers questions such as how many, how far, how fast, and how long?

Based on her accomplishments, Julie's PLP statement would read as follows:

Julie can underhand serve a volleyball trainer by stepping toward the net with the foot opposite her serving arm while holding the ball in the palm of her hand and pushing the ball forward with her serving hand [process]. She can do this independently from midcourt [parameter] in 2 out of 5 attempts [product].

Employ the Universal Design for Learning in the game to coincide with a student's present level of performance by using a modified ball or moving the student up to half-court.

Annual Goals and Short-Term Objectives

Once the PLP statement is documented, you can develop annual goals and short-term objectives (if applicable) that correspond with the student's present level of performance. Annual goals are **long-term goals** that can be reasonably accomplished in 1 year. For students with severe disabilities, **short-term objectives** must also be included in the IEP. Not all students are required to have short-term objectives, but if they are needed, they should be written in increments to attain the annual goal. Annual goals and short-term objectives must be written in objective, observable, and measurable terms. By adhering to the 3Ps, you can achieve this. The following annual goal is aligned with Kiera's earlier PLP statement based on TGMD 3 assessment data:

Kiera will be able to reach the 16th percentile on locomotor skills and the 16th percentile on object control skills on the TGMD 3.

If Kiera is provided opportunities to improve her locomotor and object control skills over the course of the year and can increase her TGMD 3 score by several points, she will reach the 16th percentile. For Zoe, the following is an appropriate annual goal related to the PACER test:

Zoe will be able to complete 12 laps on the 15-meter PACER test independently as measured with the Brockport Physical Fitness Test and will meet the healthy fitness standard.

If Zoe increases her number of laps on the PACER test, she will meet the healthy fitness standard.

Finally, returning to Julie, the following is an appropriate annual goal:

Julie will be able to independently serve a volleyball trainer using a mature pattern from the serving line in 4 out of 5 attempts.

If Julie needs a short-term objective to reach this standard, it might look like this:

Julie will be able to independently underhand serve a volleyball trainer by stepping toward the net with the foot opposite the serving arm, holding the ball in the palm of her hand and making a fist with the serving hand, shifting her weight forward, contacting the ball in front of her body, and following through with her serving arm from midcourt in 3 out of 5 attempts.

The process has been expanded; Julie is expected to perform all components of the underhand volleyball serve. The parameter is the same (from midcourt), and the product for successfully executing the skill is more rigorous.

List of Special Education and Related Services

This section on the IEP requires a list of services that will be provided to the student and the individual responsible for providing the service. For example, adapted physical education taught by Ms. Michele Walsh would be identified as a special education service, while physical therapy taught by Mr. Robert Martinez would be identified as a related service.

Support Services and Supplementary Aids

Support services and supplementary aids may be needed to instruct students with disabilities. This section outlines the forms of support that can be made available to students based on their unique needs; two typical types are *personnel* and *equipment* support.

Personnel support ensures that individualized instruction or behavioral intervention is available as needed to provide safe and successful educational experiences for learners. Personnel support can include APE consultants, teacher aides and paraeducators, interpreters for deaf students, and trained peer tutors. This is further discussed in chapter 7.

Equipment support ensures that specialized or adaptive equipment is available that allows students to experience high degrees of participation and success. For example, Julie needed a volleyball trainer to successfully serve the ball over the net. Maddie needed a beeper on the basket for basketball. Equipment needs should be based on IEP goals; you must consider what items will be necessary to support the curriculum over the course of a year. Once these areas of support are agreed on, the district is responsible for supplying the requested resources. Specialized equipment can include beep balls, adjustable basketball goals, modified bicycles, bowling ramps, and switches that move or propel objects. Most of this equipment can be purchased through physical activity catalogs and even in the sports section of some local stores.

The student's IEP may specify assistance from a peer tutor.

Participation in General Physical Education

IDEIA (2004) requires that students be educated with their typically developing peers to the extent possible. Only when the nature and extent of a student's disability prevent safe and successful experiences should he or she be removed from the general education setting. Each IEP will have an area that addresses the extent to which the child will participate in the general education curriculum, including in physical education. Even students who are eligible for adapted physical education must be considered for placement in the general education setting. The placement of a student with a disability in adapted physical education can be one of the most difficult decisions a district makes (see chapter 3). IEP team members should look at specific variables that can point them toward placing the student in the LRE that enables success. Variables to consider include the students' sensory needs (i.e., the effect that acoustics, spatial relationships, and class size may have on the student's performance), individual skill sets (e.g., motor skills and physical fitness), and behavioral factors (e.g., ability to work independently or with peers). It is not appropriate, however, to determine placements based on the wishes of the teacher. Lack of training or inexperience should not factor into the decision-making process.

Although legislation requires students with disabilities to receive physical education equal to their typically developing peers, students with disabilities can spend additional time in physical education if it is feasible and if they would benefit. In some cases, students have physical education in inclusive class environments, modified settings, and small-group or self-contained settings. Some students with severe disabilities or medical or behavioral conditions may require self-contained placements to fully benefit from the class, and the IEP should include documentation to justify this.

Schedule of Services

As previously indicated, students with disabilities can receive adapted physical education in a variety of settings. The IEP's schedule of services must identify the nature, frequency, duration, and setting of services that the student will receive. It should also identify groupings for instruction, such as individual, small-group, or whole-class instruction. The schedule for Jamal, a student who can benefit from an inclusive setting and a self-contained, small-group setting, might be as follows:

Jamal will receive adapted physical education 2 times a week for 30 minutes in the general class setting and 2 times a week for 30 minutes in a small-group, self-contained setting. Ms. Walsh, the APE specialist, will accompany Jamal in the general PE setting and provide support as needed and will provide direct instruction to Jamal in the small-group, self-contained setting.

There are situations in which typically developing peers are not required to take physical education (IDEIA, 2004). If it can be demonstrated that lack of physical education will cause a regression of skills for a student with a disability, this justification can be used to ensure that the student receives uninterrupted physical education throughout the year regardless of whether typically developing peers are receiving it. In addition, if a student's disability is such that a break from physical education in the summer months would cause regression, the student might qualify for extended-year services (i.e., 12-month PE instruction).

Procedures for Evaluation

Procedures for evaluation are used to describe and document student progress toward meeting goals. These procedures allow you to recognize when goals and objectives are met or when they are no longer appropriate. If a goal is deemed inappropriate because the student has made little to no progress, the goal can be rewritten. Most schools require teachers to examine and update IEP goals and objectives on a quarterly basis. Examples of evaluation methods include teacher-made tests, rubrics, authentic assessments, standardized tests, criterion-referenced tests, teacher observations of specific skills, and checklists (see chapter 2 for more on these types of assessment).

This part of the IEP also states how parents will be informed about the child's progress. By law, the school must send reports to parents at least as often as their same-age peers' reports are sent home. For example, if a school sends out quarterly report cards, then parents of a child with a disability must also receive progress reports on the same schedule. The school can issue a report card or a progress report or hold quarterly meetings with the student's parents. The physical educator must share student progress at least as often as the progress of peers is shared.

Participation in State- and District-Wide Assessment

With the strong push for accountability, more students with disabilities are being required to participate in state- and district-wide assessments. For students who cannot be assessed in a traditional manner or who cannot participate in state- or district-wide assessments, the law allows for alternative assessments. In these cases, the IEP must include a statement about why the default assessment is not appropriate for the student and identify alternative strategies. Chapter 2 provides more information on alternative assessments for students with severe disabilities.

Transition Services

Transition services are a component of the IEP that addresses life after school with goals related to vocational training, activities for daily living, and recreational programming. You should consider the physical activity and recreational opportunities available in the community after formal schooling is over and embed those activities in the curriculum. Current legislation requires that transition services begin by the time the student is 16 years of age (IDEIA, 2004). Transition services in physical education emphasize lifelong activities and community-based physical activities and address the life skills that will enable students to access these opportunities after they leave school. Examples of transition activities in physical education include hiking at a park, swimming at a public pool, ice skating at a local rink, exercising at the YMCA, or rock climbing at a public facility. See chapter 8 for more information on transition.

Parental Reporting

Finally, the IEP will include a schedule detailing the dates when progress reports will be distributed to parents or guardians. In addition, the schedule will outline dates for IEP annual review meetings.

Electronically Generated IEPs

Time is a restraint for many people, so school districts often use electronically generated IEPs. One popular program, IEP Direct, maintains a goal bank for all curricular subject areas. A **goal bank** is a system in which you choose predetermined numbered goals, objectives, and evaluation procedures and identify the number(s) on a standard grid sheet. Based on the numbers identified on the grid sheet, the computer generates the goals, objectives, and evaluation criteria for each student.

This procedure is controversial because IEPs need to be individualized, and sometimes needed goals and objectives are not included in the goal bank. In addition, you should refrain from using the same goal bank numbers for every student with a disability; you must put thought and effort into your use of a goal bank. If needed goals and objectives are not identified in the goal bank, IEPs should be written up without the goal bank or new goals and objectives should be added to the bank. See the Advantages and Disadvantages of Using Goal Banks sidebar for more information.

Advantages and Disadvantages of Using Goal Banks

Advantages

- Accessibility: Professionals have quick access to files from home or school.
- Continuity: All paperwork is similar in nature in terms of format but individual goals, objectives, and criteria will vary depending on the individual student.
- Efficiency: Goals are easy to track. Multiple professionals can work on one IEP at the same time.
- Quantity: There is an extensive library of goals.
- Consistency: Use of the goal bank ensures consistency of language and minimizes redundancy and errors.

Disadvantages

- Generality: There is a possible lack of fit between goals and individual students' needs.
- Lack of flexibility: Existing goals can't be modified (although you can create new ones).
- Complexity: The program is difficult to navigate.
- Lack of training: There is too little training and insufficient ongoing support.

(Kowalski, McCall, Aiello, & Lieberman, 2009)

Physical Educator's Role in the IEP Process

The thought of being involved in the IEP process for physical education may make even the most enthusiastic teacher uneasy. The time required to participate in meetings and write the IEP adds to an already busy schedule. However, the IEP is a useful tool in securing the supports and services needed to provide high-quality programs for students with disabilities, and as such, it can become your best ally. General physical educators are often left out of the IEP process and therefore do not gain its intended benefits. For example, Block (2016) and Samalot and Lieberman (2017) found that general physical educators were often

- unaware of the existence of an IEP for a particular student,
- aware that the student had an IEP but were given no input in developing it,
- aware of an IEP but not encouraged to review goals and objectives from past IEPs,
- familiar with the IEP but hindered by the fact that it did not address physical education,
- excluded from IEP meetings and the process in general, or
- not seen as part of the multidisciplinary team.

The students are also often unaware of their PE goals and objectives. Researchers found that of surveyed students who were blind or visually impaired, only those who were totally blind were aware that they had IEPs with PE goals and objectives. Students with low vision (i.e., who had travel vision or were legally blind) were less aware of their IEP PE goals and objectives. Furthermore, fewer than 40 percent of the students surveyed knew they had IEP goals and objectives related to physical education, and fewer than 25 percent knew what those objectives were (Lieberman, Robinson, & Rollheiser, 2006).

You have several roles in the IEP process. As previously discussed, you may be called upon to conduct assessments, determine eligibility for services, and report these findings during the IEP meeting. The dates and times of IEP meetings are available from the Office of Special Education in each school district. You should be informed of the meeting dates and times for students under your care. If this information is not readily transmitted, you are encouraged to contact the appropriate personnel and find out for yourself. If you are unable to attend IEP meetings, you should provide written recommendations to the classroom teacher or other individuals, such as parents or guardians, who can speak on behalf of physical education. Other options include having a colleague with a free period teach your PE class or combining classes so that one member of the PE staff can attend the meeting. Districts can also provide substitute teachers if multiple meetings are scheduled in one day (Kowalski, Lieberman, & Daggett, 2006). If physical education is not clearly represented at IEP meetings (whether in written form or by in-person attendance), chances are you will not receive the necessary supports to successfully include these students.

Some school districts require that IEP team members address only those issues and recommendations that relate to the student's present level of performance. During the meeting, the team, especially the parents, can give valuable information and insight about the child's performance, and all this information is taken into consideration when writing the IEP goals and objectives. In other instances, a teacher's draft of the IEP is brought to the meeting, and necessary adjustments are made based on the meeting results. After this meeting, the team has 10 days to complete the full IEP for the parents to review and approve. Only after the team has met and agreed on the student's performance do the members write the IEP. Administrators, parents, and all teachers who participated in writing the IEP must sign the written document to signify agreement.

You should bring the following to an IEP meeting:

- List of student's strengths and weaknesses
- Description of student's learning style
- Assessment results for the student's PLP
- Suggestions for goals and short-term objectives
- Suggestions about extent of inclusion in general physical education
- Suggestions for supports needed in physical education
- Suggestions regarding transition services (if applicable)
- Report on assessment modifications
- Suggested evaluation schedule
- Note-taking materials
- A positive, open mind

After the IEP is approved, the final stage of the process is implementing what is set forth in the IEP in the classroom.

Incorporating Goals and Objectives Into the General Physical Education Class

You are responsible for creating goals and objectives for all your students. Objectives may include improving motor skills, fitness, balance, endurance, cooperation, and teamwork. What happens when a student with a disability has goals and objectives that differ from the rest of the class? This is a common dilemma for teachers of inclusive classes who do not want to separate students with disabilities from their peers. Regardless of the type of lesson or the structure of the class, good physical educators constantly modify and change activities to meet goals and objectives. This process can be used to incorporate a student's IEP goals into class activities. Once you know the student's IEP goals, you can look for situations in which tasks can be incorporated within the current lesson or unit, such as during the class warm-up or cool-down. If the original lesson, game, or activity does not work with a student's goals, you can modify equipment, add a challenge or task, or change a rule to allow the student to work toward his or her goals. Table 4.1 provides examples of how to embed IEP goals into the GPE curriculum.

Incorporating modified games, such as sitting volleyball, into a unit can help meet IEP goals and objectives.

TABLE 4.1   Incorporating IEP Goals in the Inclusive Physical Education Curriculum

IEP goal	Unit	Activity	Description	Equipment and modifications
Improve eye-hand coordination	Volleyball	Toss, set, bump	1. Student 1 (with disability) tosses a ball to student 2, who sets or bumps it back to student 1. 2. Student 1 catches or retrieves the ball to start over. 3. Student 1 takes a turn setting or bumping the ball back to student 2.	Beach balls, volleyball trainers, 8-inch (20-centimeter) playground balls, volleyballs Vary the height of the net.
		Newcomb	1. Students on opposite teams throw and catch the ball over the volleyball net. 2. Students on one side of the net serve the ball over the net to the other side, and players on the other side catch the ball.	Beach balls, volleyball trainers, 8-inch (20-centimeter) playground balls, volleyballs Vary the height of the net.
	Skill theme: catching and throwing	Stations	1. Student 1 (with disability) tosses or throws a ball to student 2, who catches or retrieves it and rolls it back to student 1. 2. Students reverse roles and repeat step 1.	Tennis balls, Wiffle balls, Koosh balls, yarn balls, beanbags Vary the distance between the partners to promote success.
Improve spatial awareness	Dance	Moving in open space	1. Students move to a beat while clapping and stomping without invading other classmates' space. 2. Students perform line dances. 3. Students perform partner dances.	Emphasize the ability to move in open space, group space, and partner space using various forms of dance, beats, instruments, and music.
Improve balance	Gymnastics	Static and dynamic balance	1. Students perform stationary or static balances. 2. Students perform dynamic (moving) balances.	Mats, balance beams, balance boards Create tape lines that students can walk on. Vary the levels of the beams.
Improve upper-body strength	Fitness	Push-ups	1. Wall push-up 2. Isometric push-up 3. Knee push-up 4. Push-up	Use a short cone or therapy ball on the chest for push-ups to ensure a 90-degree angle.

Summary

The IEP is a legal document that is developed to ensure high-quality educational programming for children with disabilities. It serves a variety of purposes, including as a monitoring system to ensure that students with disabilities receive appropriate education. It also serves as a communication system between the school district and a child's family. The IEP is created based on assessment data through the collaborative efforts of a multidisciplinary team. IEPs must address physical education, and qualified students are entitled to adapted physical education. General physical educators and APE specialists play roles in educating students who need adapted physical education. They may be responsible for assessing the student, determining unique needs and eligibility for services, and developing appropriate goals and objectives for the student. Teachers may create their IEP goals and objectives on their own or may use goal banks. No matter which format is used, goals and objectives must be based on individual needs ascertained through assessment.

Managing Student Behavior

Chapter Objectives

After reading this chapter, you will

▶ know how to use proactive strategies to avoid behavioral problems;

▶ be able to determine the purpose of inappropriate behavior;

▶ know how to use positive behavioral supports to improve behavior; and

▶ understand how to implement intervention strategies for managing student behavior.

Deepika is 12 years old and has an attention-deficit/hyperactivity disorder. When she enters the gym, she becomes very excited and wants to move to a new station every 30 seconds. When you talk to her about staying on task, she stares blankly at you.

Tina is 8 years old and has autism; she does not use words to communicate. When she enters the gym, she begins to cry and hit herself on the side of the head.

Doug is 14 years old and has a behavioral disability. During a small-sided game of floor hockey, a puck gets past him and goes into the goal. Doug becomes very angry, runs over to John (the goalie), and starts yelling and cursing at him.

The three opening scenarios suggest the range of behavioral situations that you can face at any given time in a PE class. Being able to positively manage student behavior is an essential component of teaching. Without order, no real teaching can occur. Research has shown that teachers often lack the skills necessary to effectively manage behavior (Lavay, Guthrie, & Henderson, 2014; Lavay, Henderson, French, & Guthrie, 2012). The next section provides strategies to equip you to better handle the behaviors that may occur in a PE class.

Strategies to Avoid Behavior Problems

Teachers who are focused, interested, and skilled at using appropriate pacing greatly reduce the incidence of behavior problems in their classrooms. Ensuring that students are challenged and providing feedback and recognition for skilled and on-task behavior are also key instructional approaches. Even teachers who follow best practices will have incidents of inappropriate student behavior in class, whether due to disability, home life, or other factors (Cothran, Kulinna, & Garrahy, 2009); however, most students (80 percent or more) do not have any major behavioral episodes (Collier, 2007).

You can minimize the chances of such incidents by being proactive in behavior management. The key to effective management is structured teaching. From the beginning, students need to understand what is expected of them (Alstot & Alstot, 2015). For example, students should know

This student was rewarded with an activity she enjoys—playing on a therapy ball—after completing a less-preferred task.

- entry and exit routines,
- signals for stops and starts,
- rules of acceptable behavior, and
- consequences for unacceptable behavior.

Determining, reviewing, and posting class rules and consequences can help you be consistent in handling situations as they arise. You should be a role model by exemplifying the good behavior you would like to see in your students. You can also reduce the chances of inappropriate behaviors by providing developmentally appropriate activities that meet the needs of typically developing learners and learners with disabilities, thus promoting active engagement by all students. Students are much more likely to engage in off-task or inappropriate behavior if the classroom is marked by disorganization, long periods of waiting, or skill demands that are too hard or too easy.

You also need to establish a positive climate for learning, and one way to do this is to provide positive reinforcements for behavior and skill performance. Most researchers believe that 80 to 90 percent of reinforcement should be positive (Lavay, French, & Henderson, 2016). **Positive reinforcement** is offering something of value (e.g., praise, rewards, awards) as a result of a desired behavior in an attempt to increase the frequency of that behavior. For positive reinforcement to be effective, the **reinforcer** must be perceived as valuable to the individual. Something that students consider desirable one day may not be as desirable another day; therefore, you should have a variety of reinforcers available and switch them around from time to

Best Practices
for Administering Positive Reinforcement

- Positive reinforcement should be used when the appropriate behavior is demonstrated.
- Reinforcers must be valued and age appropriate.
- Physical activity should be used as a reinforcing reward and not as a punishment. For example, on successful completion of a task or activity, students can be rewarded with 5 minutes of free jump-rope time at the end of class.
- Initially, reinforce more to achieve the desired goal; then, gradually reduce reinforcers so the appropriate behavior is demonstrated without the reliance on reinforcers (Lavay et al., 2016).

time. Reinforcers can be used as a whole-class or an individual strategy to manage behavior. The sidebar Best Practices for Administering Positive Reinforcement addresses this topic.

You can also promote a positive learning environment by employing a behavior management strategy known as the **Premack Principle**, which essentially uses high-probability activities to reinforce low-probability activities. For the Premack Principle to be effective, you need to be aware of activities that students enjoy (e.g., roller-skating, shooting baskets) that can be used as reinforcers for activities that students don't enjoy. For example, Tina, who was mentioned earlier, enjoys rolling on a therapy ball, but she does not like to do fitness activities. The instructor tells Tina that after she completes 10 curl-ups, she can roll on the therapy ball. Tina completes her curl-ups and is then permitted to roll on the ball. Use various reinforcers so the preferred activity does not become a neutral or less-preferred activity. You should not strictly rely on the Premack Principle to elicit appropriate behaviors because not all nonpreferred actions are reinforced with preferred actions.

A final strategy for mitigating inappropriate behavior is using **negative reinforcement**, in which a negative outcome or aversive stimulus is presented as the consequence for inappropriate behavior. For example, negative reinforcement is being applied if a student perceives detention as aversive, if it is clear to the student that inappropriate behavior will lead to detention, and if the student refrains from inappropriate behavior to avoid detention. In essence, avoiding the aversive stimulus yields appropriate behavior.

Despite using best practices to manage student behavior, you will be faced with students who exhibit inappropriate behaviors. All inappropriate behavior has a communicative function. You must determine what message the behavior is conveying in order to minimize or eliminate it (Alstot & Alstot, 2015). The following section deals with understanding the purpose of the behavior. Often if we can determine why a student is doing what he or she is doing, we can create environments and situations to avoid these behaviors.

Understanding the Purpose
of Inappropriate Behavior

Two methods for determining the purpose of inappropriate behavior are the ABC model and positive behavior support.

The ABC Model

Determining the purpose or the "why" of an inappropriate behavior usually involves some detective work. One common method is known as the **ABC model**, which is based on the principle of applied behavior analysis (ABA). In the ABC model, you first examine the *antecedent* (A), which is what was happening right before the incident occurred; second, you note the actual *behavior* (B); and third, you note the *consequence* of the behavior (C), which is what happened right after the behavior occurred. Detecting the antecedent enables you to modify that variable to eliminate or reduce the recurrence of the inappropriate behavior.

For example, if you determine that when Josh stands in the back of the room he pokes at his peers, moving him to the front of the room may alleviate the inappropriate poking. In addition, you must also note the consequence to see if it positively reinforces the behavior (e.g., if students laugh at Josh's behavior, this may be positively reinforcing him). To see changes in behavior, consequences must be such that the student avoids the behavior to avoid the perceived aversive or undesirable consequence. Inappropriate behaviors will continue if consequences are reinforcing. So if Josh were to poke a peer and his classmates criticize him for the behavior rather than laugh, Josh is less likely to continue the behavior. Or if the consequence for poking a peer is having lunch with his teacher, and Josh perceives that to be nonrewarding, he is likely to refrain from the behavior.

Positive Behavior Support

In addition to the ABC model, **positive behavior support (PBS)** is another behavior management system used to understand the purpose of challenging or inappropriate behavior exhibited by students. PBS is also known as *positive behavioral intervention support* (PBIS), and it provides intervention strategies to remediate challenging or inappropriate behaviors. PBS emerged as an outgrowth of the need for further behavior management in schools. PBS relies on the use of person-centered interventions to modify environments, teach alternatives to inappropriate behavior, and employ meaningful consequences when inappropriate behaviors occur (Wheeler & Richey, 2005). PBS is tied to a **functional behavioral assessment** (FBA), which is a form of assessment used to inform professionals about the function of the behavior. The FBA uses structured interviews with key individuals (e.g., parents, teachers, students) and observations of the student in various settings to gain more information about the behaviors that are exhibited by the student (i.e., what is the function or purpose of the behavior?). Interview questions might include the following: What triggered the behavior? What does the student get out of the behavior? How often does the behavior occur? Who are the individuals present when the behavior occurs? Are there settings where the behavior does not occur? Based on the information gleaned from the FBA, professionals and parents collaborate to problem-solve effective educational programs that teach students more appropriate alternative behaviors (Block, Henderson, & Lavay, 2016). An FBA allows you to

- identify the targeted behavior,
- identify conditions that yield or prevent the targeted behavior,
- identify consequences of the targeted behavior,
- hypothesize about what motivates the targeted behavior, and
- gather baseline data regarding the targeted behavior.

Once information about the targeted behavior is gathered, person-centered interventions are established.

Interventions and Strategies to Improve Behavior

The goal of an intervention strategy is either to increase the occurrence of appropriate behaviors or to decrease or eliminate the occurrence of inappropriate behaviors. Four commonly used procedures for increasing appropriate behaviors are shaping, chaining, prompting, and fading. **Shaping** reinforces approximations that lead to the desired terminal or final behavior. Approximation means any behavior that resembles the desired behavior or takes the person closer to the desired behavior. **Chaining** reinforces a series of related behaviors of the terminal or desired behavior. Chaining is based on task analysis where skills or behaviors are broken down into smaller sequential steps, and steps in the process are reinforced as they are demonstrated. **Prompting** involves giving cues prior to any output. Prompts serve as reminders of what *is* expected and appropriate before any action occurs. **Fading** is the process of gradually removing prompts or reinforcers so that appropriate behaviors occur naturally.

The consequences for inappropriate behaviors should be tailored to the unique characteristics of students. What serves as a displeasing consequence to one student may be appealing to another. For example, if a student who does not like physical education forgets her sneakers and is given the consequence of going to study hall, the consequence is likely to *increase* the chance that she will forget her sneakers again. With this in mind, you should consider an array of consequences and choose those that will be most effective in promoting positive student behaviors.

Time-Outs

One consequence that is overused in education (and elsewhere) is the **time-out**, which is the removal of a child from an environment in which unacceptable behavior occurred. For a time-out to be effective, the student must consider the removal an aversive or undesirable consequence for inappropriate behavior. For example, if a student does not enjoy physical education, removing him from class activity or from the gymnasium might positively reinforce his behavior rather than alleviate it. Experts agree that time-outs should not be viewed only as punishment (Lavay et al., 2016). Instead, they can be used and self-regulated by students who feel that they are about to lose control; prior to taking inappropriate action, the student has the opportunity to regroup and regain composure. In this case, a time-out is not a punishment.

In current practice, however, time-outs are often the only strategy that teachers use to manage behavior, and they are used even for minor infractions. Before using a time-out as a method to manage student behavior, consider the following:

• **What is the purpose of the time-out?** It can be a cooling-off time, an opportunity to regain composure after a blow-up, or a punishment when inappropriate behavior occurs. You should discuss the purpose with students in advance.

• **Where will students go to take the time-out?** A designated area should be set up in the gymnasium so it is clear to students where they will go for a time-out. You must be sure you can always see the student during the time-out.

• **How long will the student need to stay in the time-out?** Some suggest a ratio of 1 minute for each year of the child's age, but we do not recommend this strategy; in a typical 30- to 40-minute PE class, a child who is 10 years old could miss one-third of the class. You need to determine how long a time-out should last for each infraction. Similarly, in situations where students are using the time-out to self-regulate behavior, they should have the opportunity to determine for themselves (within reason) the time needed to serve the purpose. Even 30 seconds sitting out of a preferred activity can be a long time to a third grader.

- **What type of infraction will lead to a time-out?** Make sure that the punishment fits the crime. For example, Mahmoud pushed his peer while waiting in line for a game. He was given one warning, but he did it again. Because Mahmoud likes the game and it was his first time exhibiting that behavior, he was given a 30-second time-out. After he apologized, he was allowed back in the game. Don't overuse time-outs by assigning them for minor infractions. Identify which behaviors will lead to time-outs.

- **How will the student know when to return to the activity?** Once a time limit has been established, have a stopwatch or timer available so that the student can see when it is time to return. Sometimes teachers inadvertently leave students in time-out for too long because they forget.

- **What happens after the time-out has been served?** The final step in effectively using a time-out is to plan to debrief with the child after the time-out. You should discuss what happened that led to the time-out and help the student develop strategies for handling the same situation if it arises again. Teaching alternatives to inappropriate behavior is the key to managing student behavior.

Token Economy

A **token economy** deploys tokens as positive reinforcers for appropriate behavior. Tokens can be plastic chips, stickers, checkmarks, or any other item that can be collected or tallied and redeemed for something of value to the student. For a token economy to be effective, you must make students aware of the targeted acceptable behavior and the number of tokens needed to gain the privilege or item of interest (Loovis, 2017).

Contracts

The use of contracts relies heavily on consequences. Contracts are written documents that outline terms of acceptable behavior and consequences for acceptable and unacceptable behavior. Contracts are signed by the student, the teacher, and, in some cases, the parents. Ensure that the contract is achievable (i.e., with appropriate support the student can meet the terms of the contract). Approximations of the desired behavior should also be included in the contract to ensure that goals are realistic. If it becomes apparent that the contract goals are unattainable, then the contract can be renegotiated.

Strategies to Decrease Inappropriate Behavior

There are several other behavioral intervention strategies that can be tailored to the unique characteristics of students and will contribute to the maintenance of a positive climate.

- **Differential reinforcement of other behaviors.** In this approach you provide reinforcement to a student who exhibits any appropriate behavior and does not perform the unacceptable behavior. For example, if the unacceptable behavior is banging equipment on the floor, the student is reinforced for demonstrating an activity, answering a question, or helping a peer as long as the student was not banging the equipment on the floor.

- **Differential reinforcement of incompatible behaviors.** This strategy can be used when a student engages in behaviors that are the opposite of the unacceptable behavior. For example, if talking out is an unacceptable behavior that has been targeted for change, the student is reinforced every time he or she raises a hand to ask or respond to a question.

- **Differential reinforcement of low rates of behavior.** This approach is used when a student reduces unacceptable behaviors or increases acceptable behaviors. For example, if the unacceptable behavior is refusal to participate in activities, then each time the student participates in any form of appropriate activity, he or she is reinforced.

Summary

This chapter provides strategies for managing student behavior in PE classes. The proactive strategies herein will help you create environments that reduce the chance of inappropriate behaviors. Even the best class managers will encounter students who engage in inappropriate behaviors (due to disability or other risk factors), and this chapter presents intervention strategies that use a positive behavior support model. Interventions are tailored to the individual interests of students to help them positively modify their behavior.

Universal Design for Learning

Chapter Objectives

After reading this chapter, you will

▶ know the Universal Design for Learning (UDL) approach and how it is used in physical education;

▶ understand self-determination theory and promoting the rights of all students;

▶ incorporate differentiated instruction to promote Universal Design for Learning in physical education;

▶ know the process and methods for adapting activities;

▶ understand and be able to implement variations related to equipment, rules, environment, and instruction; and

▶ infuse the Paralympic games into the physical education curriculum.

Mrs. Starble is an elementary PE teacher. She has a kindergarten class that includes one child with diplegia cerebral palsy (Mayumi) and one child who has a visual impairment (Enrique). The district uses a common online curriculum that does not provide Universal Design for Learning options; therefore, Mrs. Starble needs to come up with ways to accommodate all the students in her class. Mrs. Starble plans all her lessons with the universal design approach. She provides various skill levels for each activity, numerous equipment choices, and various ways to execute assessments. For example, during a jump-rope unit she ties one end of a rope to a tree at 2 feet (0.6 meters) and slopes the rope to the ground; children can jump over the rope at the level at which they feel comfortable. In addition, when students are doing yoga poses, Mrs. Starble allows them to use the wall or a fence for balance. During activities students also get to choose the equipment they feel most comfortable using. Mrs. Starble has 100 percent participation in her class, and she embraces the Universal Design for Learning approach.

Universal Design for Learning (UDL) emerged from the field of architectural design. When federal legislation began requiring universal access to buildings and other structures for individuals with disabilities, architects began to design universally accessible buildings rather than retrofitting standard structures. Building on this architectural principle, UDL is a strategy for eliminating barriers to student learning, and it includes Universally Designed Instruction (UDI), Universally Designed Curriculum (UDC), and Universally Designed Assessment (UDA) (Meyer & Rose, 2000; Rapp, 2014; Rose & Meyer, 2002). There are numerous examples of UDL in our everyday lives. For example, a curb cut enables a person who uses a wheelchair to access a sidewalk. It also makes travel easier for individuals who use walkers, strollers, and bicycles or who are having trouble negotiating curbs. Closed-captioned television programming is another example. It helps persons who are hard of hearing or deaf to follow TV programs. It also helps people with typical hearing who are watching TV in a noisy room or have the volume turned down. Finally, universal symbols that communicate function, such as those on traffic signs, are helpful to individuals who have trouble reading or do not speak the local language (Spooner, Baker, Harris, Ahlgrim-Delzell, & Browder, 2007). These principles can easily be applied to physical education.

Universal Design in Physical Education

Universal design is a concept, a set of principles, a framework, and a frame of mind that supports accessibility for the heterogeneity found in classrooms today and encourages teachers to explore new ways of delivering instruction and assessment (Bowes & Tinning, 2015). The UDL curriculum in physical education provides students with disabilities access to the same learning outcomes as their typically developing peers. The opening scenario demonstrates that games and activities can be adapted and still be fun and effective in helping all students meet their PE goals. The adjustments Mrs. Starble made were ideal for Mayumi and Enrique, as well as for all learners, and it was not difficult to come up with a few variables to ensure inclusion of everyone. Many teachers feel ill equipped to accommodate students with disabilities in their classes. The goal of this chapter is to provide you with teaching strategies for including students with disabilities by making the curriculum accessible and ensuring the success of all students.

The UDL curriculum in physical education gives all students access to the same learning outcomes.

Creating a UDL Curriculum in Physical Education

In a recent review of the literature, Haegele and Sutherland (2015) found that students with disabilities were bullied and socially isolated by their typically developing peers (Healy, Msetfi, & Gallagher, 2013; Moola, Fusco, & Kirsh, 2011). As a teacher, you have control over the curriculum you provide, and you can make modifications to promote the success of all students, which in turn minimizes negative behaviors exhibited by peers. Modifications can decrease concerns about the competence of students with disabilities and reduce negative peer interactions because the modifications make task completion easier and do not draw attention to deficits. Research has shown that modifying the curriculum reduces skill-level discrepancies and improves student attitudes (Brian & Haegele, 2014; Coates & Vickerman, 2008; de Schipper, Lieberman, & Moody, 2017; Spencer-Cavaliere & Watkinson, 2010).

Self-Determination Theory Applied to Physical Education

All people should get to make their own choices. In doing so, self-determination is promoted. **Self-determination theory** posits that people have three basic psychological needs: competence (need to feel capable and have control over the outcome of a situation), connectedness (need for relationships with others), and autonomy (need for control over their life, or independence) (Deci & Ryan, 1983). Creating situations that give all students equal opportunities for participation and allow them to make choices to have success over the outcome will enhance self-determination. For example, if Mayumi's peers are taught 13 units, then Mayumi should be involved in the same 13 units, although it is appropriate to make modifications and adjustments to meet her needs. Considering what Mayumi may need to be successful in the unit is the premise behind Universal Design for Learning.

When individuals with disabilities are included with their peers in normal activities, they are viewed as valued in society (Wolfensberger, 1972). The practice of valuing all persons can be promoted by offering units in which all students can participate and succeed. The underlying principle of UDL is the consideration of the range of student abilities at the curriculum design stage; the curriculum then includes the necessary accommodations for students with and without disabilities (Lieberman, Lytle, & Clarcq, 2008; Rapp & Arndt, 2012). To ensure that all students are being valued, ask yourself whether students with disabilities have the same choices and options as their typically developing peers. If the answer is no, then adaptations will need to be made.

Differentiated Instruction

UDL-PE ensures that the physical, social, and learning environments are designed so that diverse learners are supported through variations in the teaching and learning process (Perez, 2014). Universal design is achieved by modifying teaching to meet the needs of every student; this concept is also referred to as **Differentiated Instruction**. Differentiated Instruction provides alternative methods of teaching students that tap into their preferred learning modality such as visual, auditory, or kinesthetic. It also makes accommodations with regard to materials and equipment used and allows for students to respond in a variety of ways to demonstrate their abilities (Odem, Brantlinger, Gersten, Thompson, & Harris, 2005; Rapp, 2014).

When teachers fail to create a UDL environment and are unwilling to differentiate instruction, students suffer. For example, students have expressed that activities that are not modified for their needs can be too challenging for their physical ability levels and the speed of activities in physical education can be too fast for them, creating a stressful experience and undermining their self-determination. The inability to keep up in activities can lead to embarrassment and further negative social interactions with peers (Bredahl, 2013; Healy et al., 2013). Experiences like these can be avoided if you are willing to adapt and modify your classroom activities based on the needs of all students before the unit starts. Adapting activities so students with disabilities feel like they contribute to the success of the class is essential in creating an inclusive environment (Spencer-Cavaliere & Watkinson, 2010).

Universal design uses instructional materials and activities that allow achievement of learning goals by individuals with wide differences in their abilities to see, hear, speak, move, read, write, understand English, attend, organize, engage, and remember. Designing this curriculum before instruction begins enables you to provide each student with appropriate physical education without having to make spur-of-the-moment adaptations to meet student needs. Equipment, instructions, rules, and environmental variations that meet the standards of UDL help students learn. These variations support motivation to learn by offering multiple ways to engage with the lessons, which enables learners with various preferences and abilities to find avenues that match their needs (Block, Hutzler, Barak, & Klavina, 2013; Lieberman & Block, 2016). As demonstrated in the opening scenario, the variables offered by Mrs. Starble provided enough variation to ensure that all students in the class could participate. This environment was set up ahead of time with all students in mind, which created a welcoming and encouraging learning space for all. The Instructional Methods That Employ the Principles of Universal Design sidebar can make your class content accessible to students with a wide range of abilities.

Instructional Methods That Employ the Principles of Universal Design

- **Inclusiveness.** Create a classroom environment that respects and values diversity. Avoid stigmatizing or segregating any student (Rapp & Arndt, 2012).
- **Physical access.** Ensure that classrooms, gymnasiums, fields, pools, and courts are accessible to individuals with a wide range of physical abilities. In addition, provide a wide range of equipment options (e.g., a variety of rackets, balls, bats, flotation devices, mats) (Hodge, Lieberman, & Murata, 2012).
- **Delivery modes.** Use multiple modes to deliver content. Alternate your methods of delivering instruction by using demonstrations, posters, discussions, explanations, videos, hands-on activities, and multisensory approaches. Ensure that each mode is accessible to students with a wide range of abilities, interests, and previous experiences (Rapp, 2014).
- **Interaction.** Encourage various ways for students to interact with each other and with you, such as class questions and discussions, group work, individual demonstrations, routines, station work, and group dances and demonstrations (Rapp, 2014).
- **Feedback.** Provide appropriate feedback based on student output. Feedback can be given on skill performance as well as behavior. Use both positive and corrective feedback to shape desired outcomes.
- **Assessment.** Provide multiple ways for students to demonstrate knowledge, understanding, and skills. In addition to traditional tests, consider group work, demonstrations, routines, station work, portfolios, and presentations (Rapp, 2014).

Process of Adapting Activities

You must consider the entire class before you engage in planning. Individual units in the curriculum must be fluid in their makeup, instruction, and implementation, and the modification of equipment, rules, and instructions is integral in planning for units and lessons. To ensure that each student is fully included in the class, answer the following preplanning questions (Bowes & Tinning, 2015; Getchell & Gagen, 2006; Rapp, 2014):

- What can the student see?
- What can the student hear?
- Does the student have additional disabilities?
- How does the student ambulate?
- Are any activities contraindicated based on the student's disability?
- What is the student's previous experience in physical activity?
- What can the student do related to motor skills and fitness?
- How does the student perform?
- What does the student like?

Next, determine the goal of the game or unit (Grenier, Dyson, & Yeaton, 2005), such as endurance, upper-body strength, cooperative learning, or skill development. You must also consider specific objectives and how they relate to the student's IEP (Kowalski, Lieberman, Pucci, & Mulawka, 2005). Recall Enrique, who was mentioned in the chapter opener and has a visual impairment. Enrique can run with a guide, along a wall, or with a guidewire. He also has good upper-body strength. These capabilities represent Enrique's function (e.g., how he moves and manipulates objects). IEP goals for Enrique are related to his areas of need, such as abdominal strength, endurance, independence, and socialization. By participating in a modified soccer game using scooters and a bright Omnikin ball, Enrique can work on abdominal strength, endurance, independence, and socialization with his peers. All students, no matter their abilities, must be held to high expectations so they can reach their full potential.

The benefits of employing UDL cannot be underestimated. They include

- full access to content for all,
- increased motivation in all learners,
- increased active participation by all learners,
- increased learning of curricular content,
- increased acceptance of students with disabilities by their peers,
- reduced time spent figuring out how to accommodate various learners once the unit has begun, and
- reduced frustration for all parties.

See the Basic Principles for Adapting Activities sidebar.

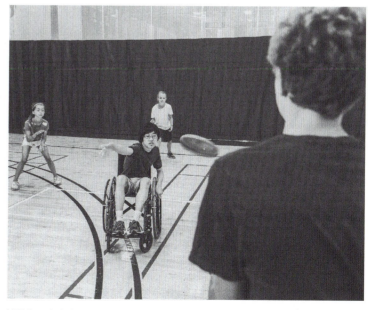

UDL leads to increased active participation of all students.

Basic Principles for Adapting Activities

- When possible, include students with disabilities in adaptation decisions. Some students will not mind having the activity modified to ensure success. In middle school and high school, however, many students with disabilities prefer to fit in rather than be successful, and they may not welcome an adaptation that makes them seem different. You must first consider the student's attitude toward the activity, peers, and him- or herself. Universal Design for Learning applies to *all* students, so if the modifications are for all students then students with disabilities may not feel as marginalized as if the modifications were just for them.
- Give the student as many choices as possible. The more types of equipment, teaching styles, rule modifications, and environmental options you provide, the greater the chance that the student can make a choice that will enable him or her to be successful in the activity. You can also discuss all options with the student prior to the unit and allow him or her to try out a few to make the best decisions. This way, the student can start the unit with success, and you can make further adaptations if needed (Haegele & Sutherland, 2015).
- Physical assistance is acceptable and is preferred over sitting out of an activity. Physical cues, hand-over-hand aid, and total physical assistance are appropriate to ensure participation in the activity. The amount of assistance should be decreased when possible (Grenier & Lieberman, 2018).
- If a modification is not working, change it as soon as possible to facilitate success.
- Students with disabilities should be offered the same variety of sports, games, and recreational activities as their peers. This approach maximizes the chance that students will learn lifetime activities and a variety of skills.
- Community-based activities should be included in the curriculum whenever possible. Practice these activities in a community setting (e.g., ice skating at a public rink) to increase the likelihood that students will continue the activity outside of class (Samalot & Aiello, 2018; Samalot & Lieberman, 2016).
- Adaptations should be continually evaluated and changed as needed. As a student's independence increases, or if the student becomes frustrated or embarrassed, modify the adaptation to meet the student's need (Block et al., 2013).
- Determine all modifications of the lesson plan at the beginning of the unit. Consider all students in the class when developing lessons; do not adapt as an afterthought.

Types of Adaptation

Many students with disabilities need adapted environmental variables so they can be successful, and these adaptations help them attain control over their lives (Grenier, Rogers, & Iarrusso, 2008). For example, if equipment, rules, environment, and instruction had not been modified, Mayumi and Enrique would have had fewer activities available to them; however, because basic principles for adapting activities were applied, Mayumi and Enrique know how to play the same games as their peers. This contributes to their self-determination, which will ultimately empower them to make decisions, advocate for their needs, and enjoy a better quality of life.

In many cases, parents are the strongest advocates for their children, and they should be consulted for functional ideas when you are incorporating modifications into lessons at the beginning of the school year (Perkins, Columna, Lieberman, & Bailey, 2013). In addition, you should share successful modifications with parents so they can implement them during leisure time.

The following sections address four types of modifications: equipment, rules, environment, and instruction (Lieberman et al., 2008). Some variables fit into more than one area, so we tried to put each in the most appropriate section.

Equipment Modifications

Equipment modifications allow the participant to be more successful than he or she would be using the unmodified equipment. Equipment modifications are among the most common modifications that you can make to encourage desired movement (Getchell & Gagen, 2006). Students with disabilities may need to have equipment adapted for any number of reasons, including limited mobility, limited grip strength, lack of vision or hearing, decreased cognitive function, or inability to attend for a long period (Bevans, Sanchez, Fitzpatrick, & Forrest, 2010). Examples of equipment modifications include the use of beeper balls, guide wires, Velcro mitts, longer rackets, and softer balls. Remember that equipment should be age appropriate. Research has shown that using modified equipment does not hinder students' performance on motor skills (Lieberman, Haibach, & Wagner, 2014); therefore, modified equipment can be used by the whole class, which supports inclusion of students with disabilities.

As the following scenario involving Tamiqua shows, a few minor equipment modifications and rule changes can greatly improve the opportunities for students with disabilities:

Tamiqua is a ninth-grade girl with a spinal cord injury; her legs are paralyzed, but she has full use of her arms. She uses a wheelchair to ambulate, and she can move her chair independently. Before the tennis unit, the PE teacher worked with Tamiqua, the paraeducator, and Tamiqua's mother to identify necessary modifications. They decided to try using a badminton racket and Nerf tennis balls to build strength and coordination. At first Tamiqua could not get the timing right and became frustrated, so they switched to a balloon. By the second week of the unit, they switched back to the Nerf tennis ball and used a two-bounce rule. Over time, Tamiqua transitioned to a tennis racket and tennis ball, and she has begun playing tennis with her brothers on weekends. These adaptations enabled Tamiqua to be successful in her PE class, and now she also has an activity she can participate in with family and friends.

In this case, modifications led Tamiqua down a path toward beginning tennis. There are no limitations on how much she can improve her tennis skills and her upper-arm strength, mobility, and speed.

Rule Modifications

A rule modification can involve any deviation from the original or accepted rules of the game. You must create an atmosphere of flexibility among all participants. There are many ways to play a game, and all players must be open-minded and willing to try new things.

Examples of rule modifications include slowing down the pace of a game, allowing more chances, taking away rules, not using a defender, limiting or adding responsibilities, and making sure all players are involved

Tamiqua participates in tennis with a rule modification that allows two bounces instead of one.

Finnigan is successfully included in the softball unit with some minor rule adaptations.

before a team can score. You can also change a task for a specific skill; for example, offering the option of throwing a ball instead of striking it or kicking a stationary ball instead of a rolling ball. Low-organized games with few rules lend themselves to accommodating many students (White, Casebolt, & Hull, 2004).

For many students, inclusion in a game with traditional rules would be impossible; therefore, you must consider alternative rules to ensure inclusion of all students in general physical education. Consider the following example:

Finnigan is a fifth grader with mild cerebral palsy. He can run, but he is slower than his peers because he has a scissors gait. The class completed a disability awareness unit and learned how Finnigan functions in different situations. Before each unit, the PE teacher, Mr. Short, allows all students in the class (including Finnigan) to brainstorm appropriate adaptations for Finnigan and the class. In the softball unit, for example, Finnigan uses the option to bat off a tee, runs, and fields on his own, but he also uses the option to score a run for every base he touches (e.g., if he runs to second base before being called out, he scores two runs). This simple rule modification accommodates his mild disability, and a few other students took advantage of these choices as well. The class is very accepting, and they fight over which team Finnigan will be on! Finnigan considers himself a good softball player, and he plans to join a summer league so he can continue to play the game.

Environmental Modifications

Environmental modifications may be needed to successfully include students with disabilities. Often, necessary modifications are not conceived of until a problem arises, but it is never too late to modify the environment to increase a person's success (Block et al., 2013; Petersen & Piletic, 2006). Environmental modifications include decreasing distractions, increasing visual cues, limiting noise, changing lighting, and increasing accessibility of the playing area. Modifications can also address access to facilities (Petersen & Piletic, 2006). Environmental modifications can greatly increase the involvement of students with disabilities in physical education (Healy et al., 2013; Menear & Davis, 2007). In the following case of Nikolai, swimming in the designated area was not possible or conducive to his learning:

Nikolai is a third grader who moved to a new school district midyear. Nikolai has autism and limited communication skills. The IEP team found no goals related to physical education, even though adapted physical education was checked off on the front page of his IEP. They had no idea what Nikolai could do or what he needed in terms of instruction. The PE teacher, Mr. Wilkinson, wanted Nikolai to receive his APE program in the GPE class. The class was working on a 3-week swimming unit, and Nikolai's mother signed the permission form for swimming and indicated that he swims at an intermediate level. Mr. Wilkinson was happy about that and allowed Nikolai's paraeducator, Ms. Bernstein, to go into the pool with him. While Mr. Wilkinson was instructing all students on rhythmic breathing in the shallow end, Nikolai began screaming and pushing away from his paraprofessional. He continually tried to swim away from the group toward the deep end. He would not calm down. Because he had no verbal communication skills, the teachers didn't know what was wrong. After 15 minutes of struggling to keep

Nikolai in the shallow end, Mr. Wilkinson instructed Ms. Bernstein to allow him to swim away from the group as she shadowed him. This was the answer to the problem. Nikolai's autism made him hypersensitive to the noise and distractions of his peers. He could not tolerate swimming in the shallow end with the other students. With a simple modification in the environment (using the deep end of the pool), Nikolai was able to follow Ms. Bernstein's directions, and his swimming improved greatly during the 3-week unit. He even started using a trained peer tutor in the deep end, and this tutor became his friend.

Keep in mind that changing the environment is not always as simple as it was in Nikolai's case; oftentimes, you must have additional permission or personnel (e.g., another lifeguard). Other examples of environmental manipulations include changing lighting, closing folding doors, covering windows that create glare, or minimizing decorations that distract. The increased involvement of students with disabilities is the reward for the extra work of changing the environment.

Instructional Modifications

You can modify the way you teach a class to better accommodate all learners. In some cases, teaching in small groups or using individualized instruction can help students (Lieberman, Cavanaugh, Haegele, Aiello, & Wilson, 2017). In other cases, you may have to modify your method of teaching a skill. The following four teaching methods are listed from least invasive to most invasive:

1. Use verbal cues to explain what you want the student to do. Your cues should be
   - clear, specific, concise, and free of jargon and slang;
   - communicated in a way the student understands;
   - repeated in a different way if the student does not understand the first time;
   - used with demonstration to ensure understanding (if the student has usable vision); and
   - given in such a way that the student has time to process them.
2. Demonstrate or model (through pictures or actions) what you want the student to do (Waugh, Bowers, & French, 2007). Your demonstrations should be
   - in the student's field of vision;
   - done by someone close to the student's size and ability; and
   - shown in a whole-part-whole manner when possible (i.e., demonstrate the whole skill, then the task-analyzed parts, then the whole skill again).
3. Physically assist or guide the student through the desired skill or movement. Your assistance should be
   - thoroughly documented (i.e., where you physically assisted, how much assistance you gave, how long you assisted);
   - preceded by telling the student you are going to touch him or her; and
   - decreased to normal touch cues when possible.
4. Allow the learner to feel you (or a peer) while you execute a skill or movement that the student didn't understand using the three previous approaches (Lieberman & Cowart, 2011; Lieberman, Ponchillia, & Ponchillia, 2013). Be sure to
   - tell the student where and when to feel you (or a peer) executing the skill;
   - document when and where the student touched you (or a peer) and why;
   - repeat the actions as many times as necessary to ensure understanding; and
   - combine this with other teaching methods to increase understanding.

In some cases, these techniques need to be paired (e.g., verbal cueing and modeling). You can also modify your instructional approach; some common approaches include the following:

- **Direct instruction.** Tell students what to do and how to do it; then, actively observe the learners and provide feedback.

- **Task teaching.** Use a series of task cards (which can be written in braille or rendered in pictures, if needed) to show the steps that lead to the achievement of an instructional objective. Task teaching allows different students to practice different tasks at the same time. A similar approach is used in station teaching or learning centers.

- **Guided discovery.** Use a series of questions or short statements to guide students in a series of steps that result in the discovery of a movement solution that meets the intended criteria.

- **Problem-solving.** Use a series of questions to generate multiple solutions to a given problem. For example, ask the class how many different ways they can balance on three points, two points, and then one point.

These instructional approaches should be varied depending on the task demands and intended outcomes.

You can also consider changing the class organization for a lesson. Besides whole-class instruction, organization forms can include small groups or squads, stations, pairs, and individual work.

You can also use a multisensory approach when providing instructions in which you tap into the students' preferred learning modes (e.g., auditory cues, visual demonstrations, tactile methods). This combination approach ensures that all students' learning modes are addressed. This complies with the concept of teaching with a universal design in mind.

Infusing the Paralympics Into the Curriculum

Another approach to universally designing the curriculum is to infuse Paralympic sports. The 2016 Paralympics brought intense excitement with 23 Paralympic sports. There were 528 events over the course of 11 days of competition that yielded 225 medals for women, 265 for men, and 38 mixed medals. Around 4,350 athletes from more than 160 countries traveled to Rio de Janeiro, Brazil. The individuals who competed in the Paralympics had disabilities that included impaired muscle power (e.g., paraplegia and quadriplegia, muscular dystrophy, post-polio syndrome, spina bifida), impaired passive range of movement, limb deficiency (e.g., amputation or dysmelia), leg length difference, short stature, hypertonia, ataxia, athetosis, vision impairment, and intellectual impairment.

Many students are not familiar with the disability sports offered at the Paralympics or the level of athleticism of the elite athletes who participate. Infusing the Paralympics into physical education can increase awareness of geography of countries participating, sociology of cultures related to disability, history of sports and countries' participation in the Paralympics, and understanding of the triumph of the human spirit (Grenier, Wright, Collins, & Kearns, 2014). Adding Paralympic content into the physical education curriculum is not difficult and only takes some time and creativity (Grenier & Kearns, 2012; Tepfer & Lieberman, 2012).

Infusing Paralympic sport into the physical education curriculum allows students to gain an understanding of a variety of Paralympic sports and how they are played. Please be aware that individuals in the disability community do not support disability simulations for their own sake (Lalvani & Broderick, 2013; Leo & Goodwin, 2016).

These disability sport experiences must be introduced with sensitivity and respect in mind. Do not promote pity, misfortune, or a superhero attitude. The emphasis should be on the experience of playing the sport, the skills involved in the sport, and ability of each individual to perform and compete in the activity.

Paralympic sports are primarily typical sports slightly modified to accommodate the competing individuals and their disability classification. Many Paralympic sports mirror the content taught in a physical education curriculum such as track and field, swimming, archery, soccer, wheelchair basketball, quad rugby, and sitting volleyball. Infusing Paralympic sports into the curriculum could involve including a day or two of the sport during the specific unit being taught. For example, when the unit is volleyball, include a day of sitting volleyball; for basketball, include a day of wheelchair basketball (if you have access to wheelchairs); for soccer, include a day of 5-a-side soccer (visual impairment) or soccer for people with cerebral palsy; for boccia, have a day of boccia from a seated position or wheelchair or offer alternative ways of tossing the ball. In doing so, students learn how the sport is played in the Paralympics. There are a few sports that are unique to the specific disability and to the Paralympics such as goalball. This can be taught as its own unit and would be a more significant curricular change. For the rules and ways to infuse these sports, see Davis (2011) or visit the United States Association of Blind Athletes website (usaba. org) (Lieberman, 2016).

Providing students with a visual of the sport, such as a YouTube video or a video of the sport being played at an elite level, allows students to fully comprehend the skill and intensity involved in the sport. This approach also allows the instructor to explain the rules and strategies of the game. The 2016 Paralympics were the most televised in history. NBC and NBCSN showed 66 hours of coverage from the Paralympic Games in Rio de Janeiro, Brazil, an increase of 60.5 hours from the coverage of the London 2012 Paralympic Games. These videos and others are easily found through web searches (Lieberman, 2016).

Add a Paralympic Day or Week to the Curriculum

Another option would be to add a Paralympic day, week, or unit to the curriculum. In this approach students would experience a variety of Paralympic sports in a short time frame. Students would get an overview of several sports as well as the opportunity to see the sports being played before they play. One suggestion is to divide classes into different countries in order to compete for medals or recognition (i.e., one class represents the United States, another class represents Mexico, a third class represents Japan, and so on).

Offer a Paralympic Night at Your School

During a Paralympic night families can be invited to listen to an overview of Paralympic sports and watch or participate in competition. Students can practice the sports before the event so they can show their families how the sport is played.

Topics can include the history of the sport, the country of origin, and medal winners. If possible inviting Paralympians to the event can create excitement and educate all about possibilities in sport.

Bring in Role Models to Speak

There is nothing like the experience of the Paralympics from the voice of a Paralympian. This can be done in person if the athlete lives nearby or through online video chat if the Paralympian lives farther away. Meeting a Paralympian brings the

Martha Ruether

Martha Ruether is a first-time Paralympic swimmer with a visual impairment. She is from western New York and is part of the U.S. team. See www.teamusa.org/para-swimming/athletes/Martha-Ruether for more information.

Photo courtesy of Maureen Ruether.

Paralympics to life and shows the participants what can be accomplished, disability or not (Lieberman, 2016). See the Martha Ruether sidebar for an example.

Keep in mind that if there is a student in the class with a specific disability it is always a good idea if the sports offered and role models selected include that particular disability. Children with disabilities have the right to see athletes similar to themselves and play sports specifically designed for individuals such as themselves. All children also need to see athletes of all abilities and skills. An added benefit is that their peers will then see them playing a sport, being the leader, and truly having no barriers in competition.

This is a perfect way to infuse Paralympic content into the curriculum to raise awareness and infuse geography, history, and sociology. It is also a time that everyone can celebrate the accomplishments of all athletes and imagine a future where everyone can participate in sports at their level (Lieberman, 2016).

Summary

UDL can assist you in teaching students with disabilities in inclusive PE classes. The principles for adapting activities are based on UDL literature and self-determination theory. Keep in mind that UDL stresses preplanning for every unit and every lesson. The adaptation strategies presented here (i.e., equipment, rules, environment, and instruction) allow students with disabilities to achieve their IEP goals and objectives. By facilitating success in physical education, you can empower students with disabilities to consistently involve themselves in physical activities, sports, and recreation with friends and family. Lastly, it is always exciting and fun to infuse Paralympic sports into the curriculum to aid in awareness and understanding and increase enjoyment for everyone!

7

Support Personnel

Chapter Objectives

After reading this chapter, you will

- ▶ be able to determine what types of support personnel are needed to help individualize instruction in an inclusive PE class;
- ▶ understand the advantages of using peer tutors, paraeducators, senior citizens, and college students; and
- ▶ know how to plan and implement training programs for support personnel.

Maura is a ninth grader who is blind. When Maura was in middle school, she was placed in an inclusive PE class; however, her teacher was afraid she would get hurt, so he let Maura sit in the locker room and read during class. Over the summer, Maura attended a camp for students with visual impairments, became more physically active, and made the cross-country team. She is determined to participate in physical education with her peers in high school.

Maura's PE class is scheduled at the same time as her paraeducator's mandatory break. As a result, Maura has once again been sidelined, and her hopes of participating in physical education with her peers are shattered. Maura's parents are very upset that Maura is still being excluded from physical education. They called the school and set up a meeting to discuss the situation. In addition to violating the terms of her IEP, the situation compromises the confidence Maura gained over the summer. The meeting consisted of the PE director, the PE teacher, the district's new APE specialist, the paraeducator, and Maura. They had a productive meeting and came up with several viable options to support Maura in physical education. First, they would train several of Maura's friends to serve as peer tutors in class. Second, they paired her with a different paraeducator who was available during the PE period and was also trained to work with her in physical education. With some additional modifications included in her teacher's universally designed lesson plan, Maura is now successfully participating in the inclusive PE class with her peers, and she has decided to go out for the track team in the spring.

General physical educators are increasingly expected to teach heterogeneous classes that include students with various disabilities. For these classes to be effective, trained support personnel must be involved daily to help individualize instruction and ensure successful inclusion. There are a variety of supports you can use to assist students with disabilities in physical education, such as peer tutors, paraeducators, senior citizens, and college students; all of these are discussed in this chapter.

Peer Tutors

Peer tutoring allows for individualized instruction, and it gives students with disabilities time to work on developmental skills that are vital to their involvement in physical activity. It is an appropriate and effective way to set up meaningful activity that includes high rates of motor-appropriate practice. Students also receive reinforcement and continuous feedback on performance.

Many researchers agree that implementing a peer tutor program can improve skill levels and socialization for students with disabilities (Copeland et al., 2002; d'Arripe-Longueville, Gernigon, Huet, Cadopi, & Winnykamen, 2002; Hughes et al., 2004; Wiskochil, Lieberman, Houston-Wilson, & Petersen, 2007). When students are inconsistent or do not perform skills correctly, they fail to learn the skills or they learn them incorrectly; peer tutors can help students with disabilities learn skills and practice them correctly. In addition, peer tutoring is an inexpensive way to help students with disabilities succeed in the GPE class. Peer tutors may also increase socialization in group settings (Kasser & Lytle, 2013).

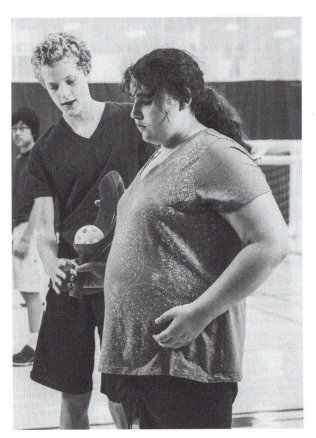

These students are involved in unidirectional peer tutoring; the trained peer tutor takes on the role of teacher, and the partner remains the student.

Types of Peer Tutor Programs

Peer tutoring is not the same as peer interaction. Peer tutors are specifically *trained* to assist in PE classes. The following presents different types of peer tutoring programs:

- **unidirectional peer tutoring**—In this approach, the trained peer tutor teaches the entire time, and the student with a disability is the tutee. This method is effective with students who have more severe disabilities, such as severe autism, intellectual disability, visual impairment, or cerebral palsy. The benefits of this option are that the tutor and tutee always know their roles, and the tutor carries the responsibility throughout the entire program. The drawbacks are that the tutee never gets to take on a leadership role and may come to resent being constantly tutored.

- **bidirectional or reciprocal peer tutoring**—In this model, a student with a disability and a student without a disability form a dyad. The students take turns at being the tutor and tutee. Roles can be switched based on the skill being taught, the class, the week, or the unit. This method is most effective with students who have mild disabilities. The main benefit of this approach is that each student has an opportunity to practice leadership while serving as the tutor.

- **class-wide peer tutoring**—This strategy involves breaking the class into dyads or small groups. Each student participates in reciprocal peer tutoring by providing the partner or group members with prompts, error corrections, and feedback. Students are given task cards to keep them focused on the objectives of the lesson (although task cards can be used any time and are not exclusively for peer tutoring). The tutor can also use task cards to keep track of skills mastered by the tutee. This method is most effective with students who have mild disabilities. Its main benefit is that it involves the entire class, so students are not singled out because of disability. Johnson and Ward (2001) revealed that class-wide peer tutoring was effective for low- and high-skilled students of both genders.

- **same-age peer tutoring**—In this approach, students in the same grade tutor each other. This can be done in the unidirectional and bidirectional models. Benefits are that peers get to know each other well and can easily relate to one another. This method is less effective in young children (below second grade) and with children with severe disabilities.

- **cross-age peer tutoring**—This strategy involves an older student tutoring a younger student. It works best when the peer tutor is interested in working with students with disabilities. A cross-age peer tutor is more effective than a same-age peer tutor when the student with a disability is very young (i.e., below second grade) or the disability is more serious (e.g., severe cerebral palsy, intellectual disability, autism). The cross-age peer tutor can be chosen based on willingness, physical skills, and availability. The main benefits of this approach are that the tutor gains valuable teaching experience and the tutee receives effective individualized instruction and feedback.

Cross-age peer tutoring allows for increased instruction and feedback.

Table 7.1 summarizes additional peer tutoring options.

Students with behavioral and learning disabilities can serve as effective cross-age peer tutors (Friend, 2014). Allowing these students to take responsibility for their tutees (especially those who are younger or have more severe disabilities) helps foster leadership, confidence, and feelings of being needed. Several characteristics or traits have been shown to yield effective tutors (see the Characteristics of a Good Peer Tutor sidebar later in this chapter).

Peer Tutor Training

Training tutors is essential to the success of the program (Houston-Wilson, Dunn, van der Mars, & McCubbin, 1997; Lieberman, Dunn, van der Mars, & McCubbin, 2000; Wiskochil et al., 2007). A peer tutor training program can take an hour or more, depending on the age of the tutor, the student's disability, and the unit of instruction. The training time should be broken into smaller sessions (15 to 30 minutes each) over the course of 1 to 2 weeks. If peer tutors are trained within a 2-week period,

TABLE 7.1 Peer Tutor Program Options

Set-up	Pros	Cons
One tutor teaches throughout the program.	There is consistency in instruction and feedback. The peer tutor develops a sense of accomplishment and pride in his or her skills. A bond is created between the tutor and the tutee.	One student is teaching the whole time, which limits opportunities for other students to tutor. Tutor-tutee relationships may vary from a strong bond to no real bond.
Two to four peers take turns tutoring. The teacher sets up a schedule for who will teach when for each quarter.	More students can be peer tutors and experience the responsibility, leadership, and pride of this role. If a tutor moves, is sick, or does not want to peer tutor for a specific unit, there are other trained peers to take over.	There is inconsistent instruction and feedback from class to class. The time between turns may be a week or two. Tutor-tutee relationships may vary from a strong bond to no real bond.
Two to four peers take turns tutoring during one class (they rotate every 5 to 10 minutes depending on the activity). The teacher or a paraeducator must oversee the program to ensure a smooth transition between tutors.	More students can be peer tutors and experience the responsibility, leadership, and pride of this role. Each child can be a peer tutor and also experience physical education without the role of a peer tutor each class. If a tutor moves, is sick, or does not want to peer tutor for a specific unit, there are other trained peers to take over.	There is inconsistent instruction and feedback during the class. Tutors may be confused about whose turn it is to teach what. Someone must oversee tutor rotation and ensure students know what is happening when they start tutoring. Time is limited to get in the rhythm of peer tutoring. The tutee may not know who their peer tutor is from moment to moment and may have a negative reaction when one tutor leaves. (This approach must be set up very carefully to ensure there are no hurt feelings.) Tutor-tutee relationships may vary from a strong bond to no real bond.

"Peer tutoring: Meeting the demands of inclusion in today's general physical education settings," C.M. Cervantes, L.J. Lieberman, B. Magnesio, and J. Wood, *Journal of Physical Education, Recreation & Dance*, 84, 43-48, 2013, adapted by permission of the Society of Health and Physical Educators, (http://shapeamerica.org).

they will be better able to retain and use the information. The areas covered in the training are disability awareness, communication techniques, instructional strategies, feedback techniques, behavior management, game modifications, and assessment and evaluation techniques. (See the example Peer Tutor Training Handout.)

Additional training on specific disabilities, the unit of instruction, or program goals will require more time. For example, if a hearing student is in a tutoring program with a Deaf child, the tutor will not only go through the basic training program but will also spend time learning important signs. If the tutor is working with a student with autism during a dance unit, the tutor will need to learn the dance steps before attempting to teach them. Training typically occurs before or after school, during lunch, during recess, as part of a PE class, or on a staff development day (tutors must choose to participate on their day off).

Following are some recommendations for establishing an effective training program. First, when possible, *include the student with the disability in the training*. This approach ensures that the tutor and tutee agree on all the instructional techniques, and the tutor will get to know and better understand the student with a disability. Second, make sure the training includes scenarios so the dyad has the opportunity to

Peer Tutor Training Handout

VERBAL CUE

A verbal cue tells someone what to do.

Examples

John, run around the cones.

Jayna, it is your turn for pull-ups.

Let's stand on the black circle.

Sara, show me the crab walk.

MODELING

Modeling is a way to demonstrate how to do the activity. If the tutee does not do the activity or does it incorrectly after you give the verbal cue, repeat the cue and demonstrate what you want the tutee to do.

Examples

Mary, hop like this.

Let's do 10 curl-ups like this.

Watch me run around the cone, then you go.

When we get to station 3, we'll do jumping jacks like this.

PHYSICAL ASSISTANCE

Physical assistance is used to help the tutee if he or she is unable to do the activity after you have given a verbal cue and modeled the activity. You should physically assist the tutee by directing his or her body parts with your hands.

Examples

Kneel in front of your tutee. Hold hands and physically assist with a curl-up by helping your tutee to pull forward.

Stand next to your tutee, bend your knees, and jump over the rope together while holding hands.

Tap your tutee on the shoulder when it is his or her turn to dribble the basketball around the cones.

(continued)

POSITIVE GENERAL FEEDBACK

Positive general feedback involves making a supportive statement about the tutee's motor skill response.

Examples

Good skipping.

Nice crab walk.

Great!

Wow!

POSITIVE SPECIFIC FEEDBACK

Positive specific feedback involves letting the tutee know exactly what was good about the motor skill response.

Examples

Nice reaching up in your jumping jacks.

Great high knees with your skip.

I like the way you use your arms in your run.

That's the way to keep your feet moving in that station!

FITNESS SKILLS

Cardiovascular endurance: running, skipping, galloping, hopping, walking, sliding

Muscle strength and endurance: curl-ups, crab walk, pull-ups, push-ups

Flexibility: side bends, toe touches, trunk twists, hurdler's stretch, butterfly, sprinter's stretch

SAMPLE SCENARIOS

Scenario 1

Tutor: cue ("Lucia, jump over the rope.")

Tutee: acceptable response

Tutor: positive specific reinforcement ("Good job bending your knees when jumping over the rope!")

Scenario 2

Tutor: cue ("Jiang, do five push-ups.")

Tutee: unacceptable response

Tutor: positive general feedback ("Good try!")

Tutor: repeat cue and model ("Jiang, do the push-ups like this.")

Tutee: acceptable response

Tutor: positive specific reinforcement ("Nice job! I like the way you bent your elbows all the way.")

Scenario 3

Tutor: cue ("Ana, do the crab walk.")

Tutee: unacceptable response

Tutor: repeat cue and model ("Ana, do the crab walk like this.")

Tutee: unacceptable response

Tutor: question the student ("Can I help you?")

Tutor: provide physical assistance (Help the student lift her hips up for a correct crab walk.)

Tutee: acceptable response

Tutor: positive specific reinforcement ("That's the way to lift your hips! Now try to do it yourself.")

From Lauren J. Lieberman and Cathy Houston-Wilson, 2018, *Strategies for inclusion* (3rd ed.) (Champaign, IL: Human Kinetics).

Characteristics of a Good Peer Tutor

- Interest in tutoring
- Same gender as student being tutored (if the tutor prefers)
- Average or above-average skill performance
- Well-behaved and reliable
- Experience with younger siblings (with or without disabilities)
- Enthusiastic and positive
- Patient
- Experience working with students with disabilities
- Experience living with learning or behavioral disabilities (may need additional guidance)

practice instruction and feedback with an upcoming unit. Last, and most important, since the tutor is just learning how to teach, he or she will need your oversight and feedback. It is your responsibility to ensure that both students are learning.

Setting up the peer tutor training program is not difficult. Our model incorporates all necessary steps for planning and implementing the program. You can add your own components as necessary. The following are the steps for the Peer Tutor Training Program:

1. Application
2. Permission
3. Disability Awareness
4. Communication
5. Instructional Techniques
6. Scenarios
7. Behavior Management
8. Test
9. Social Interaction
10. Monitor Progress

Step 1: Develop an Application Procedure   When setting up a peer tutoring program, be sure tutors *want* to participate. We believe the desire to tutor should be intrinsic, so very little extrinsic reward should be offered. It's fine to give stickers or certificates at the end of the program, but higher grades or monetary rewards are inappropriate. Some teachers throw an ice cream or pizza party at the end of the year; this is acceptable because the parties allow students to celebrate the year's accomplishments. To ensure intrinsic motivation and strong desire to tutor, many schools have tutors apply for positions (see Application to Be a Trained Peer Tutor; also available in the web resource).

Allowing students to self-select based on friendships, if possible, is ideal because students who considered themselves friends gave specific feedback at higher rates (Byra & Marks, 1993). You should choose three peer tutors for each student with a disability and rotate the tutors. If one tutor is absent or moves or there is a conflict in the tutor-tutee relationship, there are other trained peers to choose from. It is important to rotate the tutors equally so they remain in practice and maintain interest in the work. If a peer tutor wants a favorite unit off from tutoring to participate uninhibitedly, this should be accommodated.

Application to Be a Trained Peer Tutor

Name: _____

Grade: _____

Name(s) of teacher(s): _____

Periods free to tutor: _____

First choice _____

Second choice _____

Third choice _____

AVAILABILITY FOR TRAINING

Minimum of 2 hours: may involve four 30-minute periods, six 20-minute periods, or one staff development day (if you choose to participate on your day off)

____ Recess   Time _____

____ Before school   Time _____

____ After school   Time _____

____ During lunch   Time _____

____ Staff development day   Time _____

____ Study halls   Time _____

____ Portion of PE class   Time _____

____ Other time   Time _____ (be specific)

Briefly describe any experience you have working with students with disabilities:

_____

_____

_____

_____

Briefly describe why you want to be a peer tutor, and indicate whether you have a specific friend you would like to tutor:

_____

_____

_____

From Lauren J. Lieberman and Cathy Houston-Wilson, 2018, *Strategies for inclusion* (3rd ed.) (Champaign, IL: Human Kinetics).

Step 2: Obtain Permission   If the tutoring program is part of the PE program and involves out-of-class training, it is necessary to obtain permission from parents of both the tutors and tutees as well as the students involved. It is also necessary to inform building administration of the program (see Peer Tutor Parental Permission Slip).

If the entire class is involved in the tutoring program, there is no need for permissions. The administration might worry, however, that this program will replace your instruction, so it is a good idea to assure administrators that the peer tutoring program can *enhance* your instruction and increase individual attention for students who need it.

Step 3: Develop Disability Awareness Activities   An effective training program for peer tutors must ensure that the tutors understand the disabilities of the students with whom they will work. It can be difficult to describe a disability in language that students understand; you can use the simple descriptions of disabilities that appear in appendix A if they are applicable.

Step 4: Develop Communication Techniques   The next step in the training program is to teach modes of communication. For example, if a peer tutor is working with a student with limited language, the tutor should be taught the difference between expressive and receptive communication. *Expressive communication* refers to words or concepts that are spoken by the student, and *receptive communication* refers to information or cues received by the student. Children who are deaf, are hard of hearing, have autism, or have severe disabilities may have unique forms of communication. Communicating with Deaf people involves signs, and communicating with students who have autism may require the use of picture boards or tablets. Students with severe disabilities may use augmentative devices that relay computer-generated words when prompted by the user. Whatever the communication method, it is essential that time be spent on this important component of the training program.

Step 5: Teach Instructional Techniques   Training peers to teach students with disabilities requires a good understanding of a teaching process known as the **system of least prompts** (Dunn, Morehouse, & Fredericks, 1986). The goal is to allow individuals to perform skills as independently as possible. The least intensive prompt is a verbal cue, a more intensive prompt is a model or demonstration, and the most intensive prompt is physical assistance. These skills are taught to the tutor via scenarios. For example, if the tutor asks the tutee to throw a ball and the skill is executed incorrectly, the tutor should then model the skill appropriately to facilitate understanding before asking again. If the combination of verbal cue and model proves unsuccessful, the final prompt is physical assistance. This type of prompt should be used only with students with severe disabilities who need physical assistance to complete tasks or with compliant tutees who just aren't grasping certain skills.

Tutors should also be taught how to give feedback about skill performance. Verbal feedback consists of positive general statements, positive specific statements, and corrective statements. Nonverbal feedback can involve such things as a high five or a thumbs-up. Positive feedback is given after the student executes a skill correctly, and corrective feedback is given after the student executes a skill incorrectly.

Step 6: Use Scenarios to Aid in Teaching   During the training program, use realistic scenarios with the tutor to check for understanding. For example, if the peer tutor is teaching a throwing skill, indicate that the hypothetical tutee is either unresponsive or does the skill incorrectly. Then, ask the tutor what he or she would do next. The tutor should indicate that he or she would need to give a verbal cue or give the cue and model the task. If the tutee then exhibits the appropriate behavior, the tutor would give appropriate feedback. By

Encourage peers to provide positive, instructional feedback to one another.

Peer Tutor Parental Permission Slip

DIRECTIONS TO STUDENTS

Please pick up a parental permission slip from the physical education office and have your parent or guardian fill it out and sign it. Return it to the office before _____ [date]. Please check _____ 's [teacher's] door in 3 weeks for tutor placements and training schedules. Thank you for your interest in our peer tutoring program.

PARENTAL PERMISSION SLIP

Dear parents and guardians,

The physical education department would like to start a peer tutoring program. We are writing to ask your permission to allow your child to participate in this program. Your child has expressed a desire to serve as a peer tutor, and we believe that he or she will be effective. Tutors will be trained during free time and will be matched with a student who is experiencing difficulty in physical education. Your child will continue to participate in physical education activities but will also help teach and monitor skills. Your child may decide to terminate this experience with no penalty. If you agree to allow your child to participate in the peer tutoring program, please sign the permission slip below and have your child return it to _____ [teacher] by _____ [date]. In addition, please have your child fill out the enclosed peer tutoring application. If you have any questions, please feel free to contact us at _____ [phone number]. Thank you.

Sincerely,

The physical education staff

I give my child permission to participate in the peer tutoring program.

_____   _____
       Signature of parent or guardian   Date

From Lauren J. Lieberman and Cathy Houston-Wilson, 2018, *Strategies for inclusion* (3rd ed.) (Champaign, IL: Human Kinetics).

practicing such techniques in training, tutors will become confident in their abilities and will perform more effectively. Provide at least 5 to 10 different scenarios to make sure the tutor understands what he or she is being asked to do within the parameters of the program. If the tutor participates in the scenario incorrectly, go over the concept again until the tutor fully understands what is expected. If bidirectional peer tutoring is being used, all the students involved should be part of the scenario training.

Step 7: Use Behavior Management Programs   Peer tutors should be aware of any **behavioral intervention plans** that are in place for the tutee, but the tutor should not be responsible for implementing the behavior plan. It is up to the teacher, the assigned support staff, or the paraeducator to handle any behavior problems that occur during class.

Step 8: Test for Understanding   The training program can include a peer tutor test (Houston-Wilson et al., 1997) that covers information taught in your program (see Peer Tutor Quiz; it and an answer key are both available in the web resource). You can add additional test questions on your quiz as appropriate based on items you have taught and deem important. A tutor should score at least 90 percent to continue in the peer tutor program. If the child does not meet this standard, he or she should be instructed in the weak areas and take the test again.

Step 9: Ensure Social Interaction   The peer tutor can get so engrossed in the lesson and tutoring that the tutee does not interact with other peers in the class. Use specific strategies to facilitate tutee socialization with peers, such as having the tutee work with others during skill development or stretching and warming up in small groups. Encouraging interaction during small-sided games, creating dances in small groups, and changing places in squads or attendance lines to ensure a variety of social interactions are also appropriate. In addition, each tutee should have at least 2 to 4 peer tutors so he or she has in-depth and meaningful experiences with different peers.

Step 10: Monitor Progress   Peer tutors can monitor and document the progress of their tutees. It is acceptable for students to collect performance data about other students. This was deemed legal through a Supreme Court ruling; the data are not considered private information until they are recorded in the instructor's record book (Batista & Pittman, 2005). You should observe the tutors several times during each class to ensure accurate data collection and check on their progress with the tutees.

Peer tutors can collect data in several ways. One is using a process checklist, which breaks skills down into component parts (also known as a task analysis; see figure 7.1 for a sample process checklist for basketball). The peer tutor observes the tutee executing the skill and checks off the tasks that are done correctly. Another way to collect data is through rubrics (see chapter 2); the peer tutor can mark off which level the student reaches during each class period (Kowalski & Lieberman, 2011).

Another way to collect data is tallying opportunities. Any discrete skill can be tallied, such as doing push-ups, kicking a ball, walking across a beam, moving through an obstacle course, or running laps around the gymnasium. Each time the tutee accomplishes a task, the tutor makes a checkmark. This allows you to note how often the tutee is engaged in an activity. For those skills that cannot be tallied, tracking time on task (how long the student is engaged in the activity) is another way to collect data (Horvat, Block, & Kelly, 2007).

Butler and Hodge (2001) report that peer assessment yields the following benefits: enhanced feedback, increased trust, and increased time on task. Research has also shown that well-trained students from third grade through high school can assess their peers reliably (70 to 96 percent agreement with researchers) (Ward & Lee, 2005).

Monitoring the progress of the peer tutors is also essential. This can be done informally throughout the experience or before, during, or after class. A more formal method is using a Peer Tutor Evaluation Checklist. This form can be filled out during the program, at the end of the program, or at both times to give the tutor feedback on his or her performance.

Peer Tutor Quiz

Name: _____ Date: _____

Choose the correct answer from the list below for questions 1 through 5.

modeling   positive general feedback

physical assistance   verbal cue

positive specific feedback

1. A sign or signal to tell someone what to do is a _____.

2. If the student does not understand how to do the skill or is doing it incorrectly, you should use _____.

3. You should give _____ to the student only if the combination of items 1 and 2 does not work.

4. A statement that is supportive and conveys exactly what was good about a skill is called _____.

5. A statement that is supportive but does not convey exactly what was good about a skill is called _____.

Circle the correct answer for questions 6 through 10.

6. What is an example of a positive specific feedback statement?
   a. Good job.
   b. Good sliding sideways! I like the way you use your arms.
   c. Good try.
   d. Slide like this.

7. The student you are working with is unable to gallop. What is a verbal cue that you could give to help the student gallop?
   a. Slide your back foot to your front foot, then step with your front foot again.
   b. Gallop.
   c. Try again.
   d. You will get it this time.

8. After getting a verbal cue to jump with knees bent, the student is unable to do the skill correctly. What do you say?
   a. Almost! Try again.
   b. That was pretty good.
   c. Watch me! Bend your knees and jump.
   d. Good jump!

9. After you give a verbal cue and model a hurdler's stretch, the student is still unable to correctly perform it. What do you say?
   a. Is it okay if I help you? (If the student agrees, sit beside him or her and put a hand on the outstretched leg.)
   b. Do you want me to take your turn for you?
   c. Do you want to do something else?
   d. Try again; I know you will get it.

10. "Good job throwing!" is an example of a
    a. positive specific statement.
    b. corrective feedback statement.
    c. verbal cue.
    d. positive general feedback statement.

From Lauren J. Lieberman and Cathy Houston-Wilson, 2018, *Strategies for inclusion* (3rd ed.) (Champaign, IL: Human Kinetics).

FIGURE 7.1

Process Checklist for Basketball

PEER TUTORING RATING SCALE FOR DRIBBLING

Tutor: Follow these steps.

1. Tell your partner to complete task 1.
2. While your partner completes the task, rate his or her dribbling by placing a check-mark in the category that best describes his or her performance (always, sometimes, or never).
3. Move on to the next task and repeat the steps until all the tasks are finished.

TASK 1: DRIBBLE WHILE STANDING IN PLACE.

Skills	Always	Sometimes	Never
Uses fingertips			
Looks forward and not at the ball			
Knees are bent			
Dribbles at waist level			
Has control of the ball			
Can use both hands			

TASK 2: DRIBBLE WHILE WALKING.

Skills	Always	Sometimes	Never
Uses fingertips			
Looks forward and not at the ball			
Knees are bent			
Dribbles at waist level			
Has control of the ball			
Can use both hands			

TASK 3: DRIBBLE WHILE RUNNING.

Skills	Always	Sometimes	Never
Uses fingertips			
Looks forward and not at the ball			
Knees are bent			
Dribbles at waist level			
Has control of the ball			
Can use both hands			

Adapted, by permission, from L.J. Lieberman et al., 2000, *Setting up a peer tutor training program for your inclusive program,* Presentation at the New York State Association for Health, Physical Education, Recreation, and Dance Conference, Hudson Valley, NY.

Peer Tutor Evaluation Checklist

Name: _____ Date: _____

Evaluator: _____ Period: _____

Name of tutee: _____

CODE MARKS

+ Good   ✔ Progressing   − Needs work

TUTOR PERFORMANCE ASSESSMENT

___ Ability to cue appropriately

___ Ability to model appropriately

___ Ability to physically assist as needed

___ Ability to maintain data

___ Ability to work well and cooperatively with teacher and peers

Comments:

_____

_____

_____

Suggestions for improvement:

_____

_____

_____

Signature of peer tutor: _____ Date: _____

Signature of teacher: _____ Date: _____

From Lauren J. Lieberman and Cathy Houston-Wilson, 2018, *Strategies for inclusion* (3rd ed.) (Champaign, IL: Human Kinetics).

Paraeducators

It has been 50 years since teacher aides were introduced into U.S. schools to enable teachers to spend more time planning and implementing instructional activities. Initially, the duties assigned to aides were routine and included clerical tasks, monitoring students in nonacademic learning environments, duplicating instructional materials, and reinforcing lessons introduced by teachers.

Teacher aides are now also referred to as paraprofessionals, paraeducators, educational assistants, teaching assistants (TAs), and support personnel. As mentioned earlier in this book, we refer to these individuals as *paraeducators*. The term **paraeducator** derives from the concept that these professionals work with teachers in much the same way as paralegals work with lawyers and paramedics work with physicians. Today most paraeducators spend part or all of their time assisting teachers and other licensed practitioners in various phases of the instructional process, including in the delivery of direct services to learners and their parents (Haegele & Kozub, 2010).

Purpose of Paraeducators

Like peer tutors, paraeducators facilitate a more successful inclusive environment (Hodge, Lieberman, & Murata, 2012; Piletic, Davis, & Aschemeier, 2005). Because some students with disabilities benefit from one-to-one instruction, paraeducators serve an important role in inclusive physical education environments. Some paraeducators may assume their break or planning period will be during PE class, but this is not acceptable. If a child needs a paraeducator in the classroom, it is likely that the support will be even more necessary in physical education (Lee & Haegele, 2016; Lieberman, 2007). Researchers (Bryan, McCubbin, & van der Mars, 2013; Davis, Kotecki, Harvey, & Oliver, 2007; Lieberman, 2007; Piletic et al., 2005) have identified common duties assigned to paraeducators, including the following:

- Implement teacher-created lessons in small groups or one-to-one in the gymnasium or in the community.
- Carry out behavior management and disciplinary plans created by the teacher.
- Assist the teacher with assessment activities.
- Assist with activity modifications as necessary.
- Document and provide the teacher with objective information about learner performance to aid in planning.
- Assist teachers with organizing and maintaining supportive, safe learning environments.
- Assist teachers with involving parents and other caregivers in the child's education.
- Shadow the child with a disability and the child's peer tutor and give feedback and support to each.
- Help related service personnel (e.g., nurses, **physical therapists**, **occupational therapists**, and **speech therapists**) provide, implement, and generalize services.
- Physically support the instructor in tasks such as helping students with toileting, changing clothes, and adjusting adapted materials.
- Assist the child with mobility around the gym throughout the lesson.
- Participate in the development and implementation of the IEP or 504 plan.
- Share ideas with the teacher to enhance learning opportunities.

Although this list is not comprehensive, it makes it clear that paraeducators juggle multiple responsibilities, and, as with peer tutors, they need training to be effective. Researchers found that the training areas most sought after by paraeducators for physical education were activity modifications, attributes of students with disabilities, knowledge of motor skill development, safety practices, guiding techniques, teaching strategies, and information on specific disabilities (Davis et al., 2007; Lieberman & Conroy, 2013).

When paraeducators are working one-to-one with students with disabilities, they should encourage social interactions with other students in the class. Klavina and Block (2008) recommend that students with disabilities who are assigned a one-to-one paraeducator be provided with as many social interactions with other students as possible, because the one-to-one relationship can be a limiting factor in social interactions in physical education. One of the biggest problems with the use of paraeducator support is that the unnecessarily close proximity can have unintended negative social effects for the students with disabilities (Broer, Doyle, & Giangreco, 2005). Classmates tend to avoid those students who have paraeducators with them on a regular basis.

Following are a few examples of the paraeducator's proximity that can hinder social interactions between peers (Causton-Theoharis & Mamgren, 2005):

- Maintaining physical contact with the student
- Sitting directly next to the student
- Allowing the student to sit on their lap
- Accompanying the student everywhere in the school setting
- Speaking for the student

Strategies to Promote Student-to-Student Interaction

- Ensure that students with disabilities are placed in rich social environments.
- Highlight the similarities, rather than the differences, between students with disabilities and typically developing peers.
- Redirect student conversation to include students with disabilities. (Some able-bodied peers tend to talk around or over these students.)
- Directly teach and practice interaction skills in appropriate natural settings (e.g., during games, waiting time, transition time, or on the sideline).
- Use instructional strategies that promote interaction (e.g., small groups, pairs, guided discovery, task-style learning).
- Teach others (peer tutors) how to interact with students with disabilities.
- Reward social behavior (e.g., interactive games, partner activities, helping with attendance). For example, all students who increase socialization at appropriate times receive stickers or free time at the end of class.
- Give students responsibilities that allow for interaction with peers (e.g., squad leader, equipment manager).
- Systematically fade out any direct support.
- Make interdependence the goal for students (e.g., using assistance from peers rather than from the paraeducator).

Adapted from J. Causton-Theoharis and K. Mamgren, 2005, "Building bridges: Strategies to help paraprofessionals promote peer interaction," *Teaching Exceptional Children* July/August, 20.

Keep in mind that student-to-student interactions are a critical component of learning (Aiello & Lieberman, 2018; Folsom-Meek & Aiello, 2007; Ward & Ayvazo, 2006). Because GPE placements are becoming more common, seek out innovative and effective ways to support students with disabilities who are placed in classrooms with their typically developing peers (see the sidebar Strategies to Promote Student-to-Student Interaction).

In addition to helping improve social interaction, the paraeducator is part of the multidisciplinary team charged with improving behavior. You and the paraeducator must be clear on the roles that you each play in the development and implementation of the behavior management plan (Haegele & Kozub, 2010; Lee & Haegele, 2016). Table 7.2 summarizes the distribution of duties between teachers and paraeducators in this area.

If you work with paraeducators, be clear about your expectations and give appropriate direction and guidance so the support is useful. According to Mach (2000), it is helpful if paraeducators receive training in emergency procedures and participate in an orientation session that addresses the PE program in which they will be working. Failure to make expectations clear can lead to frustration for you and the paraeducator (Hauge & Babkie, 2006; Lee & Haegele, 2016). Until recently, there was no clarity about who would train paraeducators for physical education or how they would be trained. Now, there is a training manual for paraeducators to assist them in working with students with disabilities in physical education (Lieberman, 2007). A summary of this training program follows.

Training Paraeducators

The paraeducator training program is broken down into the following eight categories:

1. **Define physical education.** This part of the training reviews the purpose of physical education and addresses the SHAPE America national standards as well as state standards. Common terminology is clarified and attention is paid to teaching styles, lesson plan format, and the teacher's pedagogical philosophy.

2. **Define roles.** The various roles of the paraeducator and the teacher are reviewed and specified based on the student's age, type of disability, personal needs, and class size. Roles may vary as units change, as more paraeducators enter the classroom, and during assessment.

TABLE 7.2 Teacher and Paraeducator Roles in Behavior Management

Roles in planning and implementation	Paraeducator	Teacher
Establish classroom rules.		X
Establish class schedules and activities.		X
Observe student behavior.	X	X
Design behavior management plans.		X
Establish objectives for student behavior.		X
Select appropriate reinforcers.		X
Record and chart student behavior.	X	X
Provide consequences according to the behavior plan.	X	X
Provide praise to the student.	X	X
Evaluate intervention effectiveness.		X
Provide feedback according to appropriate behavior.	X	X

3. **Review disabilities.** Although the paraeducator usually knows the students well, he or she should review the disabilities of the students in the class. The teacher and the paraeducator can share information about the cause of a disability, characteristics of persons who have that type of disability, behaviors of the student, functional ability of the student, IEP goals for physical education, and any contraindicated activities (Aiello & Lieberman, 2018). This information is crucial for the physical educator and the paraeducator.

4. **Discuss inclusion strategies.** The teacher may use a variety of inclusion strategies, and these should be shared with the paraeducator. Inclusion strategies to review might include peer tutors; activity modifications; equipment modifications; rule modifications; instructional techniques such as cueing, prompting, modeling, and providing physical assistance; teaching styles such as command, task, guided discovery, and exploration; and provision of feedback on skills and behavior.

5. **Discuss assessment strategies.** Assessment is a critical component of instructing all students in physical education. It helps to determine what to teach, how students are progressing, and whether learning has occurred. The PE instructor will need the paraeducator's assistance in setting up the gymnasium for assessment, collecting assessment data, documenting performance, and entering data into the computer. The communication of specific expectations regarding assessment ensures an accurate, smooth, and enjoyable assessment experience for everyone.

6. **Review behavior management plans.** Each child has individual strengths and weaknesses in physical education. It is imperative that the teacher and paraeducator use the same behavior management techniques with the student. In many cases, the behavior program will be developed by a multidisciplinary team and implemented throughout the school day. In some instances, the training time gives the paraeducator the opportunity to share the plan with the physical educator. The management plan must be discussed and clarified before implementation.

7. **Discuss conflict-resolution strategies.** Teachers and paraeducators occasionally possess differing ideas on how to handle a situation, and conflicts can arise even with the best staff. Therefore, a complete training program should define the hierarchy of command and the protocol for handling conflicts. We suggest that teachers and paraeducators have an open-door policy related to issues in physical education. In other words, each party should feel comfortable sharing their opinions, issues, or problems with the other in a nonbiased, safe space. This way, conflicts are resolved quickly, honestly, and positively, thus creating a win-win situation for staff and students. Ultimately, however, it is the teacher's responsibility to ensure that best practices are followed.

8. **Share resources.** The paraeducator can share resources that he or she is aware of that might be useful in physical education, and the PE teacher can share resources that might be helpful in fully understanding physical education. These resources can include books, CDs, DVDs, websites, and journals.

When possible, this training program should be presented at the beginning of the year so all parties are on the same page. The training could occupy a day, a half day, or a regularly scheduled slot (e.g., Friday afternoons).

Many variables change throughout the school year, and good communication with the paraeducator is a must. Mauerer (2004) found that communication was one of the biggest barriers to the success of paraeducators in physical education. You must discuss with paraeducators the best ways to communicate on an ongoing basis.

Even the most well-trained and dedicated paraeducators can be overheard saying "I am only a para." Paraeducators are often paid minimum wage and do not have health benefits. They are often overworked and even work while they are sick. Feelings of inadequacy can lead to apathy, absenteeism, and inappropriate instruction. Paraeducators must feel like the dedicated, committed, and invaluable professionals they are. Without this feeling of importance, the very people the paraeducator is supposed to help will suffer the most. Following are some ideas for making paraeducators feel like valued members of the team:

- **Name on the door.** The door to the gymnasium has the name of the physical educators. Adding the paraeducators' names gives them a sense of identity and belonging in the gymnasium and in physical education.

- **Introduction.** When doing introductions at the beginning of the school year, introduce paraeducators as assistant teachers and make them feel as important as they are to the success of the class. In addition, address them as Mr., Ms., or Mrs. to suggest the same respect given to teachers.

- **Whiteboard or blackboard.** Posting a whiteboard or blackboard on the office wall provides a means of communication between the teacher and paraeducator. The teacher can put the name of the student that the paraeducator is going to work with on the board with specific cues for the day's lesson. In doing so, the teacher can save time and constant direction, which lets the paraeducator know that their time and expertise are valued.

- **Equipment assistance.** When ordering equipment, get input from the paraeducator; this will give you a more accurate idea of what is needed, and it will help the paraeducator have a sense of ownership in the program.

- **Modification ideas.** The paraeducator can help make modifications in equipment, rules, instruction, and environment at the start of each unit. Asking the paraeducator's opinion will help ensure that the lesson meets the students' needs, and it increases the paraeducator's self-value in helping implement the lesson.

- **Locker.** In many instances, paraeducators do not come to school prepared for the PE environment. Providing them with lockers where they can keep comfortable shoes or clothes helps them be more comfortable for physical education and more effective.

- **Refreshing drink or protein bar.** Providing paraeducators with a healthy snack before or after strenuous units will replenish them and let them know that you want them to do well. This small gesture can go a long way in giving them a positive perspective on your classes and their participation.

- **Recognition.** It takes great energy and effort to teach students with disabilities in physical education, and their success cannot be realized without the dedication and commitment of paraeducators. Recognize individual students' accomplishments and give credit to their paraeducators as primary instructors during IEP meetings and staff meetings, through school or PE newsletters, and on PE bulletin boards.

- **Conference attendance.** Bringing your paraeducators to a conference can make them feel valued and instill ownership in the program. In addition, what you learn together will help you all believe in the same thing and work toward common goals.

- **Thanks.** A genuine thank-you can be expressed in various forms, such as homemade cookies, a plant, a card, or a balloon. A small gesture can go a long way in ensuring that the paraeducator never feels like she or he is "only a para" in physical education.

Adapted, by permission, from R. Lytle, L.J. Lieberman, and R. Aiello, 2007, "Motivating paraeducators to be actively involved in physical education programs," *The Journal of Physical Education, Recreation, and Dance* 78: 26-30, 50.

Senior Citizens

As mentioned earlier, instruction for individuals with disabilities is often best done on a one-to-one basis. Many schools have limited resources for employing paraeducators. One often-overlooked resource is senior citizens, many of whom have plenty of energy and enthusiasm to contribute. Even if they don't have experience working with students with disabilities, these citizens can assist you in a variety of ways. They can contribute in many of the same ways as paraeducators, and they can be trained in much the same way as peer tutors. They can help adapt equipment, improve time on task, give feedback, and perform evaluations. In fact, senior citizens who are former teachers may need very little training and may welcome the opportunity to share their expertise on a less demanding schedule.

To find senior citizens to assist in physical education, send letters home with students, recruit on open-school night, make phone calls to follow up on suggestions from parents, and put up notices at senior centers. Involving senior citizens is a win-win situation, especially for students with disabilities!

College Students

University or community college students are another overlooked resource. Most university programs in special education, physical education, adapted physical education, and counseling have practicum requirements for their students. When these educators-in-training serve as support personnel, students with disabilities benefit from the individualized instruction. College students can gain teaching experience, and you can benefit from additional hands in the gym. College students can be used and trained in the same way as peer tutors or paraeducators. Some may even offer teaching methods that they have learned in class and are eager to try out with real students (with your permission).

You can find college students to assist in physical education by contacting relevant departments at local universities. You will need to create proposals that allow students to meet their specific college requirements. Ask for class syllabi to ensure that students are meeting class objectives through their work in the PE class. This approach also encourages the college to send students to the school as full-time student teachers. Again, this is a win-win situation.

A college student assists a child with a disability in physical education by providing individualized instruction.

Summary

Students with disabilities are increasingly being fully included in general physical education, and you might need additional support to facilitate the learning of all students. This chapter includes strategies for working with support personnel such as peer tutors, paraeducators, senior citizens, and college students. These individuals must be appropriately trained to assist in PE classes. The ideas and training methods presented in this chapter may at first seem time consuming, but the benefits reaped from such a program are well worth the effort.

8

Transition Planning

Dr. Amaury Samalot-Rivera

Chapter Objectives

After reading this chapter, you will

- ▶ understand the purpose of transition planning and the legal rights of students with disabilities as they relate to transition;
- ▶ be able to identify services that must be included in the transition plan;
- ▶ know how to use a functional approach in transition planning and implementation; and
- ▶ employ appropriate assessment tools, such as ecological inventories, to promote social inclusion.

Mariela is a 16-year-old with spina bifida who uses a walker to ambulate. The IEP team is holding its first transition plan meeting to start planning her postsecondary goals; these will ensure that she is ready for life after high school. Because Mariela has a disability, she can attend her local high school until the age of 21. However, transition planning needs to begin early. Her special education teacher, Mrs. Jackson, asked Mariela about her favorite activities and classes in school and what she would like to do when she graduates. Mariela said that her favorite class is physical education, and when she graduates she would like to join a gym and remain physically active. She also enjoys working with computers and may have an interest in computer technology. With this information, the team began to set some transition goals for Mariela, such as visiting and accessing community recreation centers and including a computer science class in her curriculum.

This chapter provides information about services that help students with disabilities transition from high school to life in the community, and it specifically addresses the role that adapted physical education plays in providing necessary skills for effective integration. In this chapter, community integration is referred to as *social inclusion*. You will be guided through a series of steps that will aid in a functional approach to transition and promote social inclusion. In addition, activities that can be used to promote social inclusion are discussed.

As discussed earlier, IDEIA (2004) states that all students with disabilities must be provided with a free and appropriate public education in the LRE. This law also requires that transition services be provided to these students beginning at age 16. **Transition services** are intended to prepare students with disabilities for their transition into the community and assist them in becoming independent, active, and healthy individuals. These services must be provided in school settings and are identified on the IEP through an **individual transition plan (ITP)**. This official document is used as an educational guide to help students with disabilities achieve their short- and long-term goals for life after high school, which generally concludes at age 21. IDEIA (2004) defines transition services as follows:

Transition services prepare students with disabilities to become independent and active individuals in the community.

> The term "transition services" means a coordinated set of activities for a student, with a disability, that: (A) is designed within an outcome-oriented process, that promotes movement from school to post-school activities, including postsecondary education, vocational training, integrated employment (including supported employment), continuing and adult education, adult services, independent living, or community participation; (B) is based on the student's needs, taking into account the student's preferences and interests; and (C) includes instruction, community experiences, the development of employment and other post-school objectives, and, when appropriate, acquisition of daily living skills and functional vocational evaluation.

IDEIA indicates that recreational activities are an essential part of the ITP. Recreation and physical activity may be related to personal satisfaction, healthy lifestyles, and the success of people with disabilities (Foley, Dyke, Girdler, Bourke, & Leonard, 2012). Implementing an appropriate transition plan is essential in providing students with disabilities with the necessary skills to become socially active and independent and to ensure that they become active members of society once they complete school. An effective transition plan provides them with opportunities to develop the cognitive, motor, and affective skills necessary for effective social inclusion in their communities.

Transition Services and the IEP

As mentioned, transition goals must be addressed on the IEP by the time the child turns 16; this can be done earlier if deemed appropriate by the IEP team. Measurable postsecondary goals should be developed in the following three areas:

1. Education and training
2. Employment
3. Independent living (if applicable)

The multidisciplinary team writing the transition goals must provide the support service personnel as well as any equipment that will assist the student in reaching transition goals. Transition activities should address the following: instruction to support goals, related services, community experiences, development of employment and other adult-living objectives, acquisition of daily living skills, and functional vocational assessment. Detailed information on each of these components is provided in table 8.1.

As noted, the use of recreational and physical activity facilities is part of the coordinated set of skills you can develop in the transition planning process. Physical educators play an important role in facilitating these types of transition goals. Further, physical education provides a platform in which sport, recreational activities, and physical activities can help all students develop the necessary skills to achieve their goals and improve their social inclusion. The physical educator might have to help the student with training employees at community recreation facilities on how to accommodate them successfully.

You must consider the interests and preferences of the student when developing goals and objectives for the ITP. Special education literature has shown that when students have a say in their goals, they are generally more successful in achieving them. Promoting self-determination and decision-making is essential for successful social inclusion. Self-determination incorporates skills such as goal-setting, decision-making, problem-solving, communication, self-awareness, and self-advocacy and has been found to have a significant link to quality of life. Further, self-determination has been shown to be a critical element in improving the transition from secondary school to adulthood for youth with disabilities (Foley et al., 2012).

TABLE 8.1   Coordinated Transition Activities

Instruction to support goals	Identify needed instruction that will support one or more postschool goals. Consider the need for self-determination, social, and study skills training. Consider the need for occupational skills training.
Related services	Identify professionals who can address the student's disability relative to postschool goals, such as an occupational therapist, physical therapist, or orientation and mobility expert. Consider the use of tutors, trainers, and aides to ensure an effective transition.
Community experiences (including leisure and recreation)	Identify experiences that will help the student explore or apply what is learned in class. Consider the need for work, college, and independent living experiences, including how to use recreational and physical activity facilities in the community.
Development of employment and other adult-living objectives	Provide career exploration activities or different postsecondary education options (e.g., college, junior college, technical institutes). Consider the need for guidance counseling, person-centered care, career planning, and job shadowing.
Acquisition of daily living skills	Identify activities of daily living that support performance relative to postschool goals. Social skill development is a necessary living skill that aids effective social inclusion and acceptance from others in society.
Functional vocational assessment	Identify specific evaluations relative to the student's employment goals or desired certifications. Consider evidence-based practices such as situational work and independent living assessments. Ensure that assessments are valid for the student's career maturity and cognitive levels.

Adapted from Flexer, Baer, Luft, and Simmons 2013.

Teaching students how to access and use community-based locker rooms aids in transition.

You can use sport, recreational activities, and physical activities to help students with disabilities make positive health-enhancing choices (Lieberman & Linsenbigler, 2017). These activities can also support appropriate social interactions with others in their community (Samalot-Rivera & Porretta, 2012). You can also provide age-appropriate activities that enhance personal goals and outcomes (Foley et al., 2012). Research has demonstrated that the decisions these students make regarding their use of leisure time can have a significant effect on other aspects of their lives, such as the types of extracurricular activities they engage in and the social groups they connect with (Newman et al., 2011). Through physical education activities, you can help students with disabilities develop skills such as following directions, turn-taking, and sportsmanship, and these can be generalized to situations in the community.

Table 8.2 provides examples of physical activities and the corresponding skills that would need to be taught to facilitate transition for students with disabilities. Returning to the example of Mariela, it was determined that one of her goals upon graduation is to be able to ice skate at her community ice rink. What skills does Mariela need to learn to be able to do this? First, she needs to learn how to access the rink. She will need to sign in and out (and pay or swipe a card, if necessary), identify her proper skate size, put her skates on and lace them, and put her items in a locker. Next, she will need to learn the basics of skating. She will need to learn how to enter the ice rink on skates, maintain balance, and skate comfortably. Analyzing the requisite skills needed to complete an activity facilitates development of transition goals for the ITP. A functional approach to implementing transition plans is discussed in the next section.

Functional Approach in Transition Planning

The functional approach in transition planning is used to create appropriate goals in physical education. This model is based off the work of Flexer et al. (2013) and incorporates legal requirements and best practices in special education. When creating transition goals, consider the following:

- The student's needs, interests, and preferences
- How achievement will be measured
- Coordinated activities that can be included
- How the goals promote movement from school to community

Figure 8.1 provides the steps for creating a transition program in physical education. Through this process, you can assist students with disabilities in preparing for healthy, active lives in the community. Figure 8.2 provides an example of a suggested ITP in adapted physical education that aligns with the six steps presented in figure 8.1.

TABLE 8.2 Transitional Physical Activities and Prerequisite Skills

Transition activity	Skills needed
Hiking	• Putting on hiking boots • Map-reading • Carrying a backpack or hip pouch with water and snacks
Swimming at a YMCA or university or community pool	• Paying the entrance fee or swiping a membership card • Going through a turnstile • Changing clothes in a locker room • Showering in a locker room • Taking turns in a swim lane
Ice skating	• Paying the entrance fee or swiping a membership card • Renting skates and helmet (know skate and helmet sizes) • Taking shoes off and putting skates on • Skating with or without support • Turning in skates and helmet
Bowling	• Paying the entrance fee or swiping a membership card • Requesting bowling shoes (know size) • Changing shoes • Identifying assigned alley • Selecting the correct ball size • Identifying name on the screen • Taking turns and playing the game • Turning in bowling shoes
Participating in a sport (e.g., basketball, softball)	• Learning how to follow the game schedule and calendar • Selecting proper sport clothing and equipment prior to the game • Changing in a locker room or designated area • Learning skills related to the sport • Identifying positions to play • Listening to the coach's instructions and following them
Using a fitness center	• Swiping a membership card • Changing in a locker room • Identifying machines to use based on established routine • Establishing goals for each fitness activity • Cleaning equipment with a designated towel
Biking	• Wearing proper protection (e.g., helmet) • Identifying the bike and checking that it is properly working (tire pressure, brakes, chain) (Lieberman & Linsenbigler, 2017) • Riding in a designated area • Following proper biking rules for the road • Returning the bike to the assigned place for storage
Participating in other activities (e.g., martial arts or yoga classes)	• Selecting the proper attire • Changing in a designated location • Following instructor guidance for routines and exercises

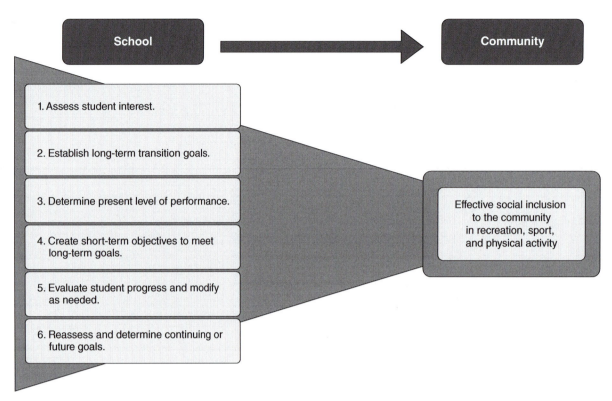

Figure 8.1 Functional approach to transition planning.

Step 1: Assess student interest.

- Determine the availability of programs, services, and facilities related to sport, recreation, and physical activities in the community.
- Ask students about their interests in sport, recreation, and physical activities (provide various options and examples to assist students in the assessment process).
- Ask parents about the interests and goals they have for the child regarding sport, recreation, and physical activities.

Step 2: Establish long-term transition goals.

- Based on the information obtained in step 1, develop long-term goals related to desired outcomes.
- Share the long-term goals with the student and family.
- If necessary, adjust goals based on feedback.

Step 3: Determine present level of performance.

- Determine the student's current level of function related to the desired outcomes.
- Evaluate the skill set needed in relation to the environment, the task, and the unique attributes of the student.

Step 4: Create short-term objectives to meet long-term goals.

- Identify sequential steps needed to achieve long-term goals.
- Readjust as necessary along the way (e.g., if the goals are too easy or too challenging).

FIGURE 8.2

Individual Transition Plan for Physical Education

Name: Mariela Rodriquez

Age: 16

Date: August 25, 2016

Characteristics (condition/diagnosis/special needs to take into consideration): Mariela has spina bifida. She uses a walker to walk from one place to another. For long distances, she uses a motorized wheelchair.

1. Self-determination: What are the sports, recreational activities, and physical activities the student enjoys and wants to participate in?

   Ice skating, aerobic exercises (riding a stationary bicycle), weight training

2. Long-term goals: What are the primary activities in the community that the student will participate in?

   - Goal 1: Independently attend a community gym.
   - Goal 2: Participate in open skate at the community ice rink with minimal support.

3. Present level of performance: What is the student's PLP related to the following activities?

   Skill 1: Physical fitness: aerobic capacity and muscular strength and endurance (assessment: Brockport Physical Fitness Test)
   - Mariela can do seven leg presses with a 20-pound (9.1 kilogram) weight with each leg.
   - Mariela can pedal a stationary bike on resistance level 3 for 5 minutes before becoming fatigued.

   Skill 2: Dynamic balance (assessment: ice-skating skills checklist)
   PLP:
   - Mariela can stand up on ice skates with assistance and maintain static balance for 10 seconds.
   - Mariela can skate forward 20 feet (6.1 meters) using short right foot-left foot strides and can stop with assistance.

   Skill 3: Personal and social behavior (assessment: teacher-made ecological inventory for social interaction at a sport facility)
   - In a role-play with her instructor, Mariela can show her ID and use proper salutation when requesting equipment.
   - Mariela can take off her sneakers and place them in a looker and put on her skates with assistance.

4. Short-term objectives: What are the main objectives to be reached during this school year?

   Skill 1: Improve physical fitness.
   - Mariela will be able to do 12 leg presses with a 20-pound weight with each leg.
   - Mariela will be able to pedal a stationary bike for 15 minutes before becoming fatigued (light level).

   Skill 2: Improve dynamic balance.
   - Mariela will be able to stand up on ice skates with assistance and maintain static balance for 20 seconds.
   - Mariela will able to skate forward 30 feet (9.1 meters) and stop independently.

   Skill 3: Enhance personal and social behavior.
   - In a role-play with her instructor, Mariela will be able to engage in light conversation when greeting staff at a fitness facility.
   - Mariela will be able to put on her skates and lace them independently.

5. Evaluation of student progress scheduled for January 15, 2017.

6. Reassessment scheduled for May 15, 2017.

This student is learning the prerequisite skills for bowling in the community.

Step 5: Evaluate student progress and modify as needed.

- Assess the student's abilities.
- If student achievement is below the established goal, modify activities to promote opportunities for success.

Step 6: Reassess and determine continuing or future goals.

- Reassess the student's performance at the end of the academic year and compare it to long-term goals.
- Identify areas that need further development.
- Identify future long-term goals if possible.

Transition Activities for Effective Social Inclusion

Finding appropriate sport, recreation, and physical activities for students with disabilities can be a daunting process, and the number of choices does not reflect the range of opportunities afforded to typically developing students. This is also true for adults with disabilities who want be involved in community-based programs. One of the biggest concerns that parents of children with disabilities have is that they don't know how to proceed once their children graduate (Aiello, 2016). Many parents worry about how their children will be integrated and active members of their communities. In addition, parents report that they do not know where to get information about available programs and services for their children; when it comes to sports and recreation, they are at a further loss (Newman et al., 2011). Unfortunately, research has demonstrated that many youth with disabilities do not actively participate in after-school programs, intramural activities, community-based programs, or social events (National Organization on Disability, 2010; U.S. Government Accountability Office, 2010). The benefits of participating in sport, recreation, and physical activities for people with disabilities are numerous; improved self-concept, allegiance to school and community, positive social behaviors, better grades and academic achievement, enhanced fitness, and significant reduction in problem behaviors are just a few of the benefits noted in the literature (Hodge, Lieberman, & Murratta, 2012).

Community-Based Programs

You must work collaboratively with parents to find appropriate activities that students with disabilities can participate in. The following steps can assist you in preparing youth with disabilities for transitions related to sport, recreation, and physical activities:

1. **See what programs are available in the community.** Connect with community recreation programs, the YMCA, or universities and colleges to determine what programs are available to students with and without disabilities. If there are

no programs available, determine whether modifications could be made to facilitate participation of students with disabilities in existing programs or if new programs could be created with the help of volunteers.

2. **Consider the student's interests.** Present various options to the student and his or her parents, and determine which activities are desirable and appropriate.

3. **Create an ITP based on these activities.** Incorporate the activities into the student's ITP. Consider the prerequisite skills needed, and teach these skills to promote student success.

4. **Evaluate progress and make adjustments as needed.** Develop an assessment plan to determine progress and areas that need improvement. Adapt and modify the ITP goals to promote success. Work with community agencies to promote familiarity so the student can independently access and participate in activities after graduation.

After-School Programs

School districts have a legal obligation to provide after-school sport programs for students with disabilities. Section 504 of the Rehabilitation Act (1973) states that

> no otherwise qualified handicapped individual in the United States shall solely by reason of his handicap, be excluded from participation in, be denied the benefits of, or be subjected to discrimination under any program receiving federal financial assistance.

It also states that

> a recipient [of federal funding] that offers physical education courses or that operates or sponsors intercollegiate, club, or intramural athletics shall provide to qualified handicapped students equal opportunities for comparable participation in these activities.

In addition, the U.S. Department of Education Office for Civil Rights (2013) wrote a letter that clarifies schools' obligations to provide extracurricular athletic opportunities for students with disabilities. A portion of this letter appears in figure 8.3. The letter also defines equal treatment of student athletes with disabilities and provides guidance on how schools can create APE programs for students with disabilities.

Assessment in Transition

As mentioned throughout this chapter, assessment is a key component of an effective transition plan for students with disabilities. (Chapter 2 provides an in-depth discussion of assessment.) Through the assessment process, you can measure students' present levels of performance and the progress they are making to achieve their long-term goals. There are several ways to assess student abilities, but one of the most useful is to create an **ecological inventory**. The best way to create an ecological inventory is to analyze the steps needed to successfully participate in a game or activity. Figure 8.4 is an ecological inventory for ice skating that includes the levels of assistance a student will need to participate. For students who are visual learners, it can be helpful to create an inventory that incorporates pictures. For students who need assistance to complete the task, the levels of assistance model is helpful. Focus on areas in which the student is not totally independent to help the student more fully integrate into his or her community.

FIGURE 8.3

Schools' Obligations to Provide Extracurricular Athletic Opportunities

A school district must

- provide students with disabilities with equal opportunities to participate in its existing extracurricular athletic programs and
- make individualized inquiries to determine whether there are reasonable modifications or necessary aids and services that would allow students with disabilities to take part in activities.

A school district must provide equal opportunities for participation by

- making reasonable modifications (policies, practices, or procedures) unless modifications constitute a fundamental alteration of the nature of the activity;
- providing aids and necessary services; and
- ensuring safe participation.

Students with disabilities have the right to

- accommodations during tryouts,
- be selected or cut from the team based solely on ability level and not disability, and
- alternatives in case they do not make the team (unified or separate sport teams).

Summary

Transition from school to community is an essential component of the IEP process. You are responsible for preparing high school students for social inclusion in sport, recreation, and physical activities. Using a functional approach to transition is an ideal way to incorporate transitional activities into the curriculum. The functional approach to transition involves researching opportunities in the community and pairing these with students' interests. An ecological inventory can be useful in determining the skills the student needs to actively participate in the activity. Ecological inventories can help you identify present levels of performance and set realistic and achievable long- and short-terms goals. Achieving sport, recreation, and physical activity goals might be the key to many students with disabilities living independent and fulfilling lives in their communities.

FIGURE 8.4

Ecological Inventory With Levels of Assistance: Ice Skating

Activity	Performed independently	Performed with some assistance	Performed with total assistance	Comments
1. Enter the building and show ID.				
2. Tell the clerk your shoe size to rent skates.				
3. Pay for the ice time and skate rentals.				
4. Remove your shoes, put your skates on, and lace them up.				
5. Enter the ice rink.				
6. Start skating by moving your arms and legs in opposition.				
7. Take a break when needed in the break area.				
8. Go to the cafeteria to get a snack and a drink.				
9. Return skates to the front desk when you are done.				
10. Exit the facility and board the bus to return to school.				

PART II

Strategies for Inclusion

Part II will enable you to set up challenging universally designed environments for students with disabilities in your inclusive PE classes. These chapters include lesson adaptations, sample assessment rubrics, and ways to document individual performance. We encourage you to use these to help you develop your own ideas. Before you plan your curriculum, you will need to address the skills and abilities of the children in your classes, the units of instruction to be taught, and the class goals and objectives.

Each chapter contains potential modifications and adaptations for each unit; these are divided into four sections: equipment, rules, environment, and instruction. For example, in a unit on soccer, you can modify the equipment by using a large ball, modify the rules by playing small-sided games, or modify the environment by changing the field size. You can also use instructional modifications to meet the goals and objectives of the unit and address the unique needs of students. You can inform students of some of the available universally designed options; they are more likely to be invested and motivated in a unit if they have some input on variable selection.

Each chapter also offers at least one sample rubric per unit. For example, the soccer unit has dribbling, passing, and game play rubrics; you will need to create additional rubrics for defense and other game skills. The rubrics fit into the assessment process by documenting the level at which each child performs. The rubrics in chapter 9 are divided into 14 levels that are represented by different colors; red is the simplest and bronze is the most difficult. Because these units are for younger children, we used the colors of the rainbow to designate each level of the rubrics. The rubrics in chapters 10, 11, and 12 are represented by colors used in martial arts; white is the simplest and black is the most difficult. The martial arts colors are in ascending order according to the belt color, and this is understandable with older children. The task description in each rubric addresses the skill the student will execute for the authentic assessment, and the scale components indicate what the child is being evaluated on.

All adaptations and rubrics are provided on the web resource at www. HumanKinetics.com/StrategiesForInclusion. The adaptation charts are modifiable and have clickable check boxes so you can save and adapt them for each student.

9

Basic Skills

Purpose: The importance of fundamental motor skills cannot be overlooked in elementary physical education. These are the prerequisites for participation in more advanced movement skills, sports, and recreational activities. Introducing these skills at the appropriate developmental level is essential for successful performance in middle and high school.

Unit adaptations: There are many ways to adapt the curriculum for students with disabilities, and modifications for each student must be specific to his or her needs. For example, if a student has athetoid cerebral palsy and moves slower than his peers, you can slow down the activity, use a different teaching style to focus on individual movement, or use a technique that slows down the movement of the student's peers.

Assessment options: Each unit includes at least one rubric for evaluating the process or product of movements; you can also create your own rubrics. In addition, you can create checklists and rating scales and have students keep journals. All of these can be included in the students' portfolios (see chapter 2).

This chapter contains ideas you can use to teach various physical activities. For each activity, we address equipment that can be used, rule modifications, environmental alterations, and instructional variations. Check off those modifications that apply to the learner. For example, if a child benefitted from *using a wall for support* when balancing, then that would be checked off in the modifications table. Once this is checked off, any subsequent lessons relating to balance can be replicated with the variables that worked as part of the Universal Design process.

BALANCE

Potential Modifications and Adaptations

Equipment	Rules	Environment	Instruction
☐ High beam	☐ Use wall for support	☐ Small space	☐ Verbal cues
☐ Low beam	☐ Holding hands, walk forward	☐ Large space	☐ Demonstration
☐ Narrow beam	☐ Holding hands, walk sideways	☐ Balance stations	☐ Modeling
☐ Wide beam	☐ Holding hands, walk backward	☐ Sequence centers	☐ Tactile modeling
☐ Balance boards	☐ Holding hands, step over object	☐ Obstacle course	☐ Physical assistance
☐ Tilt boards	☐ Holding hands, step in object (hoop)	☐ Pictures and videos	☐ Task cards (enlarged if needed)
☐ Tires	☐ Holding hands, step out of object		☐ Pictures
☐ Steps	☐ Hands free, walk forward		☐ Guided discovery
☐ Hula hoops	☐ Hands free, walk sideways		☐ Problem-solving
☐ Thin mats	☐ Hands free, walk backward		☐ Task analysis
☐ Thick mats	☐ Hands free, step over object		☐ Proximity (instructor stands close to student with disability)
☐ Low trampolines	☐ Hands free, step in object		☐ Individualized (one-to-one)
☐ Benches	☐ Hands free, step out of object		☐ Sign language
☐ Beanbags			☐ Feedback
☐ Lines on the floor			☐ Audio transitions (clapping)
☐ Jump ropes on the floor			☐ Peer tutor
			☐ Paraeducator
			☐ Interpreter

Balance Beam

Task	Student walks forward and backward on the balance beam for the distance of the beam.
Scale components	(a) Assistance, (b) height of beam

Rubric level and color	Rubric descriptors
1. Red	Student balances with assistance on low beam (_____ inches [centimeters] from floor).
2. Orange	Student walks sideways with assistance on low beam.
3. Yellow	Student walks forward with assistance on low beam.
4. Green	Student walks backward with assistance on low beam.
5. Blue	Student walks sideways without assistance on low beam.
6. Indigo	Student walks forward without assistance on low beam.
7. Violet	Student walks backward without assistance on low beam.
8. Black	Student balances without assistance on high beam (_____ inches [centimeters] from floor).
9. White	Student walks sideways with assistance on high beam.
10. Grey	Student walks forward with assistance on high beam.
11. Platinum	Student walks backward with assistance on high beam.
12. Gold	Student walks sideways without assistance on high beam.
13. Silver	Student walks forward without assistance on high beam.
14. Bronze	Student walks backward without assistance on high beam.

Potential Modifications and Adaptations

Equipment	Rules	Environment	Instruction
☐ Mats	☐ Follow instructions	☐ Indoor or outdoor	☐ Verbal cues
☐ Gymnastics apparatus	☐ Use personal space	☐ Small area	☐ Mirroring
☐ Beanbags	☐ Keep hands to self	☐ Large area	☐ Demonstration
☐ Balloons	☐ Cooperate	☐ Obstacle course	☐ Modeling
☐ Sticks	☐ Use partner when balancing	☐ Mirrors on walls (if appropriate)	☐ Tactile modeling
☐ Ropes	☐ Small to large progression	☐ Line on floor	☐ Physical assistance
☐ Carpet squares	☐ Animal walk imitations	☐ Stations	☐ Task cards (enlarged if needed)
☐ Cones		☐ Padded walls	☐ Pictures
☐ Poly spots		☐ Pictures and videos	☐ Guided discovery
☐ Footprints			☐ Problem-solving
☐ Fun mirrors			☐ Task analysis
☐ Chalk			☐ Proximity
☐ Music player (e.g., stereo, MP3 player)			☐ Individualized
☐ Task cards			☐ Sign language
☐ iPad (as appropriate)			☐ Reinforcement and feedback
			☐ Audio transitions (clapping)
			☐ Peer tutor
			☐ Paraeducator
			☐ Interpreter

Body Awareness

Task	Student identifies body parts and performs actions (stabilize, manipulate, and move) with the body and its parts.
Scale component	(a) From comprehension to action, (b) from body to environment cues, (c) from self to external pacing
Rubric level and color	**Rubric descriptors**
1. Red	Student identifies body parts with or without assistance.
2. Orange	Student imitates or mirrors examples related to body parts and limb movements (twist, bend, high, low) with or without assistance.
3. Yellow	Student imitates or mirrors examples related to movements crossing the body midline (twisting) with or without assistance.
4. Green	Student imitates or mirrors movement directionality (forward, backward) and laterality (right, left) with or without assistance.
5. Blue	Student performs movements in an obstacle course setting with or without assistance (under, over, in, out, through, on).

HULA HOOP ACTIVITIES

Potential Modifications and Adaptations

Equipment	Rules	Environment	Instruction
☐ Hula hoops (consider size, color, texture, thickness, weight) ☐ Floor tape ☐ Cones ☐ Poly spots ☐ Carpet squares ☐ Mats	☐ Follow instructions ☐ Use personal space ☐ Cooperate ☐ Small to large progression ☐ Make noise with hoop ☐ Airplane space ☐ Free time to explore	☐ Indoor or outdoor ☐ Small area ☐ Large area ☐ Obstacle course ☐ Mirrors on walls (if appropriate) ☐ Line on floor ☐ Stations ☐ Padded walls ☐ Pictures and videos	☐ Verbal cues ☐ Mirroring ☐ Demonstration ☐ Modeling ☐ Tactile modeling ☐ Physical assistance ☐ Task cards (enlarged if needed) ☐ Pictures ☐ Guided discovery ☐ Problem-solving ☐ Task analysis ☐ Proximity ☐ Individualized ☐ Sign language ☐ Reinforcement and feedback ☐ Audio transitions (clapping) ☐ Peer tutor ☐ Paraeducator ☐ Interpreter

Hula Hoops

Task	Student maintains rhythm with hula hoop around hips, leg, wrists, arms, or foot for specific periods of time.
Scale components	(a) Assistance, (b) task difficulty, (c) momentum of hoop
Rubric level and color	**Rubric descriptors**
1. Red	Student performs various actions with the hula hoop (roll, flick, jump in and out, move in levels [high, medium, low]) with or without assistance.
2. Orange	Student creates circular motion on the floor with foot inside hoop with or without assistance.
3. Yellow	Student creates a circular motion of hula hoop with wrist with or without assistance.
4. Green	Student creates a circular motion of hula hoop with arm with or without assistance.
5. Blue	Student creates a circular motion of hula hoop with leg with or without assistance.
6. Indigo	Student creates a circular motion of hula hoop with waist with or without assistance.
7. Violet	Student meets a challenge. (How long can you maintain the momentum with each body part: 5 seconds, 30 seconds, 2 minutes?)

Potential Modifications and Adaptations

Equipment	Rules	Environment	Instruction
☐ Short ropes	☐ Follow instructions	☐ Indoor or outdoor	☐ Verbal cues
☐ Long ropes	☐ Use personal space	☐ Small area	☐ Mirroring
☐ Heavy ropes	☐ Cooperate	☐ Large area	☐ Demonstration
☐ Bright ropes	☐ Small to large progression	☐ Rope on floor	☐ Modeling
☐ Handled ropes	☐ Make noise with rope	☐ Rope suspended from cones	☐ Tactile modeling
☐ Cloth ropes	☐ Free time to explore	☐ Rope tied across chairs	☐ Physical assistance
☐ Plastic ropes		☐ Slanted rope	☐ Task cards (enlarged if needed)
☐ Beaded ropes		☐ Stations	☐ Pictures
☐ Bells on ropes		☐ Pictures and videos	☐ Guided discovery
☐ Ropes cut in half			☐ Problem-solving
☐ Handles (no rope)			☐ Task analysis
☐ Velcro glove for holding rope			☐ Proximity
☐ Floor tape			☐ Individualized
☐ Cones			☐ Sign language
☐ Poly spots			☐ Reinforcement and feedback
☐ Hula hoops			☐ Audio transitions (clapping)
☐ Music player (e.g., stereo, MP3 player)			☐ Peer tutor
			☐ Paraeducator
			☐ Interpreter

Jump Rope

Task	Student rolls, walks, hops, or jumps over a rope at any height (from the floor or suspended).
Scale components	(a) Number of jumps, (b) direction of jumps
Rubric level and color	**Rubric descriptors**
1. Red	Student crawls, rolls, walks, or jumps over a rope placed on the floor with or without assistance.
2. Orange	Student steps or jumps forward over a rope on the floor with or without assistance.
3. Yellow	Student steps or jumps forward over a rope suspended 1 to 2 feet (0.3 to 0.6 meters) off the floor with or without assistance.
4. Green	Student brings rope over head with arms and steps over the rope once with or without assistance.
5. Blue	Student brings rope over head with arms and steps over the rope more than once with or without assistance.
6. Indigo	Student brings rope over head with arms and steps over the rope backward once with or without assistance.
7. Violet	Student brings rope over head with arms and steps over the rope backward more than once with or without assistance.
8. Black	Student continuously jumps rope to music using a mixture of forward, backward, and crisscross jumps.

LOCOMOTOR SKILLS

Potential Modifications and Adaptations

Equipment	Rules	Environment	Instruction
☐ Cones	☐ Follow instructions	☐ Indoor or outdoor	☐ Verbal cues
☐ Directional arrows	☐ Use personal space	☐ Small area	☐ Mirroring
☐ Poly footprints	☐ Cooperate	☐ Large area	☐ Demonstration
☐ Poly spots	☐ Small to large progression	☐ Obstacle course	☐ Modeling
☐ Ropes	☐ Free time to explore (space, speed)	☐ Mirrors on walls	☐ Tactile modeling
☐ Hoops		☐ Lines on floor	☐ Physical assistance
☐ Tires		☐ Stations	☐ Task cards (enlarged if needed)
☐ Mats		☐ Padded walls	☐ Pictures
☐ Tunnels		☐ Pictures and videos	☐ Guided discovery
☐ Stairs			☐ Problem-solving
☐ Rails			☐ Task analysis
☐ Guide wires			☐ Proximity
☐ Ramps			☐ Individualized
☐ Carpet squares			☐ Sign language
☐ Music player (e.g., stereo, MP3 player)			☐ Reinforcement and feedback
			☐ Audio transitions (clapping)
			☐ Peer tutor
			☐ Paraeducator
			☐ Interpreter

Running

Task	Student runs from one side of the gymnasium to the other (50 feet [15.2 meters]) with or without assistance.
Scale components	(a) Flight phase, (b) arm opposition, (c) 90-degree back leg bend, (d) heel-to-toe placement

Rubric level and color	Rubric descriptors
1. Red	Student runs from one end of the gymnasium to a cone 50 feet away with or without assistance.
2. Orange	Student runs from one end of the gymnasium to a cone 50 feet away with flight phase during at least 4 rotations with or without assistance.
3. Yellow	Student runs with flight phase and arm opposition during at least 4 rotations with or without assistance.
4. Green	Student runs with flight phase, arm opposition, and back leg bent at least 90 degrees during at least 4 rotations with or without assistance.
5. Blue	Student runs with flight phase, arm opposition, back leg bent at least 90 degrees, and feet landing heel-to-toe during at least 4 rotations with or without assistance.
6. Indigo	Student runs a distance of 50 feet with flight phase, arm opposition, back leg bent at least 90 degrees, and feet landing heel-to-toe 3 out of 5 times with or without assistance.
7. Violet	Student runs for 50 feet with consistently proper form.

Potential Modifications and Adaptations

Equipment	Rules	Environment	Instruction
☐ Beanbags	☐ Follow instructions	☐ Indoor or outdoor	☐ Audio transitions (clapping)
☐ Different-sized balls	☐ Use personal space	☐ Small area	☐ Student calms self before starting
☐ Nerf balls	☐ Cooperate	☐ Large area	☐ Demonstration
☐ Sponge balls	☐ Small to large progression	☐ Lines on floor	☐ Guided discovery
☐ Wiffle balls	☐ Free time to explore	☐ Stations	☐ Individualized
☐ Brightly colored objects	☐ Airplane space	☐ Padded walls	☐ Mirroring
☐ Soft, long objects	☐ Animal walk	☐ Pictures and videos	☐ No time factor
☐ Poly spots	☐ Start and stop signal	☐ Vary distance (closer, wider)	☐ Physical assistance
☐ Carpet squares	☐ Practice moving safely	☐ Constant movement	☐ Pictures
☐ Cones		☐ Boundaries	☐ Problem-solving
☐ Scarves		☐ Bright boundaries	☐ Proximity
☐ Flags		☐ Mats on floor	☐ Reinforcement and feedback
☐ Scooters		☐ Mirrors on walls	☐ Sign language
☐ Wands		☐ Circles	☐ Small group
☐ Hula hoops		☐ Safety zone	☐ Tactile modeling
☐ Pinnies		☐ Cooperative	☐ Task analysis
☐ Radio			☐ Task cards (enlarged if needed)
			☐ Verbal cues
			☐ Paraeducator
			☐ Peer tutor
			☐ Interpreter

Cooperative Games

Task	Student interacts with large groups of peers and adults (more than 6 people) for 45 minutes.
Scale components	(a) Attention, (b) group size, (c) leadership
Rubric level and color	**Rubric descriptors**
1. Red	Student repeatedly starts and stops on command (4 to 6 times).
2. Orange	Student follows a set of instructions for 10 to 15 minutes.
3. Yellow	Student adheres to a cooperative task (such as passing balls) in a small group (6 or fewer participants).
4. Green	Student adheres to a cooperative task (such as passing balls) in a large group (more than 6 participants) some of the time.
5. Blue	Student assists, follows, and supports peers most of the time.
6. Indigo	Student adheres to a cooperative task most of the time.
7. Violet	Student provides feedback and constructive instructions to peers most of the time.

OBJECT CONTROL SKILLS

Potential Modifications and Adaptations

Equipment	Rules	Environment	Instruction
☐ Auditory balls	☐ Follow instructions	☐ Indoor or outdoor	☐ Verbal cues
☐ Balls (large, small)	☐ Use personal space	☐ Small area	☐ Mirroring
☐ Balls on ropes	☐ Cooperate	☐ Large area	☐ Demonstration
☐ Beach balls	☐ Small to large progression	☐ Lines on floor	☐ Modeling
☐ Bright balls	☐ Free time to explore	☐ Stations	☐ Tactile modeling
☐ Deflated balls		☐ Padded walls	☐ Physical assistance
☐ Nerf balls		☐ Pictures and videos	☐ Task cards (enlarged if needed)
☐ Foam balls		☐ Vary distance (closer, wider)	☐ Pictures
☐ Fuzzy balls			☐ Guided discovery
☐ Sponge balls			☐ Problem-solving
☐ Tactile balls			☐ Task analysis
☐ Velcro balls			☐ Proximity
☐ Wiffle balls			☐ Individualized
☐ Yarn balls			☐ Sign language
☐ Beanbags			☐ Reinforcement and feedback
☐ Balloons			☐ Audio transitions (clapping)
☐ Auditory bases			☐ Peer tutor
☐ Baskets and buckets (laundry, garbage)			☐ Paraeducator
☐ Basketball rim			☐ Interpreter
☐ Lowered basketball rim			
☐ Lowered volleyball net			
☐ Attachment to the basketball rim (retrievable, funnel)			
☐ Large bats			
☐ Light bats			
☐ Fat bats			
☐ Wiffle bats			
☐ Batting tee			
☐ Catcher's mitts			
☐ Velcro mitts			
☐ Gloves			
☐ Large rackets			
☐ Small rackets			
☐ Foam rackets			
☐ Long-handled rackets			
☐ Short-handled rackets			
☐ Large-face rackets			
☐ Small-face rackets			
☐ Cones			
☐ Flags			
☐ Hoops			
☐ Noodles			
☐ Paddles			

Kicking

Task	Student kicks a stationary ball.
Scale components	(a) Use a three-step approach, (b) incline trunk backward during contact, (c) swing opposite arm forward, (d) follow through

Rubric level and color	Rubric descriptors
1. Red	Student kicks stationary ball with any form with or without assistance.
2. Orange	Student kicks stationary ball with a three-step approach, walking or running, 3 out of 5 times with or without assistance.
3. Yellow	Student kicks stationary ball with a three-step approach and trunk inclined backward during contact 3 out of 5 times with or without assistance.
4. Green	Student kicks stationary ball with a three-step approach, trunk inclined backward during contact, and forward swing of opposite arm 3 out of 5 times with or without assistance.
5. Blue	Student kicks stationary ball with a three-step approach, trunk inclined backward during contact, forward swing of opposite arm, and follow-through and propels the ball 30 feet (9.1 meters) 3 out of 5 times with or without assistance.
6. Indigo	Student kicks stationary ball with a three-step approach, trunk inclined backward during contact, forward swing of opposite arm, and follow-through and propels the ball 60 feet (18.3 meters) 3 out of 5 times with or without assistance.
7. Violet	Student kicks the ball with consistently proper form.

Underhand Roll

Task	Student rolls a ball underhand to a peer.
Scale components	(a) Step with opposite foot, (b) release in front, (c) shift weight forward, (d) follow through

Rubric level and color	Rubric descriptors
1. Red	Student attempts to roll a ball underhand to a peer standing 10 feet (3 meters) away with or without assistance.
2. Orange	Student rolls a ball underhand and steps with the opposite foot 3 out of 5 times with or without assistance.
3. Yellow	Student rolls a ball underhand, steps with the opposite foot, and releases in front of the body 3 out of 5 times with or without assistance.
4. Green	Student rolls a ball underhand, steps with the opposite foot, releases in front of the body, and shifts weight forward during the throw 3 out of 5 times with or without assistance.
5. Blue	Student rolls a ball underhand, steps with the opposite foot, releases in front of the body, shifts weight forward during the throw, and follows through 3 out of 5 times with or without assistance.
6. Indigo	Student rolls a ball underhand to a partner 10 feet away, steps with the opposite foot, releases in front of the body, shifts weight forward during the throw, and follows through 3 out of 5 times with or without assistance.
7. Violet	Student rolls a ball to a partner with consistently proper form.

Potential Modifications and Adaptations

Equipment	Rules	Environment	Instruction
☐ Large parachute	☐ Decrease number of shakes	☐ Indoor or outdoor	☐ Verbal cues
☐ Small parachute	☐ Increase number of shakes	☐ Large space	☐ Demonstration
☐ Bright parachute	☐ Limit range of motion	☐ Small space	☐ Modeling
☐ Tactile parachute	☐ Increase range of motion	☐ Smooth surface	☐ Tactile modeling
☐ Straps on chute	☐ Change parachute chair height	☐ Grass	☐ Physical assistance
☐ Ace bandages	☐ Two hands on parachute	☐ Mats on floor	☐ Task cards (enlarged if needed to describe the different ways to use parachute in games)
☐ Bells on chute	☐ One hand on parachute	☐ Circle marked on floor	☐ Pictures
☐ Wrist straps on chute	☐ Walk	☐ Tactile boundaries	☐ Guided discovery
☐ Towels	☐ Move in own space	☐ Roped boundaries	☐ Problem-solving
☐ Sheets	☐ Big waves		☐ Task analysis
☐ Assorted balls	☐ Small waves		☐ Proximity
☐ Auditory balls	☐ Name game, change places		☐ Individualized
☐ Poly spots	☐ Animal movements, change places		☐ Sign language
☐ Music player (e.g., stereo, MP3 player)			☐ Feedback
			☐ Peer tutor
			☐ Paraeducator
			☐ Interpreter

Parachute

Task	Student holds the parachute at a medium level and advances to a high or low level on cue.
Scale components	(a) Change levels, (b) follow cues
Rubric level and color	**Rubric descriptors**
1. Red	Student holds on to a parachute at a medium level using any grip with or without assistance.
2. Orange	Student holds on to a parachute at a medium level using an overhand grip.
3. Yellow	Student holds on to a parachute at a medium level using an overhand grip and takes his or her part of the parachute to a low level and back to a medium level.
4. Green	Student holds on to a parachute at a medium level using an overhand grip and takes his or her part of the parachute to a high level and back to a medium level.
5. Blue	Student holds on to a parachute at a medium level using an overhand grip and takes his or her part of the parachute to any level on cue.
6. Indigo	Student holds on to a parachute at a medium level using an overhand grip and takes his or her part of the parachute to any level multiple times.

RHYTHMIC SKILLS

Potential Modifications and Adaptations

Equipment	Rules	Environment	Instruction
☐ Beanbags	☐ Animal walks	☐ Mirrors on walls	☐ Visual aids
☐ Balls	☐ Start and stop signal	☐ Lines on floor	☐ Verbal cues
☐ Different-sized balls	☐ L test	☐ Smaller lines	☐ Direct
☐ Balloons	☐ Mimicking	☐ Tactile lines	☐ Indirect
☐ Rubber chickens	☐ Sub-upper body	☐ Flat surface	☐ Feedback
☐ Cones	☐ Locomotor patterns and skills	☐ Small groups	☐ Demonstration
☐ Poly spots	☐ Participate with peers	☐ Boundaries	☐ Physical assistance
☐ Footprints	☐ Link arms	☐ Circles on floor	☐ Counting beats
☐ Wrist bands	☐ Bounce to the beat	☐ Smaller circles	☐ Slow movement
☐ Lummi sticks	☐ Toss to the beat	☐ Mats on floor	☐ Mirroring
☐ Sticks	☐ Clap on the beat	☐ Targets	☐ Proximity
☐ Bright wands	☐ Have peer toss ball	☐ Small boxes	☐ Teach with or without music
☐ Scarves	☐ Shorter time on task	☐ Smaller foot position	☐ Task analyze
☐ Tambourines	☐ Dance in groups	☐ Slower tempo	☐ Command style
☐ Maracas	☐ Change partners	☐ Small groups	☐ Tactile modeling (child feels the teacher or peer conducting the activity)
☐ Drums	☐ Lie or sit	☐ Small dance area	☐ Peer tutor
☐ Keyboards	☐ Braille movements	☐ Happy environment	
☐ Boxes	☐ Create own steps	☐ Bright posters	
☐ Radio	☐ Movements to music	☐ Quiet when music is on	
	☐ Start and stop music	☐ No clutter	
	☐ Time limitations	☐ Well-lit area	
		☐ Obstacle course	
		☐ Music player (e.g., stereo, MP3 player)	
		☐ Colorful	
		☐ Cooperative	

Rhythmic Skills

Task	Student marches and claps to a beat.
Scale components	(a) March to 4- and 8-count beats, (b) clap to 4- and 8-count beats, (c) march and clap to 4- or 8-count beats.

Rubric level and color	Rubric descriptors
1. Red	Student claps to a rhythmic song (4-count beats).
2. Orange	Student marches to a rhythmic song (4-count beats).
3. Yellow	Student claps and marches to a rhythmic song (4-count beats).
4. Green	Students claps to a rhythmic song (8-count beats).
5. Blue	Student claps and marches to a rhythmic song (8-count beats).

SCOOTER BOARD ACTIVITIES

Potential Modifications and Adaptations

Equipment	Rules	Environment	Instruction
☐ Scooter boards	☐ Use all general space	☐ Volleyball court	☐ Task analysis
☐ Alternate boards	☐ Must pass end lines	☐ Basketball court	☐ Verbal cues
☐ Small scooters	☐ Use feet or hands to dribble while moving	☐ Parking lot	☐ Large groups
☐ Beanbags	☐ Use hands or feet to move	☐ Boundaries	☐ Small groups
☐ Soccer balls	☐ Down and back two times before switch	☐ End-line boundaries	☐ Individualized
☐ Soft foam balls	☐ Lower target	☐ Small boundaries	☐ Teacher help
☐ Soft balls	☐ 10-second rule	☐ Flags mark end lines	☐ Direct
☐ Bright balls	☐ Touch rule	☐ Lines on floor	☐ Indirect
☐ Hula hoops	☐ Sharing	☐ Cones	☐ Guided discovery
☐ Hoops	☐ Start and stop signal	☐ Ropes	☐ Shaping
☐ Mats	☐ Bumpers up	☐ Large area	☐ Feedback
☐ Jump ropes	☐ Airplane space	☐ Railing assistance	☐ Visual aid
☐ Ropes	☐ Partner tag	☐ Flat surface	☐ Demonstration
☐ Pillow polo sticks	☐ Time rule	☐ Different surface	☐ Modeling
☐ Soft sticks	☐ Use partner	☐ Safety zone	☐ Stress safety
☐ Noodles	☐ Pull with string	☐ Flags	☐ Peer work
☐ Whistle	☐ One pushes and one pulls	☐ Quiet while instructing	☐ Increase time
☐ Poly spots	☐ Have two pull one	☐ Padded walls	☐ Use all senses
☐ Cones	☐ Make train	☐ Obstacles	☐ Use braille
☐ Bright cones	☐ Group work	☐ Circuit obstacles	☐ Work in pairs
☐ Scarves	☐ Direction		☐ Relay races
☐ Pinnies	☐ Speed		☐ Peer tutor
☐ Radio	☐ Mode of movement		
	☐ Sit or lie down		
	☐ Personal space		
	☐ Use peer guides		
	☐ Different positions		
	☐ Support body parts		

Scooter Board

Task	Student pulls him- or herself prone on a scooter board.
Scale components	(a) Pulling motion, (b) distance, (c) speed (optional)
Rubric level and color	**Rubric descriptors**
1. Red	Student pulls self prone on a scooter board using a rope with intermittent knots along the wall for 5 feet (1.5 meters) with or without assistance.
2. Orange	Student pulls self prone on a scooter board using a rope with intermittent knots along the wall for 10 feet (3 meters) with or without assistance.
3. Yellow	Student pulls self prone on a scooter board through four cones placed 5 feet apart one time.
4. Green	Student pulls self prone on a scooter board through four cones placed 5 feet apart two times.
5. Blue	Student pulls self prone on a scooter board through eight cones placed 5 feet apart two times.
6. Indigo	Student pulls self prone on a scooter board through a 50-foot (15.2-meter) course that consists of around, through, and over obstacles one time.
7. Violet	Student pulls self prone on a scooter board through a 50-foot course that consists of around, through, and over obstacles at least two times.

Sport Skills

Purpose: The importance of sport skills and teamwork cannot be overestimated in secondary physical education. The framework of good sporting behavior, basic skills, and problem-solving will help students not only in class but also in the world of work. Introducing these skills at the appropriate developmental level is essential for successful performance in adulthood.

Unit adaptations: There are many ways to adapt the curriculum for children with disabilities, and modifications for each child must be specific to his or her needs. For example, if a child has spina bifida and uses a wheelchair, you can allow more bounces in tennis or more hits in volleyball, use a bigger ball for soccer, or modify the rules for badminton.

Assessment options: Each unit includes at least one rubric for evaluating the process or product of movements; you can also create your own rubrics. In addition, you can create checklists and rating scales and have students keep journals. All of these can be included in the students' portfolios (see chapter 2).

This chapter contains ideas you can use to teach various physical activities. For each activity, we address equipment that can be used, rule modifications, environmental alterations, and instructional variations. Check off those modifications that apply to the learner. For example, if a child benefitted from *serving closer to the net* in volleyball, then that would be checked off in the modifications table. Once this is checked off, any subsequent lessons relating to volleyball can be replicated with the variables that worked as part of the Universal Design process.

Potential Modifications and Adaptations

Equipment	Rules	Environment	Instruction
☐ Beeper balls	☐ Hit off tee	☐ Ropes leading to bases	☐ Verbal cues
☐ Auditory balls	☐ Hit off ground	☐ Guide rails	☐ Demonstration
☐ Bell balls	☐ Hit hanging ball	☐ Chalk lines to bases	☐ Modeling
☐ Tactile balls	☐ All students bat before switching	☐ Tactile lines	☐ Tactile modeling
☐ Bright balls	☐ Vary number of strikes	☐ Auditory lines	☐ Physical assistance
☐ Nerf balls	☐ Vary number of people in the outfield	☐ Bright lines	☐ Task cards (enlarged if needed)
☐ Wiffle balls	☐ Vary number of people in the infield	☐ Cones next to bases	☐ Pictures
☐ Softballs	☐ Two bases only	☐ Clap behind bases to add auditory cue	☐ Guided discovery
☐ Velcro balls	☐ Point for each base	☐ Short base distance	☐ Problem-solving
☐ Big balls	☐ Boundary limitations	☐ Short pitching distance	☐ Task analysis
☐ Light balls	☐ Time limitations		☐ Proximity
☐ Colored balls	☐ No tag-outs		☐ Task analyze
☐ Buzzer on bases	☐ Tag-outs on bases (tag the base to get someone out)		☐ Individualized
☐ Flat bases	☐ Peer runner or guide		☐ Sign language
☐ Thick bases	☐ No score		☐ Feedback
☐ Big bases	☐ No double play		☐ Peer tutor
☐ Safety bases	☐ Two extra tosses to field players (add rule that ball must be thrown to two people in the field before they can attempt an out)		☐ Paraeducator
☐ Wiffle bats	☐ Ground pass		
☐ Fat bats	☐ Out in air or on bounce		
☐ Short-handled bats	☐ Throw ball to make an out to a base before the runner gets there		
☐ Long-handled bats			
☐ Regulation bats			
☐ Batting tees			
☐ Gloves and catcher's mitts in different sizes and textures			
☐ Helmets			
☐ Pinnies			

Throwing

Task	Student throws the ball from shortstop to first base.
Scale components	(a) Form of throw, (b) distance, (c) accuracy
Rubric level and color	**Rubric descriptors**
1. White	Student throws the ball from shortstop position to second base most of the time with or without assistance.
2. Yellow	Student throws the ball with opposite-foot step, weight shift, hip rotation, and a follow-through across the body from shortstop position to second base most of the time with or without assistance.
3. Orange	Student throws the ball with proper form from shortstop position to second base with or without assistance in 3 out of 5 attempts.
4. Green	Student throws a ball with proper form from shortstop position to first base with or without assistance in 3 out of 5 attempts.
5. Blue	Student throws a ball with proper form from shortstop position to first base in 3 out of 5 attempts.
6. Purple	Student throws a ball with proper form from shortstop position to first base with accuracy in 3 out of 5 attempts.

Fielding

Task	Student shows proper form and skill in fielding the ball.
Scale components	(a) Proper form, (b) percentage of stopped balls
Rubric level and color	**Rubric descriptors**
1. White	Student takes stance in ready position with or without assistance most of the time.
2. Yellow	Student keeps knees bent and eyes on the ball most of the time when the ball is hit to him or her.
3. Orange	Student keeps knees bent, eyes on the ball, and glove down on the ground when the ball is hit to him or her in 3 out of 5 attempts with or without assistance.
4. Green	Student keeps knees bent, eyes on the ball, glove down on the ground, body behind the ball, and nonglove hand covering the ball when the ball is hit to him or her in 3 out of 5 attempts with or without assistance.
5. Blue	Student uses proper form for fielding a ball and slides right or left to field any ball hit near him or her in 3 out of 5 attempts with or without assistance.
6. Purple	Student uses proper form for fielding a ball, slides right or left to field any ball near him or her, and stops at least 50 percent of the balls that come near in 3 out of 5 attempts.
7. Brown	Student uses proper form for fielding a ball, slides right or left to field any ball near him or her, and stops at least 80 percent of the balls that come near in 3 out of 5 attempts.

(continued)

Batting

Task	Student bats a ball from a tee or when it is pitched to him or her.
Scale components	(a) Form, (b) hitting percentage
Rubric level and color	**Rubric descriptors**
1. White	Student hits a ball off a tee with the shoulder to the outfield and the nondominant foot forward in 3 out of 5 attempts with or without assistance.
2. Yellow	Student hits a ball off a tee with the shoulder to the outfield, nondominant foot forward, and weight shift to front foot in 3 out of 5 attempts with or without assistance.
3. Orange	Student hits a ball off a tee with the shoulder to the outfield, nondominant foot forward, weight shift to front foot, and ball contact in front of front foot and follows through with the bat in 3 out of 5 attempts with or without assistance.
4. Green	Student hits a ball off a tee with the shoulder to the outfield, nondominant foot forward, weight shift to front foot, and ball contact in front of front foot and follows through with the bat in 3 out of 5 attempts without assistance.
5. Blue	Student bats a ball with proper form from a pitch and contacts the ball 3 out of 5 attempts.
6. Purple	Student bats a ball with proper form from a pitch and contacts the ball 4 out of 5 attempts.

VOLLEYBALL

Potential Modifications and Adaptations

Equipment	Rules	Environment	Instruction
☐ Volleyballs	☐ One bounce	☐ Indoor or outdoor	☐ Physical assistance
☐ Large balls	☐ Two bounces	☐ Racquetball court	☐ Teach signs
☐ Small balls	☐ Catch instead of hit (i.e., Newcomb)	☐ Tactile boundaries	☐ Individualized
☐ Light balls	☐ Walk with ball	☐ Visual boundaries	☐ Task analyze
☐ Heavy balls	☐ Three passes	☐ Limit distractions	☐ Slow down
☐ Beach balls	☐ Four passes	☐ Success-oriented	☐ Demonstration
☐ Balloons	☐ Unlimited passes	☐ Limit space	☐ Modeling
☐ Trainer balls	☐ Server closer to net	☐ One game at a time	☐ Feedback
☐ Auditory balls	☐ Limited space responsibility	☐ Many games at a time	☐ Task style
☐ Colored balls	☐ Cooperation versus competition	☐ People out of the way	☐ Use universal signs
☐ Raised net	☐ More than one hit	☐ All students help	☐ Constant encouragement
☐ Bright net	☐ Everyone must serve	☐ Communication	☐ Command style
☐ Wall	☐ Modify serve	☐ Stations	☐ Cognitive cues
☐ Spike machine	☐ Serve from anywhere	☐ Wall volleyball (Wallyball)	☐ Verbal explanation
☐ Remove arm rests from wheelchair for ease of movement	☐ Overhand or underhand serve	☐ Flat surface	☐ Shadowing
☐ Rope	☐ Pay attention	☐ Decrease boundaries	☐ Problem-solving
☐ Bench	☐ Less skilled in front	☐ Textured floor markings	☐ Verbal analysis
☐ Bright-colored tape	☐ Call name before passing ball	☐ Make signs or banners	☐ Direct
☐ Whistle	☐ Shorter service line		☐ Indirect
☐ Flip cards	☐ Tutor may catch		☐ Reciprocal
☐ Task cards	☐ No rotation		☐ Inclusive
☐ Wheelchair if a child has difficulty playing standing up	☐ No hit limits		☐ Peer tutor
	☐ No carry rule		☐ Certified personnel
	☐ No punching ball		☐ Use videos for instruction
	☐ No jumping for people with shunts		☐ Play sitting volleyball
	☐ No spikes		
	☐ No blocks		

(continued)

Serve

Task	Student hits a serve in a volleyball game.
Scale components	(a) Form, (b) number of performances, (c) success
Rubric level and color	**Rubric descriptors**
1. White	Student serves the volleyball from half-court.
2. Yellow	Student serves the volleyball from half-court with shoulder facing the net and proper ball position (held in nondominant hand in front of front foot) and contacts ball in front of the body most of the time.
3. Orange	Student serves the volleyball from half-court with shoulder facing the net and proper ball position and contacts ball in front of the body, shifts weight, and follows through most of the time.
4. Green	Student serves the volleyball from half-court with shoulder facing the net and proper ball position, contacts ball in front of the body, shifts weight, follows through, and gets the ball over the net 5 out of 10 times.
5. Blue	Student serves the ball from half-court with proper form and gets the ball over the net 8 out of 10 times.
6. Purple	Student serves the ball from the service line with proper form during a game and gets the ball over the net 7 out of 10 times.
7. Brown	Student serves the ball from the service line with the proper form during a game and gets the ball over the net 9 out of 10 times and in the desired area 5 out of 10 times.

Bump

Task	Student makes a bump shot in a volleyball game.
Scale components	(a) Form, (b) number of performances, (c) success
Rubric level and color	**Rubric descriptors**
1. White	Student bumps a volleyball tossed underhand by a peer 8 feet (2.4 meters) away.
2. Yellow	With both palms up, one hand over the other, and arms out straight, the student bumps a volleyball tossed underhand by a peer 8 feet away most of the time.
3. Orange	With both palms up, one hand over the other, arms out straight, and knees bent, the student bumps a volleyball tossed underhand by a peer 8 feet away most of the time.
4. Green	With both palms up, one hand over the other, arms out straight, and knees bent, the student bumps a volleyball tossed underhand by a peer 8 feet away, contacts it in front of the body, and follows through most of the time.
5. Blue	Student properly bumps a volleyball tossed underhand by a peer from half-court and gets the ball over the net or to a setter 8 out of 10 times.
6. Purple	Student properly moves to bump a volleyball tossed anywhere on the court by a peer on the opposite side of the net and gets the ball back over the net or to a setter 8 out of 10 times.
7. Brown	Student properly bumps a volleyball from anywhere on the court during a scrimmage and gets the ball back over the net or to a setter 7 out of 10 times.

Game Play

Task	Student participates in a game of volleyball.
Scale components	(a) Choice of shots, (b) percentage of successful shots

Rubric level and color	Rubric descriptors
1. White	Student participates in a game of volleyball and uses the bump and set shots correctly 50 percent of the time.
2. Yellow	Student participates in a game of volleyball and uses the bump, set, overhead smash, and dig shots correctly 50 percent of the time.
3. Orange	Student participates in a game of volleyball and uses the bump, set, overhead smash, and dig shots correctly 75 percent of the time.
4. Green	Student participates in a game of volleyball and uses the bump, set, overhead smash, and dig shots correctly 75 percent of the time and gets the ball over the net 50 percent of the time.
5. Blue	Student participates in a game of volleyball and uses the bump, set, overhead smash, and dig shots correctly 75 percent of the time and gets the ball over the net 75 percent of the time.
6. Purple	Student participates in a game of volleyball and uses the bump, set, overhead smash, and dig shots correctly 90 percent of the time and places the ball in the desired spot 50 percent of the time.
7. Brown	Student participates in a game of volleyball and uses the bump, set, overhead smash, and dig shots correctly 95 percent of the time and places the ball in the desired spot 75 percent of the time.

BASKETBALL

Potential Modifications and Adaptations

Equipment	Rules	Environment	Instruction
☐ Basketballs	☐ Increase number of fouls allowed	☐ Cones as boundaries	☐ Verbal cues
☐ Large balls	☐ Eliminate 3-second rule	☐ Bright boundaries	☐ Demonstration
☐ Small balls	☐ Eliminate double-dribble rule	☐ Ropes as boundaries	☐ Modeling
☐ Bright balls	☐ Can walk with ball without dribbling	☐ Beeper or auditory boundaries	☐ Tactile modeling
☐ Textured balls	☐ Different points awarded for baskets	☐ Visual shooting line	☐ Physical assistance
☐ Heavy balls	☐ Extra step on layup	☐ Smooth surface	☐ Task cards (enlarged if needed)
☐ Light balls	☐ Undefended	☐ Modify court size	☐ Pictures
☐ Foam balls	☐ No defense for certain number of seconds	☐ Stations	☐ Guided discovery
☐ Nerf balls	☐ Free shooting (no defense)		☐ Problem-solving
☐ Beach balls	☐ Everyone touches ball before a shot is attempted		☐ Task analysis
☐ Deflated balls	☐ Pass certain number of times before a shot is attempted		☐ Proximity
☐ Auditory balls	☐ Vary game length		☐ Individualized
☐ Buzzer basket	☐ Limit boundaries		☐ Sign language
☐ High basket	☐ Small-sided games (e.g., 3 on 3)		☐ Feedback
☐ Low basket	☐ Increase number of players		☐ Peer tutor
☐ Bright basket			☐ Paraeducator
☐ Wide basket			☐ Interpreter

Dribbling

Task	Student dribbles a basketball around cones or inactive defensive players.
Scale components	(a) Form, (b) control
Rubric level and color	**Rubric descriptors**
1. White	Student dribbles in place using fingertips at waist height; ball contacts the floor in front (or outside) the foot on the same side as the dribbling hand in 3 out of 5 attempts with or without assistance.
2. Yellow	Student dribbles while walking around eight cones placed 5 feet (1.5 meters) apart using fingertips at waist height; ball contacts the floor in front (or outside) the foot on the same side as the dribbling hand in 3 out of 5 attempts with or without assistance.
3. Orange	Student dribbles with proper form while walking around eight cones placed 5 feet apart and controls the ball 50 percent of the time with or without assistance.
4. Green	Student dribbles with proper form while jogging around eight cones placed 5 feet apart and controls the ball 50 percent of the time with or without assistance.
5. Blue	Student dribbles with proper form while jogging around eight cones placed 5 feet apart and controls the ball 80 percent of the time.
6. Purple	Student dribbles with proper form while jogging around eight cones placed 5 feet apart and controls the ball 80 percent of the time with dominant hand and 50 percent of the time with nondominant hand.
7. Brown	Student dribbles with proper form while jogging around eight stationary defenders placed 5 feet apart and controls the ball 80 percent of the time with either hand.

Foul Shot

Task	Student shoots foul shots from the foul line.
Scale components	(a) Form, (b) accuracy

Rubric level and color	Rubric descriptors
1. White	Student shoots foul shot from 5 feet (1.5 meters) in front of the foul line in 3 out of 5 attempts with or without assistance.
2. Yellow	Student faces the basket from 5 feet in front of the foul line with knees bent, dominant hand palm up under ball, and nondominant hand supporting ball from side in 3 out of 5 attempts with or without assistance.
3. Orange	Student faces the basket from 5 feet in front of the foul line with knees bent, dominant hand palm up under ball, nondominant hand supporting ball from side, and knee and arm extension during the shot in 3 out of 5 attempts with or without assistance.
4. Green	Student shoots foul shot with proper form from the foul line in 3 out of 5 attempts.
5. Blue	Student shoots foul shot with proper form from the foul line and hits the rim in 3 out of 5 attempts.
6. Purple	Student shoots foul shot with proper form from the foul line and makes 5 out of 10 shots.
7. Brown	Student shoots foul shot with proper form from the foul line and makes at least 8 out of 10 shots.

Game Play

Task	Student is evaluated on offensive skills during game play.
Scale components	(a) Use of passes, dribbling, and shooting; (b) ability to retain ball on offensive side or score

Rubric level and color	Rubric descriptors
1. White	Student properly uses bounce pass and chest pass during game play some of the time.
2. Yellow	Student properly uses the triple threat by obtaining possession and then dribbling, passing, or shooting, according to the appropriate option, 50 percent of the time.
3. Orange	Student uses the triple threat by obtaining possession and then dribbling, passing, or shooting, according to the appropriate option, 75 percent of the time.
4. Green	Student dribbles around defenders and retains possession, completes passes, and shoots accurately (i.e., hits basket rim or backboard or makes the shot) 50 percent of the time.
5. Blue	Student dribbles around defenders and retains possession, completes passes, and shoots accurately 75 percent of the time.
6. Purple	Student assists others in shooting by passing to an open teammate 75 percent of the time.
7. Brown	Student properly uses triple threat and displays appropriate skills 95 percent of the time and accuracy in passing, shooting, and dribbling at least 50 percent of the time.

SOCCER

Potential Modifications and Adaptations

Equipment	Rules	Environment	Instruction
☐ Soccer balls	☐ Hands permitted for protection	☐ Cones as boundaries	☐ Verbal cues
☐ Large balls	☐ No heading	☐ Bright boundaries	☐ Demonstration
☐ Small balls	☐ Walk with ball	☐ Ropes as boundaries	☐ Modeling
☐ Bright balls	☐ Peer places ball on ground for kick	☐ Beeper or auditory boundaries	☐ Tactile modeling
☐ Textured balls	☐ Undefended	☐ Visual shooting line	☐ Physical assistance
☐ Heavy balls	☐ No defense for certain number of seconds	☐ Smooth surface	☐ Task cards (enlarged if needed)
☐ Light balls	☐ Free shooting (no defense)	☐ Modified field size	☐ Pictures
☐ Foam balls	☐ Everyone touches ball before shots on goal	☐ Stations	☐ Guided discovery
☐ Nerf balls	☐ Pass certain number of times before shots on goal		☐ Problem-solving
☐ Beach balls	☐ Vary playing times		☐ Task analysis
☐ Deflated balls	☐ Limit boundaries		☐ Proximity
☐ Auditory balls	☐ Lane soccer		☐ Individualized
☐ Bell balls	☐ Small-sided games		☐ Sign language
☐ Balls on strings			☐ Feedback
☐ Front bumper on chair			☐ Peer tutor
☐ Bells on net			☐ Paraeducator
☐ Buzzer on net			☐ Interpreter
☐ Wide goal			
☐ Small goal			
☐ Bright goal			
☐ Flags			
☐ Cones			
☐ Shin guards			

Dribbling

Task	Student dribbles using inside and outside of foot against a defender.
Scale components	(a) Form, (b) velocity of performance, (c) radius of direction change, (d) number of defenders

Rubric level and color	Rubric descriptors
1. White	Student dribbles with dominant foot and nondominant foot in 3 out of 5 attempts with or without assistance.
2. Yellow	Student dribbles with inside of each foot through 10 cones located 7 feet (2.1 meters) apart, up and back, with control in 3 out of 5 attempts.
3. Orange	Student dribbles fast with outside of each foot through 10 cones located 7 feet apart, up and back, with control in 3 out of 5 attempts.
4. Green	Student dribbles fast with inside and outside of each foot through 10 cones located 5 feet (1.5 meters) apart, up and back, without losing the ball 75 percent of the time.
5. Blue	Student dribbles against a defender with inside and outside of foot for 30 yards (27.4 meters).
6. Purple	Student dribbles against two defenders for 30 seconds within a 20-yard (18.3-meter) radius using the inside and outside dribble without losing the ball 75 percent of the time.

Passing

Task	Student performs an exact pass using the inside or outside of the foot to a standing or moving partner.
Scale components	(a) Form, (b) number of performances, (c) motion
Rubric level and color	**Rubric descriptors**
1. White	Student passes with dominant foot or nondominant foot in 3 out of 5 attempts with or without assistance.
2. Yellow	Student passes with inside of the foot to a partner standing 10 feet (3 meters) away using each foot 10 times.
3. Orange	Student passes with outside of the foot to a partner standing 10 feet away using each foot 10 times.
4. Green	Student passes with inside or outside of the foot to a partner standing 20 feet (6.1 meters) away 10 times (5 with the inside foot and 5 with the outside foot).
5. Blue	Student passes with only the inside of the foot to a partner moving up and down the field and has control most of the time.
6. Purple	Student passes with only the outside of the foot to a partner moving up and down the field and has control most of the time.
7. Brown	Student passes to a partner 20 yards up field, leading the receiver on the run, and keeping the ball within 5 feet (1.5 meters) of the receiver's foot 8 out of 10 times.

Game Play

Task	Student is an active participant in a soccer game.
Scale components	(a) Dribbling, (b) passing, (c) defense, (d) shooting (all performed consistently during a scrimmage or game)
Rubric level and color	**Rubric descriptors**
1. White	Student participates in a 3-on-3 game, demonstrates a dribble and a pass when on offense, and shows knowledge of defense when his or her team is on defense.
2. Yellow	Student participates in a 3-on-3 game, consistently demonstrates a dribble and a pass when on offense, and consistently shows knowledge of defense when team is on defense.
3. Orange	Student participates in a 5-on-5 scrimmage, consistently demonstrates a dribble and a pass when on offense, and consistently shows knowledge of defense when team is on defense.
4. Green	Student demonstrates all previous skills, cuts for a pass, and shoots on goal 50 percent of the time when a shot is available.
5. Blue	Student demonstrates all previous skills, consistently cuts for a pass, and consistently shoots on goal 80 percent of the time when a shot is available.
6. Purple	Student participates in a full-field soccer game with consistent offensive and defensive skills for at least 10 minutes.
7. Brown	Student participates in a full-field soccer game with consistent offensive and defensive skills for at least 15 minutes.

TENNIS

Potential Modifications and Adaptations

Equipment	Rules	Environment	Instruction
☐ Tennis balls	☐ Hit off tee for serve	☐ Play against wall	☐ Verbal cues
☐ Large balls	☐ Bounce serve	☐ Extended boundaries	☐ Demonstration
☐ Bright balls	☐ Two-step serve	☐ Limited boundaries	☐ Modeling
☐ Heavy balls	☐ Unlimited steps for serve	☐ Cones as boundaries	☐ Tactile modeling
☐ Light balls	☐ More than one bounce	☐ Bright boundaries	☐ Physical assistance
☐ Foam balls	☐ Vary points awarded	☐ Ropes as boundaries	☐ Task cards (enlarged if needed)
☐ Nerf balls	☐ Bounce the ball and hit it with a racket to specific areas on opposite side for points	☐ Beeper or auditory boundaries	☐ Pictures
☐ Beach balls		☐ Varied playing surfaces (e.g., dirt, smooth, grass)	☐ Guided discovery
☐ Auditory balls			☐ Problem-solving
☐ Wiffle balls			☐ Task analysis
☐ Tetherball			☐ Proximity
☐ Large rackets			☐ Individualized
☐ Small rackets			☐ Sign language
☐ Wide rackets			☐ Feedback
☐ Short rackets			☐ Peer tutor
☐ Foam rackets			☐ Paraeducator
☐ Strap for rackets			☐ Interpreter
☐ No net			
☐ Lowered net			

Forehand Shot

Task	Student hits a forehand shot in a tennis game.
Scale components	(a) Form, (b) number of performances, (c) placement
Rubric level and color	**Rubric descriptors**
1. White	Student hits a drop-bounce ball with a forehand shot in 3 out of 5 attempts with or without assistance.
2. Yellow	Student hits a tennis ball thrown with a bounce from 6 feet (1.8 meters) away with a forehand shot in 3 out of 5 attempts.
3. Orange	Student hits a ball thrown with a bounce with body turned sideways, makes contact in front of body, and distinctly shifts weight forward in 3 out of 5 attempts.
4. Green	Student hits a thrown ball with body turned sideways, makes contact in front of body, shifts weight forward, and follows through in 3 out of 5 attempts.
5. Blue	Student hits a forehand with proper form from a toss and gets the ball over the net 8 out of 10 times.
6. Purple	Student hits a forehand with proper form during a game and gets the ball over the net 8 out of 10 times.

Serve

Task	Student hits a serve in a tennis game.
Scale components	(a) Form, (b) number of performances, (c) success
Rubric level and color	**Rubric descriptors**
1. White	Student serves the ball from half of the half-court in 3 out of 5 attempts with or without assistance.
2. Yellow	Student serves the ball from half of the half-court with shoulder facing the net, makes proper toss above head, and makes contact out in front of the body in 3 out of 5 attempts.
3. Orange	Student serves the ball from the service line with shoulder facing the net, makes proper toss above head, makes contact out in front of the body, shifts weight, and follows through in 3 out of 5 attempts.
4. Green	Student serves the ball from the service line with shoulder facing the net, makes proper toss above head, makes contact out in front of the body, shifts weight, follows through, and gets the ball over the net 5 out of 10 times.
5. Blue	Student serves the ball from the service line with proper form and gets the ball over the net 8 out of 10 times.
6. Purple	Student serves the ball from the service line with proper form during a game and gets the ball over the net and into the service box 7 out of 10 times.
7. Brown	Student serves the ball from the service line with proper form during a game and gets the ball over the net 9 out of 10 times and in the proper service box 5 out of 10 times.

Game Play

Task	Student participates in a game of tennis.
Scale components	(a) Choice of shots, (b) percentage of successful shots
Rubric level and color	**Rubric descriptors**
1. White	Student participates in a game of tennis using the forehand and backhand shots correctly 50 percent of the time.
2. Yellow	Student participates in a game of tennis using the forehand, backhand, drop, and overhand smash shots correctly 50 percent of the time.
3. Orange	Student participates in a game of tennis using the forehand, backhand, drop, and overhand smash shots correctly 75 percent of the time.
4. Green	Student participates in a game of tennis using the forehand, backhand, drop, and overhand smash shots correctly 75 percent of the time and gets the ball over the net 50 percent of the time.
5. Blue	Student participates in a game of tennis using the forehand, backhand, drop, and overhand smash shots correctly 75 percent of the time and gets the ball over the net 75 percent of the time.
6. Purple	Student participates in a game of tennis using the forehand, backhand, drop, and overhand smash shots correctly 90 percent of the time and places the ball in the desired spot 50 percent of the time.
7. Brown	Student participates in a game of tennis using the forehand, backhand, drop, and overhand smash shots correctly 95 percent of the time and places the ball in the desired spot 75 percent of the time.

BADMINTON

Potential Modifications and Adaptations

Equipment	Rules	Environment	Instruction
☐ Birdies	☐ Points for landing in a certain area	☐ Indoor or outdoor	☐ Task analysis
☐ Bright birdies	☐ Vary points needed to win	☐ Wide court	☐ Feedback
☐ Oversize birdies	☐ Points awarded for hitting birdie	☐ Short court	☐ Demonstration
☐ Beeping birdies	☐ Allowed to hit birdie twice	☐ Reduce court size	☐ Visual aids
☐ Wiffle balls	☐ Unlimited bounces	☐ Narrower sidelines	☐ Routine
☐ Tetherball	☐ Shorter service line	☐ Stations	☐ Verbal cues
☐ Balloons	☐ Two chances to serve	☐ Bright lights	☐ Physical assistance
☐ Fleece balls	☐ No service box	☐ Placement markers	☐ Command style
☐ Badminton rackets	☐ Alternate serve	☐ Small groups	☐ Universal signs
☐ Large rackets			☐ Hand signals
☐ Small rackets			☐ Reciprocal
☐ Short-handled rackets			☐ Direct
☐ Long-handled rackets			☐ Peer tutor
☐ Racket straps			
☐ Lowered net			
☐ Wide net			
☐ No net			
☐ Music from MP3 player or sound system			

Forehand

Task	Student hits a forehand shot in a badminton game.
Scale components	(a) Form, (b) number of performances, (c) placement
Rubric level and color	**Rubric descriptors**
1. White	Student hits a self-dropped forehand shot in 3 out of 5 attempts with or without assistance.
2. Yellow	Student hits a thrown birdie and makes contact in front of the body in 3 out of 5 attempts.
3. Orange	Student hits a thrown birdie and makes contact in front of the body with a distinct weight shift forward in 3 out of 5 attempts.
4. Green	Student hits a thrown birdie, makes contact in front of the body with a distinct weight shift forward, and follows through in 3 out of 5 attempts.
5. Blue	Student hits a forehand shot from a toss with proper form and gets the birdie over the net 8 out of 10 times.
6. Purple	Student hits a forehand shot with proper form during a game and gets the birdie over the net 7 out of 10 times.
7. Brown	Student hits a forehand shot with proper form during a game and gets the birdie over the net to a designated place 8 out of 10 times.

Serve

Task	Student hits a serve in a badminton game.
Scale components	(a) Form, (b) number of performances, (c) success

Rubric level and color	Rubric descriptors
1. White	Student serves the birdie from half-court in 3 out of 5 attempts with or without assistance.
2. Yellow	Student serves the birdie from half-court and makes contact in front of the body in 3 out of 5 attempts.
3. Orange	Student serves the birdie from half-court and makes contact in front of the body with a distinct weight shift forward in 3 out of 5 attempts.
4. Green	Student serves the birdie from half court, makes contact in front of the body with a distinct weight shift forward, and follows through in 3 out of 5 attempts.
5. Blue	Student serves the birdie from half-court with proper form and gets it over the net 8 out of 10 times.
6. Purple	Student serves the birdie with proper form from the service line during a game and gets it over the net 7 out of 10 times.
7. Brown	Student serves the birdie with proper form from the service line during a game and gets it to a designated area 8 out of 10 times.

Game Play

Task	Student participates in a game of badminton.
Scale components	(a) Choice of shots, (b) percentage of successful shots

Rubric level and color	Rubric descriptors
1. White	Student participates in a game of badminton and uses forehand and backhand shots correctly 50 percent of the time.
2. Yellow	Student participates in a game of badminton and uses forehand, backhand, drop, and overhand smash shots correctly 50 percent of the time.
3. Orange	Student participates in a game of badminton and uses forehand, backhand, drop, and overhand smash shots correctly 75 percent of the time.
4. Green	Student participates in a game of badminton and uses forehand, backhand, drop, and overhand smash shots correctly 75 percent of the time and gets the birdie over the net 50 percent of the time.
5. Blue	Student participates in a game of badminton and uses forehand, backhand, drop, and overhand smash shots correctly 75 percent of the time and gets the birdie over the net 75 percent of the time.
6. Purple	Student participates in a game of badminton and uses forehand, backhand, drop, and overhand smash shots correctly 80 percent of the time and gets the birdie to the desired spot 50 percent of the time.

FLAG FOOTBALL

Potential Modifications and Adaptations

Equipment	Rules	Environment	Instruction
☐ Footballs	☐ Two flags on chair	☐ Indoor or outdoor	☐ Peer tutor
☐ Large footballs	☐ 3-foot (0.9 meter) cushion area	☐ Small environment	☐ Command style
☐ Bright balls	☐ More points for running	☐ Wide field	☐ Universal signs
☐ Nerf balls	☐ 10 seconds before rushing	☐ Narrow field	☐ Demonstration
☐ Beeper balls	☐ Three completions to get first down	☐ Short field	☐ Task analyze
☐ Velcro balls	☐ Rotate positions	☐ Use cones	☐ Visual aids
☐ Long flags	☐ Have to pass ball	☐ Boundaries	☐ Individualized
☐ Short flags	☐ Vary pass patterns	☐ Everybody included	☐ Proximity
☐ Bright flags	☐ No late hitting	☐ Short goal post	☐ Teach signs
☐ Only one flag	☐ Certain number of time-outs	☐ Close goal post	☐ Direct
☐ Bright cones	☐ Cooperation	☐ Low noise	☐ Small-group work
☐ Whistle	☐ Alternate running	☐ Play on a gym floor or parking lot surface	☐ Lesson plan on board
☐ Helmets	☐ Must get both flags	☐ No distractions	☐ Clear explanation
☐ Mouth guards	☐ Blindfold half of the class	☐ No sun in eyes	
☐ Bright pinnies	☐ Buddy catches		
☐ Task cards	☐ Three time-outs		
☐ Flip cards	☐ Smaller-sided games		

Defense

Task	Student defends opponent in game of flag football.
Scale components	(a) Form, (b) proximity, (c) interceptions
Rubric level and color	**Rubric descriptors**
1. White	Student slides sideways, runs forward, runs backward, and slides again for the distance of one football field.
2. Yellow	Student practices guarding opponent by shadowing through zigzag drills at half speed and staying with opponent most of the time.
3. Orange	Student practices guarding opponent by shadowing through zigzag drills at three-quarters speed and staying with opponent most of the time.
4. Green	Student practices guarding opponent by shadowing through zigzag drills at full speed and staying with opponent 75 percent of the time.
5. Blue	Student stays within 8 feet of opponent 75 percent of the time during a game.
6. Purple	Student stays with opponent 75 percent of the time and intercepts 75 percent of the balls that come near him or her during a game.
7. Brown	Student stays with opponent 80 percent of the time and intercepts 75 percent of the balls that come near him or her during a game.

Passing

Task	Student passes to teammate while running.
Scale components	(a) Form, (b) distance, (c) accuracy
Rubric level and color	**Rubric descriptors**
1. White	Student throws with proper form (step with opposite foot, shift weight, rotate hip, and follow through) most of the time.
2. Yellow	Student throws 10 feet (3 meters) with proper form and spirals the football most of the time.
3. Orange	Student throws 10 feet with proper form and spirals the football to a stationary teammate most of the time.
4. Green	Student throws 10 feet with proper form and spirals the football to a teammate running toward him or her most of the time.
5. Blue	Student throws 10 feet with proper form and spirals the football to a running teammate 50 percent of the time.
6. Purple	Student throws 10 feet with proper form and spirals the football to a running teammate 75 percent of the time.
7. Brown	Student throws 10 feet with proper form and spirals the football to a running teammate with a defender 75 percent of the time.

Potential Modifications and Adaptations

Equipment	Rules	Environment	Instruction
☐ Large heads	☐ Limit distance	☐ Uncluttered (no sand or ponds)	☐ Explanation
☐ Large golf balls	☐ Add distance	☐ Limit distractions	☐ Demonstration
☐ Auditory balls	☐ Count every other or every third hit	☐ Predictable	☐ Physical assistance
☐ Bright balls	☐ Move ball to preferred spot	☐ Play on a cloudy day	☐ Visual aids
☐ Plastic balls	☐ Pair up with a buddy	☐ Play at night with a bright ball	☐ Command style
☐ Beeper balls	☐ Play in teams	☐ Practice at a range	☐ Use of first name for children with autism or children who need help paying attention
☐ Large grips	☐ No score	☐ Supportive	☐ Task style
☐ Short clubs	☐ Frisbee golf	☐ Directional arrows	☐ Problem-solving
☐ Light clubs	☐ Make up own course	☐ Targets are marked	☐ Allow practice
☐ Hockey sticks	☐ Play at own pace	☐ Positive atmosphere	☐ Diagram course
☐ Thicker shafts for better grip	☐ Wait for command	☐ Short instruction	☐ Task analyze
☐ String tied to ball and club	☐ Points for certain area	☐ Short fairways	☐ Cooperative games
☐ Golf cart with driver	☐ Take any number of shots	☐ Close tees	☐ Use braille
☐ Flags	☐ No out of bounds	☐ Open field	☐ Feedback
☐ Small basket for hole	☐ Student not required to perform	☐ Cage	☐ Reciprocal
☐ Music with MP3 player or a sound system	☐ Mulligan redo	☐ Nets	☐ Shaping
☐ Tactile board description of course	☐ Add two strokes	☐ Large holes	☐ Universal signs
	☐ Two swings at hazard	☐ Decrease distractions	☐ Peer tutor
	☐ Shorter green flags	☐ No sun in eyes	
	☐ Larger number for par		
	☐ Be quiet		
	☐ Personal space		

Drive

Task	Student drives a golf ball.
Scale components	(a) Form, (b) distance
Rubric level and color	**Rubric descriptors**
1. White	Student attempts a drive shot with a proper club.
2. Yellow	Student attempts a drive shot while standing with shoulder to desired direction, feet shoulder-width apart, and knees bent.
3. Orange	Student attempts a drive shot while standing with shoulder to desired direction, feet shoulder-width apart, and knees bent and holding club with 10-finger grip most of the time.
4. Green	Student attempts a drive shot while standing with shoulder to desired direction, feet shoulder-width apart, and knees bent; holding club with 10-finger grip; shifting weight; and following through most of the time.
5. Blue	Student hits a drive shot with proper form 10 to 20 feet (3 to 6.1 meters) most of the time.
6. Purple	Student hits a drive shot with proper form 10 to 20 feet in desired direction 8 out of 10 times.
7. Brown	Student hits a drive shot with proper form at least 20 feet in desired direction 8 out of 10 times.

Putt

Task	Student putts a golf ball.
Scale components	(a) Form, (b) accuracy

Rubric level and color	Rubric descriptors
1. White	Student attempts a putt, choosing the proper club 3 out of 5 times.
2. Yellow	Student attempts a putt, choosing the proper club all the time, while standing with shoulder to desired direction, feet shoulder-width apart, and knees bent.
3. Orange	Student attempts a putt while standing with shoulder to desired direction, feet shoulder-width apart, and knees bent and holding club with reverse overlap grip (index finger of the top hand overlaps between the little finger and the ring finger of the bottom hand, bottom hand palm covers the top hand thumb on the shaft) most of the time.
4. Green	Student attempts a putt while standing with shoulder to desired direction, feet shoulder-width apart, and knees bent; holding club with reverse overlap grip; shifting weight; and following through most of the time.
5. Blue	Student hits a putt with proper form 5 to 10 feet (1.5 to 3 meters) most of the time.
6. Purple	Student hits a putt with proper form 10 to 20 feet (3 to 6.1 meters) in desired direction 8 out of 10 times.
7. Brown	Student hits a putt with proper form at least 10 to 20 feet in desired direction and in 5-foot (1.5-meter) square area 8 out of 10 times.

TRACK AND FIELD

Potential Modifications and Adaptations

Equipment	Rules	Environment	Instruction
☐ Bright lane lines	☐ Set number of trials	☐ Indoor or outdoor	☐ Physical assistance
☐ Carpet squares	☐ Time limitations	☐ Bright boundaries	☐ Eye contact
☐ Soft hurdles	☐ Boundary limitations	☐ Throwing line	☐ Verbal cues
☐ Low hurdles	☐ Guide runner	☐ Tactile lines	☐ Proximity
☐ Ropes	☐ Cooperation versus com-petition	☐ Auditory lines	☐ Sign language
☐ Tethers	☐ Limited space	☐ Cones	☐ Use braille
☐ Auditory jump boards	☐ Clap in target areas	☐ Ropes	☐ Bright clothing for stu-dents with visual impair-ment to follow during running
☐ Tactile jump boards	☐ Look before throwing	☐ Jumping line	
☐ Sand pit	☐ Clear surface	☐ Success-oriented	
☐ Track	☐ Warm up	☐ Limited distractions	
☐ Batons	☐ Help others	☐ Open and friendly	☐ Cognitive cues
☐ Mats	☐ Wait for others to finish	☐ Safe, clean surfaces	☐ Individualized
☐ Various throwing objects	☐ No jumping with shunts	☐ Water is accessible	☐ Slow down
☐ Beanbags	☐ Bigger ring for shot put	☐ Long distance	☐ Demonstrate
☐ Shots	☐ Throw in any manner	☐ Short distance	☐ Feedback
☐ Soft shots	☐ Lines closer to target	☐ Chalk lines instead of hurdles	☐ Direct
☐ Small shots	☐ Shorter fly zone		☐ Run with partners
☐ Light shots	☐ Adjust times	☐ Wide vector	☐ Play-by-play action
☐ Discuses	☐ Shorter approach	☐ Obstacle course	☐ Inclusive
☐ Soft discuses	☐ Head start	☐ Use music	☐ Sequential
☐ Light discuses	☐ Checklist of activities	☐ Controlled group	☐ Activity analysis
☐ Weights	☐ Ability grouping	☐ Divided for safety	☐ Guided discovery
☐ Whistle	☐ Run time rather than dis-tance	☐ Large lane lines	☐ Use of first name for chil-dren with autism or chil-dren who need help paying attention
☐ Lanes		☐ Smooth surface	
☐ Score sheets	☐ No time on field events		
☐ Task cards	☐ Throw with good tech-nique		
☐ Parachute (for training)			☐ Task analysis
☐ Visual aids	☐ Hand signals		☐ Peer tutor
☐ Tape measure	☐ Run at own pace		
☐ Timing device	☐ No high-jump bar		
	☐ Auditory start		
	☐ Auditory high jump		

High Jump (Flop Approach)

Task	Student performs a high jump with moderate speed on the approach and obvious flow from the approach to the jump, leads the jump with the shoulders and head and all other body parts following, and lands on the upper back or shoulder area over a 3-foot (0.9-meter) pole.
Scale components	(a) Flow, (b) form, (c) speed, (d) height
Rubric level and color	**Rubric descriptors**
1. White	Student uses slow speed on the approach and there is no obvious flow from the approach to the actual jump; student leads the jump with the side or feet and all other body parts following and lands on a 2-foot-high (0.6 meter) pit mat.
2. Yellow	Student uses medium speed on the approach and there is no obvious flow from the approach to the actual jump; student leads the jump with the side or feet and all other body parts following and lands on a 2-foot-high pit mat.
3. Orange	Student uses moderate speed on the approach with obvious flow from the approach to the actual jump, leads the jump with the side or feet and all other body parts following, and lands on a 2-foot-high pit mat sometimes.
4. Green	Student uses moderate speed on the approach with obvious flow from the approach to the actual jump, leads the jump with the side or feet and all other body parts following, and lands on a 2-foot-high pit mat most of the time.
5. Blue	Student uses moderate speed on the approach with obvious flow from the approach to the actual jump, leads the jump with shoulders or head and all other body parts following, and lands on a 2-foot-high pit mat (pole at the 2-foot mark).
6. Purple	Student uses previous approach with the pole at the 2.5-foot (0.8-meter) mark.
7. Brown	Student uses previous approach with the pole at the 3-foot mark.

Hurdles

Task	Student jumps over regulation-height hurdles using proper form.
Scale components	(a) Form, (b) height, (c) speed (optional)
Rubric level and color	**Rubric descriptors**
1. White	Student runs flat-footed during preflight, uses arms and legs on the same side to initiate flight, jumps over a plastic pole 1 foot (0.3 meters) high, and lands unbalanced.
2. Yellow	Students runs with mature form during preflight, uses arms and legs on the same side to initiate flight, leads with one distinct foot, jumps over a plastic pole 1 foot high, and lands unbalanced.
3. Orange	Students runs with mature form during preflight, uses arms and legs on opposite sides to initiate flight, leads with one distinct foot, jumps over a plastic pole 1 foot high, and lands balanced.
4. Green	Students runs with mature form during preflight, uses arms and legs on opposite sides to initiate flight, leads with one distinct foot, jumps over a plastic pole 2 feet (0.6 meters) high, and lands balanced.
5. Blue	Student successfully jumps one regulation hurdle with mature form.
6. Purple	Student successfully jumps five regulation hurdles with mature form.
7. Brown	Student successfully runs a hurdle race at three-quarters speed with mature form.

GYMNASTICS

Potential Modifications and Adaptations

Equipment	Rules	Environment	Instruction
☐ Mats of all sizes	☐ Cooperation	☐ Lower bars	☐ Spotting
☐ Wedge mats	☐ Rubrics	☐ Lower rings	☐ Shaping
☐ Beam	☐ Have a partner	☐ Lower other equipment	☐ Peer tutor
☐ Wide beam	☐ Adequate space	☐ Use music	☐ Demonstration
☐ Horse	☐ No shoes on mats	☐ Pictures	☐ Problem-solving
☐ Short horse	☐ Varied distance	☐ Shorter approach	☐ Face students
☐ Rings	☐ Physical assistance	☐ Small space	☐ Visual aids
☐ Parallel bars	☐ Fewer floor events	☐ Boundaries	☐ Task analyze
☐ Uneven bars	☐ Attempt all activities	☐ Low noise level	☐ Feedback
☐ Springboard	☐ No activity without a tutor	☐ Large mat area	☐ Direct
☐ Trampoline	☐ Challenge by choice	☐ Break down skill	☐ Indirect
☐ Balls	☐ Personal best	☐ Bright equipment	☐ Clear
☐ Whistle	☐ Safety at all times	☐ Small groups	☐ Use braille
☐ Ribbons	☐ No horseplay		☐ Independence
☐ Loose-fitting clothing	☐ No flipping		☐ Verbal cues
	☐ One at a time		☐ Hand signs
			☐ Write out class plans
			☐ Orientation

Cartwheel

Task	Student performs side and front cartwheels two times in a row to each side in combination with other gymnastic elements.
Scale components	(a) Support (spotting), (b) type of cartwheel, (c) number of performances
Rubric level and color	**Rubric descriptors**
1. White	Student attempts a side or front cartwheel with limited success.
2. Yellow	Student performs one of the cartwheels with or without support.
3. Orange	Student performs both cartwheels without a spot.
4. Green	Student performs both cartwheels two times in a row.
5. Blue	Student performs both cartwheels two times in a row to nondominant side.
6. Purple	Student combines each of the cartwheels with other gymnastic elements in a series.

Handstand

Task	Student performs a stable handstand in combination with different gymnastic elements.
Scale components	(a) Support (spotting, wedge mat), (b) type of performance, (c) number of performances
Rubric level and color	**Rubric descriptors**
1. White	Student attempts a handstand with limited success.
2. Yellow	Student performs the handstand with a spot or a wedge mat.
3. Orange	Student performs a handstand and holds it for 1 second without a spot or wedge mat.
4. Green	Student performs the handstand, holds it for 3 seconds, and turns into a forward roll.
5. Blue	Student performs a handstand over into a bridge with controlled step out (one leg over at a time) and holds it for 2 seconds.
6. Purple	Student performs a handstand and turns into a forward roll in a pike position.
7. Brown	Student performs a backward roll into a handstand position and holds it for 2 seconds.

Balance Tasks

Task	Student controls balance on hands and knees while raising some body parts.
Scale components	(a) Laterality, (b) number of body parts raised
Rubric level and color	**Rubric descriptors**
1. White	Student is on all fours with both knees and hands on the mat and is stable.
2. Yellow	Student raises less-affected arm and hand without losing balance.
3. Orange	Student raises less-affected knee and foot without losing balance.
4. Green	Student raises more-affected arm and hand without losing balance.
5. Blue	Student raises the more-affected knee and foot without losing balance.
6. Purple	Student raises the hand or arm and knee or foot of the less-affected side without losing balance.
7. Brown	Student raises the hand or arm and knee or foot of the more-affected side without losing balance.
8. Red	Student raises the hand or arm and knee or foot of the opposite sides of the body without losing balance.

(continued)

Squat Vault

Task	Student performs a squat vault and lands with both feet and has good balance.
Scale components	Form
Rubric level and color	**Rubric descriptors**
1. White	Student stands on springboard with hands 1 foot (0.3 meters) away on horse, jumps three times, lands on horse in squat position, and jumps off horse on two feet.
2. Yellow	Student repeats previous skill with only one quick touch on top of the horse with feet before jumping down.
3. Orange	Student takes a running start with medium speed, jumps from springboard 1 foot away to top of horse, lands on feet, and jumps down onto both feet with control.
4. Green	Student runs from end of runway at moderate speed, jumps on springboard 1 foot away from horse, squats over horse without touching, and lands on both feet.
5. Blue	Student runs from end of runway at full speed, jumps on springboard 2 feet (0.6 meters) away from horse, squats over horse without touching, and lands on both feet.
6. Purple	Student runs from end of runway at full speed, jumps on springboard 2 feet away from horse, squats over horse without touching, lands on both feet with control, and raises hands over head for finish.
7. Brown	Student runs from end of runway at full speed, jumps on springboard 2 to 3 feet (0.6 to 1 meter) away from horse, squats over horse without touching, lands on both feet with control, and raises hands over head for finish 4 out of 5 times.

Potential Modifications and Adaptations

Equipment	Rules	Environment	Instruction
☐ Head gear	☐ Match skill levels	☐ Bright boundaries	☐ Task analyze
☐ Wrestling shoes	☐ Skill utilization	☐ Decrease boundaries	☐ Demonstration
☐ Elbow and knee pads	☐ Pin counts as 1	☐ Clear boundaries	☐ Guided discovery
☐ Mats of all sizes	☐ Control position	☐ Stations	☐ Cognitive cues
☐ Soft mats	☐ 5-count equals a pin	☐ Soft surfaces	☐ Verbal cues
☐ Short ropes	☐ Large number cards for children with low vision to see during competition	☐ Bright lights	☐ Personal cues
☐ Short jump ropes	☐ Time limit	☐ Technique posters	☐ Problem-solving
☐ Small stationary bike	☐ Slow down pace	☐ Safety procedures posted	☐ Minimize instruction
☐ Blindfolds	☐ Contain no inner circle	☐ Cones	☐ Small groups
☐ Tackle dummy	☐ Stop when told	☐ Padded wall	☐ Physical assistance
☐ Visual aids	☐ No half nelson	☐ Proper clothing	☐ Use braille
☐ Whistle	☐ No fireman's carry	☐ Warm room	☐ Command style
☐ Timer	☐ No shunts	☐ Low ceiling	☐ Shaping
☐ Task cards	☐ No spinal injuries	☐ Mirrors on walls	☐ Reciprocal
☐ Flip cards	☐ No body slamming		☐ Inclusive
	☐ No choke holds		☐ Peer tutor
	☐ No arm bars		☐ Use videos for instruction
	☐ No trash talking		☐ Short, simple cues
	☐ No prosthetics		
	☐ No wheelchairs		

Arm-Bar Takedown (Bottom Position)

Task	From the kneeling position, the student makes a two-handed wrist lock on the top person's right hand, brings the opponent into the body, wraps the right arm over opponent's arm, uses body weight in opposition to the opponent's, rolls to the right side, and maintains grip on the wrist throughout (done within 5 seconds).
Scale components	(a) Weight transfer, (b) weight opposition, (c) rolling, (d) speed
Rubric level and color	**Rubric descriptors**
1. White	From the kneeling position, the student makes a two-handed wrist lock on top of the person's right hand, uses body weight in opposition to the opponent's, and rolls to the right side.
2. Yellow	From the kneeling position, the student makes a two-handed wrist lock on top of the person's right hand, uses body weight in opposition to the opponent's, rolls to the right side, and maintains grip throughout.
3. Orange	From the kneeling position, the student makes a two-handed wrist lock on top of the person's right hand, brings arms into the body, uses body weight in opposition to the opponent's, rolls to the right side, and maintains grip throughout.
4. Green	From the kneeling position, the student makes a two-handed wrist lock on top of the person's right hand, brings arms into the body, wraps right arm over opponent's, uses body weight in opposition to the opponent's, rolls to the right side, and maintains grip throughout.
5. Blue	Student performs a proper takedown in less than 15 seconds.
6. Purple	Student performs a proper takedown in less than 10 seconds.
7. Brown	Student performs a proper takedown in less than 5 seconds.

11

Recreation and Leisure Skills

Purpose: The importance of recreational skills cannot be overlooked at any age. The ability to participate in enjoyable recreational activities is crucial to enjoying a high quality of life in school and beyond.

Unit adaptations: There are many ways to adapt the recreation curriculum for children with disabilities, and modifications for each child must be specific to his or her needs. For example, a 13-year-old child with an intellectual disability wants to learn to in-line skate because he and his siblings got skates for the holidays. He has never done in-line skating before, but with some physical assistance from his physical educator, he can use teaching cues to work through slow, small steps and become proficient enough to be independent at the party.

Assessment options: Each unit includes at least one rubric for evaluating the process or product of movements; you can also create your own rubrics. In addition, you can create checklists and rating scales and have students keep journals. All of these can be included in students' portfolios (see chapter 2).

This chapter contains ideas you can use to teach various recreational activities. For each activity, we address equipment that can be used, rule modifications, environmental alterations, and instructional variations. Check off those modifications that apply to the learner. For example, if a child benefitted from *holding onto the wall to begin in-line skating*, then that would be checked off in the modifications table. Once this is checked off, any subsequent lessons relating to in-line skating can be replicated with the variables that worked as part of the Universal Design process.

Potential Modifications and Adaptations

Equipment	Rules	Environment	Instruction
☐ Small packs	☐ Stay with group	☐ Trails	☐ Verbal cues
☐ Light packs	☐ Use buddy system	☐ Groomed trails	☐ Demonstration
☐ Water bottles	☐ Stay on path	☐ Accessible trails	☐ Modeling
☐ Walking sticks	☐ Modify pace	☐ Smooth walking paths	☐ Tactile modeling
☐ Rails on side of path	☐ Shorter trails	☐ Fields	☐ Physical assistance
☐ Bright trail markers	☐ Identify poison ivy	☐ Small hills	☐ Task cards (enlarged if needed)
☐ Large trail markers	☐ Drink or rest when needed	☐ Marked boundaries	☐ Pictures
☐ Bright flag markers	☐ Know basic first aid		☐ Guided discovery
☐ Color-coded maps	☐ Know and plan what to do if lost		☐ Problem-solving
☐ Large compasses	☐ Don't touch plants		☐ Task analysis
☐ Ropes for tethering or guiding	☐ Don't eat anything		☐ Proximity
☐ Proper footwear	☐ No alternative trails		☐ Individualized
☐ Proper clothing	☐ No running		☐ Sign language
☐ Change of clothes	☐ No littering		☐ Feedback
☐ Camping gear	☐ Use buddy for support		☐ Peer tutor
☐ First-aid kit			☐ Paraeducator
☐ Whistle			☐ Interpreter
☐ Toilet paper			

Backpacking and Hiking

Task	Student hikes with or without a pack.
Scale components	(a) Distance, (b) terrain, (c) weight of and distance with a pack (optional)
Rubric level and color	**Rubric descriptors**
1. White	Student walks on a flat trail in the woods that has few roots and rocks for 0.5 miles (0.8 kilometers) with or without assistance.
2. Yellow	Student walks on a flat trail in the woods that has few roots and rocks for 1 mile (1.6 kilometers).
3. Orange	Student walks on a trail with moderate hills that has some roots and rocks for 1 mile.
4. Green	Student walks on a trail with moderate hills that has some roots and rocks for 2 miles (3.2 kilometers).
5. Blue	Student walks terrain with 250- to 500-foot (76.2- to 152.4-meter) elevation that has some roots and rocks for 2 miles.
6. Purple	Student walks terrain with 250- to 500-foot elevation that has some roots and rocks for 3 miles (4.8 kilometers) or more. Optional: Student carries 10- to 25-pound (4.5- to 11.3-kilogram) pack.
7. Brown	Student walks terrain with 250- to 1,000-foot (76.2- to 304.6-meter) elevation that has abundant roots and rocks for 3 or more miles. Optional: Student carries 20- to 40-pound (9.1- to 18.1-kilogram) pack.

Potential Modifications and Adaptations

Equipment	Rules	Environment	Instruction
☐ Plastic balls	☐ Two hands if needed	☐ Indoor or outdoor	☐ Verbal cues
☐ Playground balls	☐ More than two turns at a time	☐ Directional arrows	☐ Demonstration
☐ Light balls	☐ Stand at line	☐ Guide rails	☐ Modeling
☐ Bright balls	☐ Can cross line	☐ Short distance	☐ Tactile modeling
☐ Small balls	☐ One-step approach	☐ Short lanes	☐ Physical assistance
☐ Snap-handle balls (handle snaps back in after the throw)	☐ Any number of steps	☐ Wide lanes	☐ Task cards (enlarged if needed)
☐ Colored pins	☐ Spare equals strike	☐ Sloped lanes	☐ Pictures
☐ Lighter pins	☐ Tutor recovers ball	☐ More pins	☐ Guided discovery
☐ Ramp		☐ Fewer pins	☐ Problem-solving
☐ Floor markings		☐ Have only one ball in ball return rack	☐ Task analysis
☐ Bumpers		☐ Machine keeps score automatically	☐ Proximity
☐ Rails		☐ Use Nintendo Wii bowling	☐ Individualized
			☐ Sign language
			☐ Feedback
			☐ Peer tutor
			☐ Paraeducator
			☐ Interpreter

Bowling

Task	Student bowls a ball in a bowling game.
Scale components	(a) Form, (b) accuracy
Rubric level and color	**Rubric descriptors**
1. White	Student attempts to roll the bowling ball with or without assistance.
2. Yellow	Student uses three-step approach and steps with opposite foot most of the time.
3. Orange	Student uses three-step approach, swings ball from back to front, and steps with opposite foot most of the time.
4. Green	Student uses three-step approach, swings ball from back to front, steps with the opposite foot, and releases ball in front with a smooth transition most of the time.
5. Blue	Student uses proper form with a smooth release and hits the pins without rolling the ball into the gutter 5 out of 10 times.
6. Purple	Student uses proper form with a smooth release and hits the pins without rolling the ball into the gutter 8 out of 10 times.
7. Brown	Student uses proper form and hits at least three pins in 8 out of 10 tries.

Potential Modifications and Adaptations

Equipment	Rules	Environment	Instruction
☐ Bamboo poles	☐ Sit down	☐ Calm water	☐ Verbal cues
☐ Short poles	☐ No cast	☐ No ledge to water	☐ Demonstration
☐ Long poles	☐ Multiple tries for cast	☐ Stocked pond	☐ Modeling
☐ Pole holders for belts	☐ Assistance with cast	☐ Accessible dock	☐ Tactile modeling
☐ Holders for poles	☐ Sit on boat with fixed chair		☐ Physical assistance
☐ Automatic cast-on poles	☐ No time limit		☐ Task cards (enlarged if needed)
☐ Velcro gloves for holding poles			☐ Pictures
☐ Blunt hooks			☐ Guided discovery
☐ Life jackets			☐ Problem-solving
			☐ Task analysis
			☐ Proximity
			☐ Sign language
			☐ Feedback
			☐ Peer tutor
			☐ Paraeducator
			☐ Interpreter

Casting

Task	Student casts the fishing line with bait.
Scale components	(a) Skills, (b) independence, (c) distance of the cast

Rubric level and color	Rubric descriptors
1. White	Student baits own hook with verbal prompting and some physical assistance.
2. Yellow	Student baits own hook independently and can bring rod back and cast forward without allowing reel to release.
3. Orange	Student releases the reel and gets the line out by bringing rod across the body most of the time.
4. Green	Student releases the reel, casts the line from behind the shoulder, and follows through in front; line and bait cast at least 10 feet (3 meters) some of the time.
5. Blue	Student releases the reel, casts the line from behind the shoulder, and follows through out front; line and bait cast at least 10 feet most of the time.
6. Purple	Student releases the reel, casts the line from behind the shoulder, and follows through out front; line and bait cast at least 10 feet 8 out of 10 times.
7. Brown	Student releases the reel, casts the line from behind the shoulder, and follows through out front; line and bait cast at least 15 feet (4.6 meters) 8 out of 10 times.

ROCK CLIMBING

Potential Modifications and Adaptations

Equipment	Rules	Environment	Instruction
☐ Rock wall	☐ Safety first	☐ Indoor wall	☐ Verbal cues
☐ Helmets	☐ Trust your leader	☐ Outdoor wall	☐ Demonstration
☐ Ropes	☐ Challenge by choice (child can choose more difficult part of wall if desired)	☐ Mountain	☐ Modeling
☐ Safety lines		☐ Wheelchair accessible	☐ Tactile modeling
☐ Carabiners		☐ More handholds	☐ Physical assistance
☐ Harnesses	☐ Go at own pace	☐ Sloped walls	☐ Task cards (enlarged if needed)
☐ Tandem belts	☐ Positively encourage	☐ Various rock textures	
☐ Belays	☐ Listen		☐ Pictures
☐ Cargo nets	☐ Communicate (one person gives instructions at a time)		☐ Guided discovery
☐ Ladders			☐ Problem-solving
☐ Stall bars	☐ Proper commands (specific to the climb and needs of the child)		☐ Task analysis
☐ Hand chalk			☐ Proximity
☐ Climbing shoes			☐ Individualized
☐ Gloves	☐ Lower climbs		☐ Sign language
☐ High ropes course	☐ Unlimited time		☐ Feedback
☐ Low ropes course	☐ Climb across, not up		☐ Progress with climbing to higher levels as confidence and skill improve
☐ Whistle	☐ Climb side by side		
☐ Red flags as boundaries	☐ One person climbs at a time		
☐ Cowbells	☐ Rocks close together and simply placed		☐ Small group
	☐ Adjustable surface		☐ Review safety
	☐ Belayer takes most of weight		☐ Lesson on chalkboard or whiteboard
	☐ Always have a buddy		☐ Peer tutor
	☐ Use spotters		☐ Paraeducator
			☐ Interpreter

Basic Rock Climbing

Task	Student climbs a 30-foot (9.1-meter) rock wall with harness and helmet.
Scale components	(a) Preparation, (b) attempts at climbing, (c) descent
Rubric level and color	**Rubric descriptors**
1. White	Student puts on harness and helmet with assistance.
2. Yellow	Student puts on harness and helmet and sufficiently understands the safety terminology to begin climbing.
3. Orange	Student attempts to pull body up with both hands, up to 10 feet (3 meters), and climbs down.
4. Green	Student attempts to pull body up with both hands and feet, up to 10 feet, and climbs down.
5. Blue	Student uses both hands and feet, climbs 10 to 20 feet (3 to 6.1 meters), and attempts the backward fall (the skill needed to walk down the wall).
6. Purple	Student uses both hands and feet, climbs 10 to 20 feet, and properly executes the backward fall.
7. Brown	Student uses both hands and feet, climbs 20 to 30 feet (6.1 to 9.1 meters), and properly executes the backward fall.

SKATING AND IN-LINE SKATING

Potential Modifications and Adaptations

Equipment	Rules	Environment	Instruction
☐ Wrist and knee pads	☐ Skate slowly	☐ Smooth surface	☐ Verbal cues
☐ Helmets	☐ Skate forward	☐ Soft surface	☐ Demonstration
☐ Velcro skates	☐ Skate backward	☐ Inclined surface	☐ Modeling
☐ Brakes (front and back)	☐ Skate in a circle	☐ Limited space	☐ Tactile modeling
☐ Trash can on wheels	☐ Skate with a partner	☐ Large space	☐ Physical assistance
☐ Shopping cart	☐ Skate for distance	☐ Visual boundaries	☐ Task cards (enlarged if needed)
☐ Walker on wheels	☐ Skate for time	☐ Auditory boundaries	☐ Pictures
☐ Tethers	☐ Skate and dance	☐ Use obstacles	☐ Guided discovery
☐ Bars	☐ Skate for transportation	☐ Limited number of people in the way	☐ Problem-solving
☐ Hula hoops			☐ Task analysis
			☐ Proximity
			☐ Individualized
			☐ Sign language
			☐ Feedback
			☐ Use the wall for support during instruction
			☐ Peer tutor
			☐ Paraeducator
			☐ Interpreter

Skating and In-Line Skating

Task	Student skates or in-line skates in various directions while maintaining control.
Scale components	(a) Skill ability, (b) balance and control, (c) task complexity
Rubric level and color	**Rubric descriptors**
1. White	Student skates forward, close to railing or wall, without falling for 5 minutes.
2. Yellow	Student brakes, using the brake at will, 4 out of 5 times at specific marks or cones on the floor.
3. Orange	Student skates forward on alternating feet for 20 feet (6.1 meters) without losing balance 4 out of 5 times.
4. Green	Student skates clockwise and counterclockwise in a 10- to 20-foot (3- to 6.1-meter) circle.
5. Blue	Student skates backward for 20 feet without losing balance.
6. Purple	Student skates backward in a 10- to 20-foot circle one time.
7. Brown	Student skates forward and changes to backward while moving, skates in a straight line and in a circle, and stops on command without losing balance 4 out of 5 times.

Potential Modifications and Adaptations

Equipment	Rules	Environment	Instruction
☐ Outrigger canoe	☐ Stay seated	☐ Pool	☐ Verbal cues
☐ Tactile marks on paddles	☐ Stay in pairs	☐ Calm body of water	☐ Demonstration
☐ Canoe pads for seat	☐ Vary number of students in canoe	☐ Boundary markers	☐ Modeling
☐ Flotation devices	☐ No horseplay		☐ Tactile modeling
☐ Paddles in various sizes	☐ No rocking boat		☐ Physical assistance
☐ Harnesses			☐ Task cards (enlarged if needed)
☐ Kayak paddles			☐ Pictures
☐ Thick-handled paddles			☐ Guided discovery
☐ Thin-handled paddles			☐ Problem-solving
			☐ Task analysis
			☐ Proximity
			☐ Individualized
			☐ Sign language
			☐ Feedback
			☐ Peer tutor
			☐ Paraeducator
			☐ Interpreter

Canoeing

Task	Student enters the canoe, paddles using two different strokes, and controls direction of the canoe in calm water.
Scale components	(a) Entry, (b) form, (c) control
Rubric level and color	**Rubric descriptors**
1. White	Student enters and leaves the canoe safely from a dock or landing with physical assistance as needed.
2. Yellow	Student paddles forward on one side.
3. Orange	Student paddles forward on both sides.
4. Green	Student paddles forward with partner and attempts the J stroke.
5. Blue	Student paddles forward with partner and successfully uses the J stroke.
6. Purple	Student points and steers the canoe in the desired direction most of the time.

Potential Modifications and Adaptations

Equipment	Rules	Environment	Instruction
☐ Cones	☐ Stay in own space	☐ Flat surface	☐ Verbal cues
☐ Floor tape	☐ Modify beat count	☐ Mirror	☐ Demonstration
☐ Poly spots	☐ Modify movements (e.g., walk to the beat)		☐ Modeling
☐ Footprints			☐ Tactile modeling
☐ Lummi sticks	☐ Mirror partners		☐ Physical assistance
☐ Carpet squares	☐ Similarly sized partners		☐ Task cards (enlarged if needed)
☐ Scarves			☐ Pictures
☐ Lights			☐ Guided discovery
☐ Task cards			☐ Problem-solving
☐ Boundary markers			☐ Task analysis
☐ Music			☐ Proximity
☐ Slow music			☐ Individualized
☐ Music with bass on an MP3 player or sound system			☐ Sign language
			☐ Feedback
			☐ Peer tutor
			☐ Paraeducator
			☐ Interpreter

Electric Slide

Task	Student performs the electric slide line dance.
Scale components	(a) Ability to keep the beat, (b) ability to sequence steps
Rubric level and color	**Rubric descriptors**
1. White	Student performs the moves to the electric slide with no music, in one direction, and with demonstration and verbal cues.
2. Yellow	Student performs the moves to the electric slide with music, in one direction, and with demonstration and verbal cues.
3. Orange	Student performs the moves to the electric slide with music, in two directions, and with demonstration and verbal cues.
4. Green	Student performs the moves to the electric slide with music, in all four directions, and with demonstration and verbal cues.
5. Blue	Student performs the moves to the electric elide with music, in all four directions, and with only verbal cues for the entire song.
6. Purple	Student independently performs the moves to the electric slide with music and in all four directions for the entire song.
7. Brown	Student leads the electric slide with music and in all four directions for the entire song.

Potential Modifications and Adaptations

Equipment	Rules	Environment	Instruction
☐ Mats	☐ No contact	☐ Indoor or outdoor	☐ Verbal cues
☐ Loose clothing	☐ Personal space	☐ Large space	☐ Demonstration
☐ Head gear	☐ Arm movements while sitting	☐ Matted floors	☐ Modeling
☐ Visual aids	☐ Modify moves	☐ Padded walls	☐ Tactile modeling
☐ Books to learn moves	☐ Move at own pace	☐ Flat, smooth surface	☐ Physical assistance
☐ Tubes instead of sticks	☐ Two-step cushion in distance	☐ Mirrors on walls	☐ Task cards (enlarged if needed)
☐ Props	☐ Take turns striking	☐ Posters of moves	☐ Pictures
☐ Small dummy	☐ Switch partners	☐ Small boundaries	☐ Guided discovery
☐ Punching bags	☐ Bow before technique		☐ Problem-solving
☐ Whistle	☐ Side by side with tutor		☐ Task analysis
	☐ Limit noise		☐ Proximity
	☐ Be respectful of space		☐ Individualized
			☐ Sign language
			☐ Feedback
			☐ Peer tutor
			☐ Paraeducator
			☐ Interpreter

Martial Arts

Task	Student goes through a series of martial arts moves on command.
Scale components	(a) Number of moves, (b) form, (c) level of independence

Rubric level and color	Rubric descriptors
1. White	Student executes one martial arts move with or without assistance.
2. Yellow	Student executes up to three martial arts moves correctly with or without assistance.
3. Orange	Student executes up to three martial arts moves correctly with verbal cues.
4. Green	Student executes four or more martial arts moves correctly with verbal cues.
5. Blue	Student executes four or more martial arts moves correctly without cues.

YOGA

Potential Modifications and Adaptations

Equipment	Rules	Environment	Instruction
☐ Yoga mats	☐ Use a chair if child cannot tolerate the up and down movements	☐ Indoor or outdoor	☐ Verbal cues
☐ Yoga blocks		☐ Quiet	☐ Demonstration
☐ Yoga bolsters		☐ Decrease distractions	☐ Modeling
☐ Yoga straps	☐ Modify poses to make them more or less challenging	☐ Large space	☐ Tactile modeling
☐ Yoga wedges		☐ Use music	☐ Physical assistance
☐ Blankets		☐ Mirrors on walls	☐ Task cards (enlarged if needed)
☐ Towels	☐ Use a blanket under the head to decrease neck tension	☐ Posters	
☐ Water bottles			☐ Pictures
☐ Chairs			☐ Guided discovery
☐ Yoga music	☐ Use blocks to decrease pressure on joints		☐ Problem-solving
☐ Stereo			☐ Task analysis
☐ Yoga DVDs	☐ Use the wall for those with balancing challenges		☐ Proximity
☐ TV and DVD player			☐ Individualized
☐ Comfortable clothing			☐ Sign language
☐ Yoga socks			☐ Feedback
☐ Wall			☐ Peer tutor
☐ Poly spots			☐ Paraeducator
☐ Carpet squares			☐ Interpreter
☐ Task cards			
☐ Wheelchair			
☐ Walker			

Yoga

Task	Student goes through a series of yoga poses on command.
Scale components	(a) Number of poses, (b) form, (c) level of independence
Rubric level and color	**Rubric descriptors**
1. White	Student executes one yoga pose correctly with or without assistance.
2. Yellow	Student executes up to three yoga poses correctly with or without assistance.
3. Orange	Student executes three or more yoga poses correctly with or without assistance.
4. Green	Student executes three or more yoga poses correctly without assistance.
5. Blue	Student does a 30-minute yoga class with or without assistance.
6. Purple	Student does a 30-minute yoga class independently.

Potential Modifications and Adaptations

Equipment	Rules	Environment	Instruction
☐ Cones	☐ Stay in own space	☐ Flat surface	☐ Verbal cues
☐ Floor mats	☐ Change beat count	☐ Small dance floor	☐ Demonstration
☐ Wall mats	☐ Cooperate	☐ Big area	☐ Modeling
☐ Poly spots	☐ Use short steps	☐ Music of choice	☐ Tactile modeling
☐ Footprints	☐ Walk to the beat	☐ Mirrors on walls	☐ Physical assistance
☐ Carpet squares	☐ Differentiate movements	☐ Clear boundaries	☐ Task cards (enlarged if needed)
☐ Scarves	☐ Mirror partners	☐ Lights to the beat	☐ Pictures
☐ Visual aids	☐ Use slow movements	☐ Limit noise	☐ Guided discovery
☐ Task cards	☐ Similarly sized partners	☐ Decrease distractions	☐ Problem-solving
☐ Music			☐ Task analysis
☐ Music with bass			☐ Proximity
☐ Slower music on an MP3 player or sound system			☐ Individualized
☐ Wheelchair			☐ Sign language
☐ Walker			☐ Feedback
☐ Forearm crutches			☐ Peer tutor
			☐ Paraeducator
			☐ Interpreter

Dancing

Task	Student performs a dance routine that includes Zumba moves.
Scale components	(a) Ability to keep the beat, (b) ability to sequence steps

Rubric level and color	Rubric descriptors
1. White	Student performs 1 to 3 aerobic dance moves with no music and with or without assistance.
2. Yellow	Student performs 1 to 3 original dance moves with no music and with or without assistance.
3. Orange	Student performs 1 to 3 Zumba moves with no music and with or without assistance.
4. Green	Student performs 1 or 2 aerobic moves, 1 original move (optional), and 1 or 2 Zumba moves.
5. Blue	Student performs a routine that incorporates 2 or 3 aerobic moves, 1 or 2 original moves, and 2 or 3 Zumba moves.
6. Purple	Student performs a routine that incorporates 3 or 4 aerobic moves, 2 or 3 original moves, and 3 or 4 Zumba moves.
7. Brown	Student performs a routine that incorporates 4 or 5 aerobic moves, 3 or 4 original moves, and 4 or 5 Zumba moves.

SPIKEBALL

Potential Modifications and Adaptations

Equipment	Rules	Environment	Instruction
☐ Spikeballs ☐ Auditory balls ☐ Big balls ☐ Brightly colored balls ☐ Textured balls ☐ Beach balls ☐ Balloons ☐ Spikeball net ☐ Brightly colored tape ☐ Brightly colored string ☐ Tape or chalk to mark positions on the floor	☐ Servers feet must be behind 6-foot (1.8-meter) serving line ☐ Ball must come cleanly off the net ☐ If the serving team cannot hit a legal serve on the second try, they lose the point ☐ Only the defensive player opposite the server can return the serve ☐ The server continues to serve until his team loses a point ☐ Three hits to return the ball off the net ☐ Hits must alternate between teammates ☐ Can use any part of the body for contact ☐ Rally scoring	☐ Indoor or outdoor ☐ Big area ☐ Limit noise ☐ Clearly marked boundaries	☐ Verbal cues ☐ Demonstration ☐ Modeling ☐ Tactile modeling ☐ Physical assistance ☐ Task cards (enlarged if needed) ☐ Pictures ☐ Guided discovery ☐ Problem-solving ☐ Task analysis ☐ Proximity ☐ Individualized ☐ Sign language ☐ Feedback ☐ Peer tutor ☐ Paraeducator ☐ Interpreter

Spiking

Task	Student can spike the ball during a game of Spikeball.
Scale components	(a) Skill ability, (b) cooperation, (c) task complexity
Rubric level and color	**Rubric descriptors**
1. White	Student spikes the ball from 2 feet (0.6 meters) away 10 times in a row with or without assistance.
2. Yellow	Student spikes the ball from 2 feet away 15 times in a row independently.
3. Orange	Student spikes the ball from 3 feet (0.9 meters) away seven times in a row independently.
4. Green	Student spikes the ball onto the net from 6 feet (1.8 meters) away during a game three times in a row with or without assistance.
5. Blue	Student can spike the ball onto the net from 6 feet away at the proper time during a game five times in a row with or without assistance.
6. Purple	Student can consistently spike the ball onto the net from 6 feet away at the proper time during a game.
7. Brown	Student can consistently spike the ball onto the net from 9 feet (2.7 meters) away at the proper time during a game.

Passing

Task	Student can pass a Spikeball to a teammate during a game.
Scale components	(a) Skill ability, (b) cooperation, (c) task complexity
Rubric level and color	**Rubric descriptors**
1. White	Student passes the ball back and forth at least one time without the ball hitting the ground and with or without assistance.
2. Yellow	Student passes the ball back and forth at least three times without the ball hitting the ground and with or without assistance.
3. Orange	Student passes the ball back and forth at least five times without the ball hitting the ground and with or without assistance.
4. Green	Student passes the ball back and forth at least three times in a game without the ball hitting the ground and with or without assistance.
5. Blue	Student passes the ball back and forth at least five times in a game without the ball hitting the ground and with or without assistance.
6. Purple	Student passes the ball back and forth consistently in a game without the ball hitting the ground and with or without assistance.

PADDLEBOARDING

Potential Modifications and Adaptations

Equipment	Rules	Environment	Instruction
☐ Paddleboards	☐ Two people per board	☐ Calm water	☐ Verbal cues
☐ Small paddleboards	☐ Never leave buddy	☐ Practice with the board on the gym floor to support proper strokes and positioning in a safe environment	☐ Demonstration
☐ Large paddleboards	☐ Stand up when comfortable		☐ Modeling
☐ Leashes	☐ No rocking the paddleboard		☐ Tactile modeling
☐ Paddles			☐ Physical assistance
☐ Small paddles	☐ No splashing	☐ Pool	☐ Task cards (enlarged if needed)
☐ Large paddles	☐ No horseplay	☐ No sun in eyes	☐ Pictures
☐ Double-sided paddles	☐ No jumping	☐ Decrease distractions	☐ Guided discovery
☐ Large-handled paddles			☐ Problem-solving
☐ Bathing suits			☐ Task analysis
☐ Water bottles			☐ Proximity
☐ Flotation devices			☐ Individualized
☐ Cushions			☐ Sign language
☐ Boundary markers			☐ Feedback
☐ Task cards			☐ Peer tutor
			☐ Paraeducator
			☐ Interpreter

Paddleboarding

Task	Student enters paddleboard, paddles using two different strokes, and controls direction of paddleboard in calm water.
Scale components	(a) Entry, (b) form, (c) control
Rubric level and color	**Rubric descriptors**
1. White	Student enters and leaves paddleboard safely from a dock or landing with or without assistance.
2. Yellow	Student paddles forward on one side from the kneeling position with verbal assistance.
3. Orange	Student paddles forward on both sides from the kneeling position independently.
4. Green	Student moves from kneeling position to standing up on the board while maintaining balance with or without assistance.
5. Blue	Student moves from kneeling position to standing up on the board while maintaining balance independently.
6. Purple	Student maintains balance from standing position and paddles straight independently.
7. Brown	Student maintains balance from standing position and makes turns independently.

Health and Fitness

12

Purpose: The importance of fitness skills and activities cannot be overlooked at any age. A basic fitness level is vital to enjoyment of physical activity and sports. In addition, adequate physical fitness can help prevent heart disease, high cholesterol, diabetes, and obesity. Introduction of fitness skills at the appropriate developmental level is essential for successful performance throughout life.

Unit adaptations: There are many ways to adapt the fitness curriculum for children with disabilities, and modifications for each child must be specific to his or her current fitness needs. For example, if a child is blind, he or she may use a guide wire or a guide with a tether when running, a tandem bike when riding, and a long pole with a ball on the end (to indicate the end of a lane) when swimming.

Assessment options: Each unit includes at least one rubric for evaluating the process or product of movements; you can also create your own rubrics. In addition, you can use the Brockport Physical Fitness Test (see chapter 2).

This chapter contains ideas you can use to teach various fitness activities. For each activity, we address equipment that can be used, rule modifications, environmental alterations, and instructional variations. Check off those modifications that apply to the learner. For example, if a child benefitted from *using personal flotation devices* when swimming, then that would be checked off in the modifications table. Once this is checked off, any subsequent lessons relating to swimming can be replicated with the variables that worked as part of the Universal Design process.

SWIMMING

Potential Modifications and Adaptations

Equipment	Rules	Environment	Instruction
☐ Chair lift	☐ Stop on first whistle	☐ Warm water (when possible)	☐ Verbal cues
☐ Mats	☐ Exit on two whistles in case of emergency	☐ Lane markers	☐ Demonstration
☐ Lane lines	☐ Buddy system	☐ Floating buoys as distance markers	☐ Modeling
☐ Buoys	☐ Walk on deck	☐ Mark off shallow end	☐ Tactile modeling
☐ Personal flotation devices	☐ Appropriate spacing	☐ Mark off deep end	☐ Physical assistance
☐ Water wings	☐ Swim for time and not distance	☐ Dry deck	☐ Task cards (enlarged if needed)
☐ Kickboards	☐ Modify distance		☐ Pictures
☐ Tubes	☐ No rough play		☐ Guided discovery
☐ Waist floats			☐ Problem-solving
☐ Extension pole with tennis ball at the end			☐ Task analysis
☐ Goggles			☐ Proximity
☐ Nose plugs			☐ Individualized
☐ Fins			☐ Sign language
☐ Aqua gloves			☐ Feedback
☐ Aqua joggers			☐ Teach in progressions (e.g., water adjustment, preswim skills, swim skills, lifesaving skills)
☐ Snorkels			☐ Peer tutor
☐ Aqua socks			☐ Paraeducator
☐ Deck rings			☐ Interpreter
☐ Hula hoops			
☐ Beach balls			
☐ Bright balls			
☐ Bell balls			
☐ Sinking objects			
☐ Noodles			
☐ Rescue tubes			
☐ Safety devices			
☐ Whistle			

Distance Swim

Task	Student swims 350 yards (320 meters) with appropriate form.
Scale components	(a) Distance, (b) timing (optional), (c) skill level
Rubric level and color	**Rubric descriptors**
1. White	Student swims 50 yards (46 meters) with any stroke, stopping when necessary, with or without flotation device.
2. Yellow	Student swims 100 yards (91 meters) with any stroke, stopping when necessary, with or without flotation device.
3. Orange	Student swims 150 yards (137 meters) with any stroke, stopping when necessary, with or without flotation device.
4. Green	Student swims 200 yards (183 meters) with any stroke, stopping when necessary, with or without flotation device.
5. Blue	Student swims 250 yards (229 meters) with any stroke, stopping when necessary, with or without floatation device.
6. Purple	Student swims 300 yards (275 meters) with any stroke, stopping when necessary, with or without flotation device.
7. Brown	Student swims at least 350 yards (320 meters) with any stroke, stopping when necessary. Optional: Time decreases with practice for distance of 350 yards.

AEROBICS

Potential Modifications and Adaptations

Equipment	Rules	Environment	Instruction
☐ Lines on floor	☐ No music to start	☐ Indoor or outdoor	☐ Verbal cues
☐ Poly spots	☐ Go at own pace	☐ Flat surface	☐ Demonstration
☐ Ribbons	☐ Create own dance	☐ Matted surface	☐ Modeling
☐ Scarves	☐ Modify movements	☐ Space from peers adequate for movement	☐ Tactile modeling
☐ Stretch bands	☐ Dance while sitting	☐ Bright and clear boundaries	☐ Physical assistance
☐ Mats	☐ Shadow partner		☐ Task cards (enlarged if needed)
☐ Mirrors	☐ Work with partner	☐ Steps by the wall (wall is for balance)	☐ Pictures
☐ Lights	☐ Work in groups	☐ Lights timed with the beat	☐ Guided discovery
☐ Bar for balance	☐ Repeat moves		☐ Problem-solving
☐ Steps	☐ Slow the tempo		☐ Task analysis
☐ Lower steps	☐ Low impact		☐ Proximity
☐ Light weights	☐ Modify time		☐ Individualized
☐ Modified weights			☐ Sign language
☐ Music			☐ Feedback
☐ Music with bass on an MP3 player or sound system			☐ Heart rate check
☐ DVDs or online videos			☐ Peer tutor
			☐ Paraeducator
			☐ Interpreter

Basic Aerobic Workout

Task	Student participates in a 30- to 45-minute aerobics class.
Scale components	(a) Ability to execute the skill demonstrated, (b) keeping up an 8-count beat, (c) duration of continuous exercise

Rubric level and color	Rubric descriptors
1. White	Student executes 3 or 4 aerobic moves as demonstrated by the instructor with no music and with or without assistance.
2. Yellow	Student executes 5 to 8 aerobic moves as demonstrated by the instructor with no music and with or without assistance.
3. Orange	Student continuously executes at least eight aerobic moves as demonstrated by the instructor with music to a 4-count beat for 10 minutes.
4. Green	Student continuously executes at least 10 aerobic moves as demonstrated by the instructor with music to a 4-count beat for 15 minutes.
5. Blue	Student continuously executes at least 10 aerobic moves as demonstrated by the instructor with music to an 8-count beat for 20 minutes.
6. Purple	Student continuously executes any number of moves as demonstrated by the instructor with music to an 8-count beat for 20 to 30 minutes.
7. Brown	Student continuously executes any number of moves as demonstrated by the instructor with music to an 8-count beat for 30 to 45 minutes. Optional: Student leads all or part of the workout.

WEIGHT TRAINING

Potential Modifications and Adaptations

Equipment	Rules	Environment	Instruction
☐ Bars	☐ No max weight	☐ Indoor or outdoor	☐ Verbal cues
☐ Modified bars	☐ Put equipment back where you got it (for safety)	☐ Bright atmosphere	☐ Demonstration
☐ Weights	☐ Warm up	☐ Positive feedback	☐ Modeling
☐ Wooden weights	☐ Follow individual program	☐ Padding on floor	☐ Tactile modeling
☐ Light weights	☐ Use spotter	☐ Wheelchair access	☐ Physical assistance
☐ Rubber weights	☐ Proper form	☐ Posters	☐ Task cards (enlarged if needed)
☐ Ankle weights	☐ Learn names and functions of muscles	☐ Visuals of muscles used	☐ Pictures
☐ Bright weights	☐ Strength and resistance training	☐ Different colors of posters on walls for different areas (e.g., stretching areas, free weights)	☐ Guided discovery
☐ Kettlebells	☐ Use own pace	☐ Minimal distractions	☐ Problem-solving
☐ Hand grips	☐ Do half sets		☐ Task analysis
☐ Gloves	☐ Always use a partner		☐ Proximity
☐ Straps	☐ Use personal space		☐ Individualized
☐ Velcro straps			☐ Sign language
☐ Weight belts			☐ Feedback
☐ Towels			☐ Peer tutor
☐ Stretch bands			☐ Paraeducator
☐ Fitness machines			☐ Interpreter
☐ Carpets			
☐ Everyday objects (e.g., cans, jugs)			
☐ Task cards			
☐ Music on MP3 or sound system			
☐ DVD or online video on proper technique			

Bench Press

Task	Student lifts the weight bar during a bench press and increases the maximum amount of weight from the initial pretest maximum.
Scale components	Weight increase
Rubric level and color	**Rubric descriptors**
1. White	Student bench presses weight equal to pretest maximum with or without assistance.
2. Yellow	Student bench presses weight 1 to 3 percent heavier than pretest maximum with or without assistance.
3. Orange	Student bench presses weight 4 to 6 percent heavier than pretest maximum with or without assistance.
4. Green	Student bench presses weight 7 to 9 percent heavier than pretest maximum with or without assistance.
5. Blue	Student bench presses weight 10 to 12 percent heavier than pretest maximum with or without assistance.
6. Purple	Student bench presses weight 13 to 15 percent heavier than pretest maximum with or without assistance.
7. Brown	Student bench presses weight more than 15 percent heavier than pretest maximum with or without assistance.

CROSS-COUNTRY SKIING

Potential Modifications and Adaptations

Equipment	Rules	Environment	Instruction
☐ Skis	☐ Pulled in sled	☐ Flags at trails	☐ Discuss hypothermia
☐ Short skis	☐ Stay in groups	☐ Use gym if no snow	☐ Verbal cues
☐ Light skis	☐ Follow trails	☐ Stations	☐ Demonstration
☐ Sit skis	☐ Move slowly	☐ Already-made tracks	☐ Modeling
☐ Poles	☐ Everyone skis	☐ Slight decline	☐ Tactile modeling
☐ Short poles	☐ Peer buddy	☐ Open space	☐ Physical assistance
☐ Sleds	☐ Alternative trails	☐ Small hills	☐ Task cards (enlarged if needed)
☐ Rollerblades	☐ Vary distances	☐ Short trails	☐ Pictures
☐ Scooters	☐ Head start	☐ Use large-print signs to tell skiers and guides where to go	☐ Guided discovery
☐ NordicTrack	☐ Group leader		☐ Problem-solving
☐ Cones	☐ Personal space		☐ Task analysis
☐ Tow ropes	☐ Bells on skis		☐ Proximity
☐ Proper clothing	☐ Work at own ability		☐ Individualized
☐ Sunglasses	☐ Stay on trails		☐ Sign language
☐ Ski boots	☐ No jumping		☐ Feedback
☐ Task cards			☐ Peer tutor
			☐ Paraeducator
			☐ Interpreter

Cross-Country Traditional Stride

Task	Student skis traditional stride for at least 100 consecutive yards (91 meters).
Scale components	(a) Form, (b) control
Rubric level and color	**Rubric descriptors**
1. White	Student stands with poles in ground and moves legs back and forth 1 to 5 times with or without assistance.
2. Yellow	Student steps with left foot and right-pole push and glides on both skis with control with or without assistance (one time).
3. Orange	Student steps with left foot and right-pole push and glides and then steps with right foot and a left-pole push and glides on both skis with control (one time).
4. Green	Student continues stepping and gliding on a flat surface for 50 yards (46 meters) with control.
5. Blue	Student continues stepping and gliding on a flat surface for 75 yards (69 meters) with control.
6. Purple	Student continues stepping and gliding on a slightly inclined surface for 100 yards (91 meters) with control.
7. Brown	Student continues stepping and gliding on variously inclined surfaces for at least 100 yards (91 meters) with control.

FITNESS ACTIVITIES

Potential Modifications and Adaptations

Equipment	Rules	Environment	Instruction
☐ Jump ropes ☐ Hula hoops ☐ Balls ☐ Sponge balls ☐ Beanbags ☐ Stair steps ☐ Carpet squares ☐ Poly spots ☐ Numbers on the floor ☐ Cones ☐ Mats ☐ Dyna-Bands ☐ Kettlebells ☐ Small trampoline ☐ Hand weights ☐ Music on MP3 player or a sound system	☐ Vary time per station or activity ☐ Vary number of reps per station ☐ Allow for water breaks	☐ Indoor or outdoor ☐ Circuit training ☐ Stations ☐ Adequate personal space to perform activity ☐ Clear boundaries	☐ Verbal cues ☐ Demonstration ☐ Modeling ☐ Tactile modeling ☐ Physical assistance ☐ Task cards (enlarged if needed) ☐ Pictures ☐ Guided discovery ☐ Problem-solving ☐ Task analysis ☐ Proximity ☐ Individualized ☐ Sign language ☐ Feedback ☐ Peer tutor ☐ Paraeducator ☐ Interpreter

Fitness Activities

Task	Student participates in an aerobic activity (e.g., biking, jumping rope, step aerobics, weight-training circuits, aerobic obstacle course) for time.
Scale components	(a) Time, (b) heart rate (use heart rate monitor, take pulse, or note level of exertion)
Rubric level and color	**Rubric descriptors**
1. White	Student continuously sustains 60 to 75 percent of target aerobic heart rate for 5 minutes.
2. Yellow	Student continuously sustains 60 to 75 percent of target aerobic heart rate for 10 minutes.
3. Orange	Student continuously sustains 60 to 75 percent of target aerobic heart rate for 15 minutes.
4. Green	Student continuously sustains 60 to 75 percent of target aerobic heart rate for 20 minutes.
5. Blue	Student continuously sustains 60 to 75 percent of target aerobic heart rate for 25 minutes.
6. Purple	Student continuously sustains 60 to 75 percent of target aerobic heart rate for 30 minutes.
7. Brown	Student continuously sustains 60 to 75 percent of target aerobic heart rate for 35 minutes.

Disabilities in Kid Terms

This section contains definitions of many disabilities in terms easily understood by children. Each definition includes a description of the disability, some common characteristics that kids may see in a child with the disability, and what kids can do to make sure that child feels included in his or her educational setting.

It is important to note that instructors should emphasize similarities as well as differences. Instructors can easily think of similarities, but the following example demonstrates the presentation of similarities for each child.

The instructor might tell students, "You can make sure your friend is included in games and activities in your neighborhood or on the playground by adapting the equipment, the playing area, or the rules. He is just like you in many ways. He likes to play with his friends, eat ice cream, go to games, and be included in a group. You can help him feel good about himself by understanding who he is and what he needs. He will do the same for you if you give him a chance."

Arthrogryposis

- Children with arthrogryposis have a difficult time bending their arms and legs.
- They were born with very stiff joints. Their knees, wrists, elbows, ankles, and shoulders are very stiff in everything they do.
- They have a hard time walking, moving, eating, dressing, and playing.
- Some kids may walk with crutches or a walker or use a wheelchair.
- They may be able to push their own chairs, or they may need help pushing the chair or use an electric wheelchair.
- Most of the time, these kids are able to think and talk just like anyone else.
- Sometimes you may need to be patient when they talk so that you can understand them.

Inclusion Ideas

- You can help kids with arthrogryposis by pushing their chairs if they need you to, waiting for them if they walk a little slowly, or helping them put their coats on if they need you to.
- You may need to help them get things they can't get for themselves, write down what they are thinking if they can't, or assist them in playing volleyball by helping their hands hit the ball.

- Other kids may look at them funny or tease them because of the way they look, but it is important to let others know that they are just like everyone else in more ways than not.

Asthma

- Children with asthma have a hard time breathing in certain situations. The difficulty breathing may occur after a stressful activity, such as running, or if they are scared or overly tired.
- It may also happen if the person is allergic to pollen, grass, perfume, smoke, or animals.
- Either way, the problem will start with shortness of breath and, if not taken care of, progress to wheezing, coughing, and perhaps even lack of air.
- Most people with asthma carry some type of inhaler, or breathing device, to help them when the problem starts so that it does not progress to a dangerous situation.
- This may be a very scary situation for the person who is having the attack.
- Students with asthma will not only have to temporarily leave the current activity; they may also feel embarrassed because they are different in this way and attention was focused on them.

Inclusion Ideas

- You can help kids with asthma by helping them remember to bring their inhaler or prescribed medication.
- You can also help by calming them if they do have an attack.
- Let them know that everything will be OK and it is not a big deal if they have to miss some of the class or game.
- You can put yourself in their situation and understand that it is hard to breathe and frustrating to have to sit out at any given moment.
- You can make sure the playing area is not too big if your friends have a hard time covering large areas.
- You can also make sure they get rest periods when they need them so that breathing does not get too difficult.
- It will also help if you and your friends have a signal for when a student with asthma feels as though he or she is in too much trouble with breathing and may need you to call the nurse, the teacher, or 911.

Attention-Deficit/Hyperactivity Disorder (ADHD)

- Children with attention-deficit/hyperactivity disorder have a hard time paying attention in school, at home, and in social and play situations. This is just the way they were born, and they may take medication to help them pay attention better.
- They are distracted very easily and sometimes make mistakes because they are rushing through an assignment or chore.
- They are often restless, fidgety, or hyperactive, and they may even run away from you in the middle of a game.

- Sometimes they have a hard time organizing schoolwork, their desks, or their lockers. They may interrupt a conversation or talk out of turn. They may seem lazy, unreliable, or uncaring.

Inclusion Ideas

- You can help these classmates to be organized and pay attention to what they need to do.
- If they become distracted in the middle of a game, group assignment, or conversation, then remind them of what they were doing and help them finish if possible.
- If they choose not to finish what they were doing at that time, remind them at another time, and help them remember what they had to do.
- If they run away from a game at recess, know that they will come back and welcome them when they do.
- You can understand that they may have a hard time paying attention to one thing for a long time, and perhaps help them structure their days so that they do not have to remain in one place for too long.
- Do not look at what they did not have time to do; look at what they did, and let them know they are doing a good job.
- Know that they are still your friends even if it appears that they are ignoring you, or if they run away from you.

Autism

- Children with autism have a difficult time relating to people.
- They may be more interested in playing with an object or watching their hand than in talking to a person.
- They may play in a corner all by themselves or run around for no apparent reason.
- They may have very limited communication or no communication, and what they do say may not make very much sense.
- They may be very good at some things and not be able to do other things at all.
- They may react to touch, noise, or lights very differently. Sometimes a low noise will seem very loud to them, so much that they will cover their ears.
- They may cry from a soft touch or cover their eyes from a dim light.
- Other kids may appear deaf when there is a loud noise, may seek out deep pressure or textured feelings on their skin, or may look for very bright lights to stimulate themselves.
- Each person with autism is different, and you need to understand what he or she wants and needs in order to be able to cope with the environment.

Inclusion Ideas

- You can help classmates with autism by talking clearly and asking them only one or two things at a time.
- You can help them when they don't know what to do, redirect them when they are doing the wrong activity, and help other people understand what they are good at and what they need help with.
- You can learn what makes them mad, frustrated, and happy, and you can help convey these feelings to other classmates and the teacher.

Blindness and Visual Impairment

- Children who are blind or visually impaired have difficulty seeing.
- They have this disability because of a birth accident, an accident after birth, or a sickness.
- Some kids can see a little bit and walk around by themselves; some kids can see a little bit but need some help getting around; and some kids cannot see anything and need help in getting around.
- With practice and a cane or a seeing-eye dog, kids may be able to walk around school and their neighborhood by themselves.
- These kids will eat by themselves and use the "clock system" for knowing where things are. You can tell them their milk is at 12:00, which means their milk is at the very top of the plate, and their fork is at 9:00, which means their fork is just to the left of the plate.
- These students can dress themselves, and they know which clothes are which color by reading brailled writing on the tag of the shirt.
- They find out what is happening in their environment, who is around them, and where they are going by having people tell them.
- Do not be afraid to use words like "see" or "look" in a sentence. Students with blindness or visual impairment will use these words, and you can, too.

Inclusion Ideas

- You can guide your classmates by allowing them to grab your elbow and walk one step behind you. This will allow them to let go if they want to.
- You can assist them in getting their food in the lunch line, and you can tell them where their food is on their plates.
- You can describe their environment to them, such as who is in the room, what the weather is like, and what equipment is located around the gym.
- You can answer their questions and make sure they are included in conversations.
- Do not ever leave a room without telling them you are leaving. They may want to talk to you and not know you are gone, and this is embarrassing.
- You can make sure they are included in games and activities in your neighborhood or on the playground by adapting the equipment, the playing area, or the rules.

Cerebral Palsy

- Children with cerebral palsy have a condition from birth that affects their arms and legs.
- They have this condition because their brains cannot tell their bodies what they want them to do.
- Their muscles contract and their body moves without control. This affects different kids in different ways.
- Sometimes they have difficulty walking, or they may look awkward when they walk.

- Children with cerebral palsy may walk with crutches or a walker or use a wheelchair.
- They may be able to push their own chairs, or they may need help pushing the chair or use an electric wheelchair.
- They may have difficulty with feeding themselves, getting dressed, or talking, and some kids with cerebral palsy communicate through a communication board or a voice synthesizer instead of with their voices.

Inclusion Ideas

- You can help your classmates who have cerebral palsy by pushing their chairs if they need a push or walking with them around school if they are a little slower so that they don't have to walk alone.
- You can go up the ramp or the elevator if they need to go a different way so that they do not have to go by themselves.
- You can be patient when they communicate with you and help others understand their wants and needs.

Congenital Heart Condition

- Children with a heart condition have a hard time breathing or functioning in certain situations.
- The difficulty breathing may occur after a stressful activity like running or if they are scared, if they physically stress themselves, or if they are overly tired.
- The problem will start with shortness of breath and if not taken care of will progress to weakness and fatigue; the person may even faint.
- This situation may be very scary for the person who is having the attack. The person will not only have to temporarily leave the current activity but may also feel embarrassed because he or she is different in this way and has become the focus of attention.
- Most people with a congenital heart disorder participate in activity at a slower rate or for short periods.

Inclusion Ideas

- You can help these kids by helping them remember to work at a slower pace and take rest periods.
- You can also help by calming them if they do have an attack.
- Let them know that everything will be OK and it is not a big deal if they have to miss some of the class or game.
- You can put yourself in their situation and understand that it is hard to breathe and frustrating to have to sit out at any given moment.
- You can also make sure they get rest periods when they need them so that effort and breathing do not get too difficult.
- You can sit out with them when they are resting so that they do not have to sit out alone.
- It will also help if you and your friends have a signal to use when a student with a congenital heart condition feels too much trouble with breathing and may need you to call the nurse, the teacher, or 911.

Deafness and Hardness of Hearing

- Children who are deaf or hard of hearing cannot hear like you and I can.
- They hear much less than we do, and in some cases they cannot hear at all. Perhaps this is due to a fever their mother had during pregnancy, or perhaps their parents are deaf and their children became deaf also. They may have been premature at birth, had a sickness after birth, or become deaf from an accident.
- Some kids wear hearing aids, cochlear implants, or other hearing devices to help them hear better.
- Some kids with hearing difficulty can talk clearly; you can understand them, and they can read your lips.
- Some kids communicate using hand gestures and sign language.
- Some kids with hearing difficulty are not able to talk with their voices, and they may not be able to understand everything you say.
- Some kids with hearing difficulty will prefer to talk mostly with other deaf kids; others will talk and make friends with anyone, hearing or deaf.

Inclusion Ideas

- Because your classmates with hearing difficulty cannot hear, you can help them in many ways.
- If they use their voices and read lips, you can help by making sure you are looking at each other when you talk.
- You can tap them on the shoulder to get their attention if the teacher is talking, if there is a fire drill, or if someone wants to talk to them.
- You can make sure they understand the instructions when you are in class, and you can answer any questions they have.
- If your friends are totally deaf and use signs, you can learn some signs to aid in communication; if you don't know the signs, you can look at them when you are talking, and the interpreter will interpret what you say.
- Many kids who are deaf feel lonely and left out, so it is important to try to include them in all activities, both in and out of school.
- It is also important that you do not make students with hearing difficulty feel bad if they do not understand something; instead, you can try to increase their understanding the best that you can.
- If you want to help students who are deaf or hard of hearing, always remember that you can make sure they are included in games and activities in your neighborhood or on the playground. Do this by communicating the rules, talking with them, and helping other kids understand them. They are just like you in many ways.

Dwarfism

- Children who have dwarfism are short in stature and may have shorter legs and arms than you have.
- For some kids, this happens at birth because of the way their bones are formed.
- Other kids are this way just because they did not grow as fast or as much as you.
- They may have a high voice and may have a hard time moving their arms and legs like you can.

- They may walk a little slower than you do and may have trouble moving their bodies in the ways you do.

Inclusion Ideas

- You can help kids with dwarfism by walking with them if they are at the end of the line so that they are not alone.
- You can help them reach something that is out of reach or assist them in doing an activity that may be difficult for them in class or on the playground.
- Other kids may give them funny looks or tease them because of the way they look, but it is important that you let others know that your friends are just like them in more ways than not.
- You can make sure they are included in games and activities in your neighborhood or on the playground by adapting the equipment, the playing area, or the rules.

Emotional Disability/Serious Emotional Disturbance/Behavior Disability

- Children with one of these conditions may make physical or verbal attacks toward the teacher or other classmates.
- These attacks may include swearing, pushing, shoving, or destruction of property.
- Sometimes the teacher or teacher's aide may have to physically restrain the student or take him or her out of the room.
- This behavior often affects the student's performance in class, and he or she may be out of the classroom frequently because of this behavior. This is not anyone's fault—it just happens because of outside factors.
- These students do not try to have excessive misbehavior; it is part of who they are and may remain this way for a while until teachers, parents, and administrators can figure out how to help decrease the behaviors.

Inclusion Ideas

- You can help these kids by giving them positive feedback when they are exhibiting good behavior.
- You can talk to them about everyday things and get to know who they are.
- You can be their partners when others may not want to and try to accept them after they come back from a time-out.
- Other kids may give them funny looks or tease them because of the way they act, but it is important that you let others know that your friends are just like them in more ways than not.

Intellectual Disability

- Children with intellectual disability may not be able to think the same way you do. This is because they had an accident before, during, or after they were born, involving their heads or the chemicals in their bodies.
- They will sometimes be able to understand parts of what you say but not everything. They may also react to what they are asked in an unusual way because of the lack of understanding.

- These classmates may also have trouble communicating with you, taking care of themselves (such as feeding themselves), or putting on their coats.
- They may walk away when you are talking to them or laugh for no reason. They may have trouble going out into the community on their own to do things, such as taking a bus or going shopping.
- Sometimes during the day, they may not know what they want to do, they may not be aware of danger in the environment, or they may need help to do classwork or recreational activities such as walking, riding a bike, or bowling.

Inclusion Ideas

- You can help these classmates by talking clearly and asking them only one or two things at a time.
- You can help them when they don't know what to do, redirect them when they are doing the wrong activity, and help other people understand what they are good at and how they can be helped.
- You can make sure they are included in groups, games, and activities by giving them clear instructions and demonstrations throughout the activity and praising them when they do something right.
- These kids have the same feelings you have. They are hurt when other kids don't want to play with them; just like you, they enjoy things like eating ice cream, watching cartoons, and being part of the game.

Learning Disability

- Children with learning disabilities have a difficult time in learning situations, with reading, or with comprehension. They are not stupid; their brains just have a hard time receiving information, processing information, or expressing or giving back information. This happens when they are born, and they look just like everyone else.
- These kids might also have problems with writing letters and numbers.
- These kids may have a hard time running the same way you do or playing a game in some situations. For example, they may run more slowly or have a hard time catching a ball or doing things with their upper bodies.
- Many kids with learning disabilities also have attention-deficit/hyperactivity disorder (ADHD). If they also have ADHD, please see the description of that condition to learn the characteristics and how you can help the student.

Inclusion Ideas

- You can help your classmates with learning disabilities by showing them the right way to catch a ball or run, assisting them in expressing their thoughts, and checking their writing if they need it.
- You can praise them when they accomplish their goals and encourage them when they are struggling.
- Because some activities or skills are more difficult for these classmates, you will need to be very patient and supportive.
- You can make sure that they are included in games and activities in your neighborhood or on the playground by adapting the equipment, the playing area, or the rules.

Obesity

- Children who are obese may be this way for many reasons.
- They may be on medication, they may have a glandular problem, they may have inherited much of their body composition, or they may not have learned how to balance diet and exercise.
- Whatever the reason for the obesity, it makes movement difficult.
- They have a difficult time running, moving their bodies, and perhaps being involved in activities for a long period.
- They may be afraid or embarrassed to participate in certain activities, such as gymnastics, dancing, or swimming.
- It is important to keep in mind that they can be involved in any activity with some minor modifications.
- They may need more rest time, they may need to cover less area in a game, or they may need to be involved in the activity in a different way.
- They may also need to substitute for activities that make their bodies hurt—for example, walking instead of running, hopping, or jumping, and doing log rolls instead of forward rolls.
- Swimming is an excellent activity for children who are obese. Be sure to make them feel welcome and encourage them to swim to the best of their ability.
- Students who are obese do need to be involved in activities, so it is important to allow them to modify any activity but continue to be involved to the maximum extent possible.

Inclusion Ideas

- You can help these kids by helping them remember to work at a slower pace and take rest periods.
- You can help them by giving them some positive feedback when they participate actively in a game.
- When they do something that you know is hard for them, be sure to give them a high five or thumbs-up, or just say, "Great job!"
- You can put yourself in their situation and understand that it is hard to move and frustrating not to be able to do everything that other kids are doing.
- You can make sure the playing area is not too big if your friends have a hard time covering large areas.
- You can also make sure they get rest periods when they need them, so that effort, movement, and breathing do not get too difficult.
- It will also help if you and your friends have a signal to use when students with obesity feel as though they are in too much trouble with breathing and may need you to call the nurse, the teacher, or 911.

Osteogenesis Imperfecta (Brittle Bones)

- Kids with this condition are born with very fragile bones that often break even when they are not doing anything. This is just the way their bones formed, and this will be their condition until they are teenagers.
- This condition can be very frustrating, because they always have to be careful when doing everything, and they spend a lot of time in the hospital or at home.

- They may walk with a waddling gait, with crutches, or with a walker, or they may use a wheelchair.
- They may push their own wheelchairs, need to be pushed, or use an electric wheelchair.
- They may also be overweight because they do not have the opportunity to exercise, run, and play.
- They are just as smart as other kids in your class, and they usually talk very clearly.
- It may be hard for them to reach things far away or move very fast.
- They may need to play very modified games, and they cannot participate in activities that will place them in danger of breaking more bones.

Inclusion Ideas

- You can help them by pushing them if they need a push, slowing down if they are slow walkers, walking with them in class, or going up the ramp or elevator with them.
- If something is out of reach for them, you can help by pushing it closer or getting it for them.
- You can help others understand how similar they are to you; they share your hopes and dreams for the future.

Spinal Cord Injury and Spina Bifida

- A spinal cord injury occurs at birth or results from an accident or disease after birth.
- The part of the spine affected is either partially or totally severed, and children with such a condition have total or partial paralysis from that point down.
- The children have little or no feeling in or control of their legs, abdominal area, or, in some cases, arms.
- Spina bifida happens when a person is born and part of the spine does not close all the way.
- Their spinal cord is often not covered by bone or tissue.
- This is always corrected by surgery, but the children are most often left paralyzed, either totally or partially, from that area down.
- These kids will walk with an awkward gait or use crutches, a walker, or a wheelchair.
- They may push their own wheelchairs, need to be pushed, or use an electric wheelchair.
- They may urinate through a tube into a bag, and they may also have braces on their legs.
- They are just as smart as other kids in your class, and they usually talk very clearly.
- They need to use ramps and elevators to go up or down steps and to other floors, and they will need a bigger restroom stall than kids without wheelchairs need.
- Other than these few differences, these kids are just like you.

Inclusion Ideas

- You can help these classmates by pushing them if they need a push, slowing down if they are slow walkers, walking with them in class, or going up the ramp or elevator with them.

- If something is out of reach for them, you can help by pushing it closer or getting it for them.

- You can help others understand how similar these children are to you; they share many of your hopes and dreams for the future.

Traumatic Brain Injury

- Children with traumatic brain injury have experienced a bad accident or a blow to the head.

- This causes them to have short-term memory loss; sometimes their speech is slurred, and they may say whatever is on their minds.

- Because they may not remember what does or does not hurt others' feelings, they may say something that does not make sense or is mean.

- They do not do these things intentionally; it just happens because they do not know what is appropriate.

- They may look unbalanced when they walk, or they may use a cane, crutches, or a wheelchair.

- They may push their own wheelchairs, need to be pushed, or use an electric wheelchair.

- They may have a hard time doing simple, everyday tasks such as brushing their teeth, putting their coats on, or eating. This is because they have difficulty in controlling their muscles. As a result, they may become frustrated with whatever they are doing.

- It is important for you to realize that they are not mad at you but frustrated with the situation, because they could do these simple things before but cannot do them now.

Inclusion Ideas

- You can help these classmates by being patient when they try to talk and by listening and responding. You can also help other classmates listen and understand.

- You can push them if they need a push or walk with them if they walk slowly so that they don't have to walk alone.

- You can offer them your hand if it looks as though they will lose their balance.

- You can assist them in their daily activities until they can do them independently.

- You can show them how to do the things they forget. You can remind them of the things they forget and applaud the things they remember.

- Because some activities or skills are more difficult for this classmate, you will need to be very patient and supportive.

Special Education Terminology

Different states and districts can have different terminology for the same special education approaches listed here. Be sure you know the terminology your district uses for these concepts.

Term	Definition	Implications for PE teachers
GENERAL EDUCATION		
Annual evaluation	This is another term for the annual IEP meeting.	During this meeting, you need to provide a report of the students' performance according to the goals established on the IEP.
Committee on Special Education (CSE)	The CSE is the district-level team that determines whether a student has a disability. The team typically includes district and building administrators, parents, teachers, and a school psychologist; it can also include an advocate, physical therapist, occupational therapist, speech-language pathologist, or other related service personnel (e.g., nurse).	You will be included as part of this team if you provide PE services to the child.
Common Core	The Common Core State Standards Initiative is promoted by the U.S. federal government to emphasize high standards and college and career readiness for all students. Many U.S. states have adopted the Common Core standards. The standards focus primarily on improving students' reading and writing skills.	There is increased attention on incorporating reading and writing in PE due to the attention and focus on Common Core subjects.
Consultant teacher	This term is often used to describe a special education teacher or APE teacher who meets with general education teachers (including PE teachers) about students with disabilities who attend general education classes. A consultant teacher helps determine placements and necessary levels of consultancy and provides information and support during class or outside of class. (A consultant teacher is not the same as a co-teacher.)	Find out if your district has consultant teachers for physical education. If so, seek out their support for placement decisions, assessments, IEP development, lesson planning, and training of support staff.
Differentiated instruction	Differentiated instruction occurs when the instructor considers every child's learning style and embeds variation in the lesson to meet the various needs of the students in the class.	Develop instructional strategies that meet the needs of all your students (e.g., different skill levels, strengths, types of learners).

Term	Definition	Implications for PE teachers
504 plan	This is a plan of support that was created through Section 504 of the Rehabilitation Act of 1973. These plans are provided for students who have disabilities that do not adversely affect educational performance. 504 plans provide reasonable accommodations for specific conditions. For example, a 504 plan could stipulate that a student with diabetes needs to check blood sugar before taking a test and is allowed to postpone the test if blood sugar is low or that a student who has difficulty being organized receives teacher support in gathering materials and homework.	You must follow the 504 plan accommodations and modifications; they are not optional.
Individualized education plan (IEP)	The IEP is the written plan of specific educational needs and appropriate resources for addressing those needs. (To have an IEP, a student must have one of the 14 disabilities listed in the IDEIA.) The IEP is rewritten each year. The IEP team may also meet during the year to revisit the goals and progress the student has made.	We strongly encourage you to get to know the students with disabilities that you teach and attend their IEP meetings. If that is not possible, request copies of their IEPs so you can effectively provide supports and services. The IEP must be followed; it is not optional.
IEP Direct	This is a web-based computer program that many districts use to write IEPs.	Your school may use this electronic system for writing IEPs. If so you can get trained on the software and use the program to write physical education IEPs.
Least restrictive environment (LRE)	This LRE is the environment in which the student learns best. Students with disabilities should be with their typically developing peers to the extent that this is possible. IDEIA requires that all students with disabilities be educated in the LRE.	It is imperative that the physical education teacher have a say in the placement of every child with a disability to ensure they are in the LRE for them.
One-to-one aide, teacher's aide, paraprofessional, paraeducator	These professionals work with students with disabilities individually or in small groups. They should be part of the PE support team. Their training should take place at the beginning of the year and be ongoing throughout the year.	Provide training and descriptions of roles and responsibilities during the PE class. Supervision, feedback, evaluation, and support should be given throughout the year so the support staff know what they are doing and understand how to improve.
Pull-out	This is the term for a child who is placed in inclusive classes in the general curriculum but benefits from a self-contained PE placement.	Ensure an appropriate placement in a modified or self-contained placement when the GPE class is not the LRE.
Push-in	This is the term for a child who is placed in self-contained classes in the general curriculum but benefits from a GPE placement.	Be sure to obtain all information necessary to appropriately include the child who is pushed in. Ensure that there are natural proportions of students with disabilities in your classes (e.g., about 5 percent of the general population has disabilities, so your class should not have a higher percentage than this).
Review meeting	This is the term for any meeting related to the IEP. Review meetings may be called by members of the team, including the family, during the school year to discuss concerns and make changes to the IEP.	You can request a review meeting if you believe the IEP goals identified are too easy or too difficult. Placement decisions can also be discussed during this meeting.
Self-contained class	A self-contained class is typically a small-group setting in which all children have disabilities.	A self-contained PE class can be held in a gym, weight room, field, or other location. These classes should not be relegated to inappropriate PE spaces (e.g., hallways, general classrooms).
Special education case manager	This is the person responsible for monitoring the education of a student with a disability. Case managers are typically special education teachers who manage 5 to 15 students. Case management includes monitoring IEP goals, connecting with the family, and supporting the student.	PE teachers are not typically case managers, but a PE teacher may have to discuss a student with a case manager.

(continued)

(continued)

Term	Definition	Implications for PE teachers
Test mods	Test modifications (mods) are changes to how a student takes a test. Test mods are indicated on a student's IEP.	You must know the test mods when written or other tests are given. Examples of test mods are giving the test in a separate, quiet location; reading the test aloud; or having a scribe record the answers the student gives orally.
Triennial evaluation	Students with IEPs have their performance reevaluated at least every three years.	Assess your students before this meeting and present new goals (if necessary) that need to be included on the IEP. You can also discuss continuing or ending services.
Universal Design for Learning (UDL)	UDL is a teaching approach that eliminates barriers to student learning by designing physical, social, and learning environments that support diverse learners through powerful possibilities for teaching and learning.	Make your curriculum and facilities accessible to all students by providing multiple options for equipment, rules, instruction, and the environment. Every child at every level should have equal access to each lesson.
COMMUNICATION		
Assistive technology (AT)	AT includes a vast range of technological supports to help students in school.	In physical education, AT can include walkers, standers, bowling ramps, switches, tablets, or other equipment that helps students move their bodies and perform physical skills. AT can also be used to help students focus (e.g., whiteboard to list steps of a skill or directions).
Picture exchange communication system (PECS)	A PECS is a form of alternative communication that it is used as an aid for children with autism and other specific disabilities. Many districts use the Boardmaker program to create individualized PECSs for their students.	PECS can be used as a form of communication in PE settings. Talk to classroom teachers for ideas about how to use this system during PE.
Proloquo2Go	This is an alternative communication solution for people who have difficulty speaking or cannot speak. This program can also be adapted to meet the needs of students with other disabilities. Speech is generated by tapping symbols or typing. The photos on the screen are individualized for each student's needs. It can be used for receptive and expressive communication. It is available for iPad, iPhone, and iPod touch.	This communication system should be brought with the child to physical education if they use it in the classroom. Physical education symbols should be included as part of the communication program for both expressive and receptive communication.
Social story	A social story is a written or a visual guide that describes different social interactions, situations, behaviors, skills, or concepts. Social stories are often used to address upcoming events that may be stressful or hard for students so they can be better prepared. They are often used with students with autism.	Create social stories to teach students appropriate behaviors or prepare them for an activity that will occur in the near future.
Video modeling	Video modeling allows students to observe different social interactions. Videos often address upcoming activities and demonstrate the behavior that is expected in those settings.	Create videos to teach students appropriate behaviors or prepare them for an activity that will occur in the near future.
THERAPY		
Occupational therapy	Occupational therapy enhances the student's ability to fully access handwriting or fine motor skills so the child can complete written assignments; the occupational therapist (OT) helps the child organize him- or herself in the environment (including work space in and around the desk) and works with the teacher to modify the classroom or adapt learning materials to facilitate successful participation.	You can consult with the student OT to help with fine motor goals and objectives, and class modifications.

Term	Definition	Implications for PE teachers
Physical therapy	Physical therapy is one of the related services for students who have a disability that interferes with their educational performance and ability to benefit from their education program movement and function. Physical therapists (PTs) ensure a free and appropriate education for students with disabilities to prepare them for further education, employment, and independent living. The school-based PT promotes motor development and the student's participation in everyday routines and activities that are a part of his or her program.	You can consult with the student PT to help with gross motor goals and objectives, positioning, and class modifications. If you are providing services for a student, you should be responsible for writing the IEP goals for that student.
BEHAVIORAL SUPPORT		
Functional behavioral assessment (FBA)	Functional behavioral assessment is generally considered to be a problem-solving process for addressing a student's problem behavior. It relies on a variety of techniques and strategies to identify the purposes of specific behavior and to help IEP teams select interventions to directly address the problem behavior.	Assist in this process by providing feedback about the student's behavior during class. Once the intervention is created, you should implement the behavioral intervention strategies provided by the IEP team.
Positive behavior support (PBS)/ positive behavioral intervention support (PBIS)	Positive behavior support is a continuum of positive behavior support for all students within a school. It is implemented in areas including the classroom and non-classroom settings (such as hallways, buses, and restrooms). Positive behavior support is an application of a behaviorally based systems approach to enhance the capacity of schools, families, and communities.	Be aware of these strategies utilized throughout your school so you can assist and reinforce them during the PE class.
PHYSICAL EDUCATION		
Brockport Physical Fitness Test	This is a health-related, criterion-referenced physical fitness test for youth aged 10 through 17 years, although it can be used for younger children. It is validated for children with orthopedic impairments, visual impairments, and intellectual disabilities.	The Brockport Physical Fitness Test can be used as a screening and placement tool as well as an assessment to determine progress on IEP goals.
Competency Test in Adapted Physical Education (CTAPE)	This is a curriculum-based assessment that is used in several states. It has six testing levels and is appropriate for students aged 6 years and older.	The CTAPE can be used as a screening and placement tool as well as an assessment to determine progress on IEP goals.
National Consortium for Physical Education and Recreation for Individuals With Disabilities (NCPERID)	The mission of the NCPERID is to promote research, professional preparation, service delivery, and advocacy of physical education and recreation for individuals with disabilities.	Join the Consortium if you can and be aware of the advocacy efforts undertaken by the organization and how legislature effects physical education.
SHAPE America (Society of Health and Physical Educators)	The national governing body for the field of physical education.	You should attend the SHAPE America conference to learn advocacy skills that will benefit your students.
Test of Gross Motor Development III (TGMD-3) (Ulrich, 2017)	This is a gross motor test of object control and locomotor skills. It is norm referenced and criterion referenced. It is validated for typically developing children aged 3 through 11 years and children with visual impairments aged 6 through 12 years.	The TGMD-3 can be used as a screening and placement tool as well as an assessment to determine progress on IEP goals.

Brockport
Aquatic Skills Checklist

The following aquatic skills assessment was developed by the authors of this book to evaluate swimming abilities of children with and without disabilities. The skills are presented in a hierarchical order by difficulty. In addition, the documentation of the skill can be presented by *parameter* (i.e., how the instructor sets up the environment; for example, floating on the back with support at the hips), *product* (i.e., how long, how fast, or how many; for example, floating on the back for 10 seconds), and *process* (i.e., how a skill is executed; for example, floating on the back with hips flat). This documentation system (the 3Ps) is described in chapter 4 and is a clear and replicable way of representing what the child *can* do.

Aquatic Skills Checklist

Student: _____ Age: _____ Date: _____

Instructor: _____

	Independent	Needs assistance	Total assistance
POOL PREPARATION			
Demonstrates proper behavior en route to pool			
Takes clothes off			
Hangs clothes in locker			
Puts bathing suit on			
Takes shower			
Awaits directions before entering pool			

	Independent	Needs assistance	Total assistance
POOL ENTRY			
Sits at edge of pool with feet in water			
Puts water on body			
Lowers self into pool			
Climbs down stairs and enters pool			
ADJUSTMENT TO WATER			
Splashes water around with no fear			
Holds gutter and kicks legs			
Kicks while lying on front and being towed			
Kicks while lying on back and being towed			
Moves arms and legs in swimming motion while being towed			
Blows bubbles			
Treads water for 30 seconds			
Puts whole face in water for 5 seconds			
Holds breath while submerged for 10 seconds			
Bobs up and down five times			
Engages in continuous rhythmic breathing while holding side of pool and turning head to side 10 times			
Engages in continuous rhythmic breathing from prone position while kicking with kickboard for 20 feet (6.1 meters)			
FLOATING SKILLS			
Floats while lying on front and holding kickboard with arms fully extended and face submerged			
Does front float			
Does back float			
BASIC PROPULSION			
Flutter-kicks with kickboard while on front for 15 feet (4.6 meters)			
Glides on front with push-off, holds kickboard with arms extended, and flutter-kicks for 15 feet			
Glides on front with push-off and flutter kicks with no kickboard for 15 feet			
Glides on front with push-off and flutter-kicks with face submerged and no kickboard for 15 feet			
Glides on back with push-off, holds kickboard with arms extended, and flutter-kicks for 15 feet			

(continued)

	Independent	Needs assistance	Total assistance
Glides on back with push-off and flutter-kicks with no kickboard for 15 feet			
Rolls over, front to back, while gliding			
Rolls over, back to front, while gliding			
SWIMMING STROKES			
Does freestyle stroke using arms only with face out of water for 10 strokes			
Does freestyle stroke using arms only with face submerged for 10 strokes			
Does freestyle stroke using arms and legs with face submerged for 10 strokes			
Does freestyle stroke using arms and legs with rhythmic breathing for 10 strokes			
Swims underwater for 10 feet (3 meters)			
Does sidestroke on either side for 10 feet			
Does breaststroke for 10 feet			
Does back crawl stroke using arms only for 10 strokes			
Does back crawl stroke using arms and legs for 10 strokes			
DIVING SKILLS			
Dives from a sitting position			
Dives from squatting or crouched position			
Dives from standing position with knees slightly bent			
Dives from standing position with spring and arm action			
Performs standing dive from end of low board			
WATER SAFETY AND DEEP WATER SKILLS			
Bobs 15 times			
Treads water for 30 seconds			
Performs survival floats			
Jumps feetfirst into water, surfaces, and swims back to side of pool			
Changes directions while swimming			
Changes position while floating and swimming (rolls from front to back)			
Changes from horizontal to vertical position while treading water			
Dives off side and swims underwater for 15 feet			

From Lauren J. Lieberman and Cathy Houston-Wilson, 2018, *Strategies for inclusion* (3rd ed.) (Champaign, IL: Human Kinetics).

Glossary

ABC model—Method used in behavior management in which you first examine the *antecedent* (A), which is what was happening right before the incident occurred; second, you note the actual *behavior* (B); and third, you note the *consequence* of the behavior (C), which is what happened right after the behavior occurred.

adapted physical education (APE)—PE classes that are designed to meet the unique needs of children with disabilities in the least restrictive environment.

authentic assessment—Ongoing feedback system that monitors and records student learning and outcomes under authentic conditions; gives students a chance to demonstrate skills, knowledge, and competencies in age-appropriate, functional activities; performance-based approach to testing (students are evaluated on skills directly related to outcomes of the program).

basic skills assessment—Test of motor performance, knowledge, and personal and social responsibility; students are assessed on the acquisition of individual skills at three levels (emerging, basic, and acquired).

behavioral intervention plan—Plan to support the student to change behavior; consists of multiple interventions or support strategies and is not a punishment.

bidirectional or reciprocal peer tutoring—Model in which a student with a disability and a student without a disability form a dyad; each student takes turns being the tutor while the other is the tutee; most effective with students who have mild disabilities.

chaining—Procedure for increasing appropriate behavior that reinforces approximations of the terminal behavior.

class-wide peer tutoring—Strategy that involves breaking the entire class into dyads or small groups and having each student participate in reciprocal peer tutoring by providing partners with prompts, error correction, and feedback; most effective with students who have mild disabilities.

Committee on Special Education (CSE)—Group that determines whether further testing is warranted to indicate whether a child has a disability; group is comprised of the child's teacher; a school psychologist; and a district representative qualified to provide, administer, or supervise special education.

criterion-referenced test—Assessment that compares student to pre-established standards of performance.

cross-age peer tutoring—Strategy that involves an older student tutoring a younger student; more effective than a same-age peer tutor when the student with a disability is very young (i.e., below second grade) or the disability is more serious (such as severe cerebral palsy, intellectual disability, or autism).

Differentiated Instruction—A teaching style that provides alternative methods of teaching students that tap into their preferred learning modality such as visual, auditory, or kinesthetic; it also makes accommodations with regard to materials and equipment used and allows for students to respond in a variety of ways to demonstrate their abilities.

direct services—Educational services that must be provided to all students with disabilities.

ecological inventory—List of the functional skills needed to successfully participate in a game or activity.

ecological task analysis (ETA)—Assessment in which students have choices about how they execute various skills (e.g., equipment, rules, pace) and teachers set the parameters or objectives.

effective assessment—Test that produces data that are valid, reliable, and functional; easy to administer and interpret.

equipment support—Availability of adaptive equipment that allows students to experience high degrees of participation and success.

fading—Procedure for increasing appropriate behavior in which prompts and reinforcement are gradually removed so the appropriate behavior occurs naturally.

formal assessment—Systematic, preplanned method of testing what students know.

formative assessment—Assessment conducted during a unit.

functional assessment—Test that evaluates skills students use frequently.

functional behavioral assessment—Problem-solving process for addressing student problem behavior; relies on a variety of techniques and strategies to identify the purposes of specific behavior and help IEP teams select interventions to directly address it.

goal bank—System in which teachers choose goals, objectives, and evaluation procedures and identify them by number on a standard grid sheet; goals, objectives, and evaluation criteria for each subject area are then electronically generated.

inclusion—Model of providing services to students with disabilities in the typical environment rather than removing them from the general class.

individualized education plan (IEP)—Plan for students with disabilities that identifies specific educational needs and determines appropriate resources for addressing those needs.

individual transition plan (ITP)—Educational guide to help students with disabilities achieve their short- and long-term goals for life after high school.

informal assessment—Evaluation based on observation or the use of checklists with no strict protocol; can be conducted during class and administered by the instructor, a peer tutor, a paraeducator, or support personnel.

least restrictive environment (LRE)—Class placement in which a child with a disability learns best; to the extent possible, students with disabilities should be educated with their typically developing peers unless it is not beneficial to do so.

long-term goals—Goals to be met within a year of the IEP meeting (also known as annual goals).

modified physical education class—Small PE class (10-20 students) comprised of children with disabilities and mostly children without disabilities.

negative reinforcement—Strategy for mitigating inappropriate behavior in which a negative outcome or aversive stimulus is presented as the consequence for the behavior.

norm-referenced test—Assessment that is standardized and compares students who have similar characteristics or traits (age, gender, disability).

occupational therapist—Multidisciplinary team member who applies specific knowledge to enable people to engage in activities of daily living that have personal meaning and value.

paraeducators—Support personnel who assist teachers in various phases of the instructional process, including the delivery of direct services.

parameters—Conditions under which a skill is performed (e.g., type of equipment used, distance at which the skill is executed, environmental arrangement, level of assistance). This is one of the components of the 3Ps system used for assessment and IEP development.

peer tutoring—Use of trained peers to help teach and give feedback to students with disabilities.

personnel support—Individualized instruction or behavioral intervention that provides safe and successful educational experiences for learners; personnel can include APE consultants, teacher aides and paraeducators, interpreters for deaf students, and trained peer tutors.

physical therapist—Multidisciplinary team member who works on the preservation, enhancement, or restoration of movement and physical function impaired or threatened by disability, injury, or disease.

placement—Determination, after screening and referral, of where a child will receive adapted physical education.

portfolio—Compilation of a student's best work that reflects a student's progress toward physical literacy.

positive behavior support (PBS)—Use of person-centered interventions to modify environments, teach alternatives to inappropriate behavior, and employ meaningful consequences when inappropriate behaviors occur.

positive reinforcement—Offering something of value (e.g., praise, rewards, awards) as a result of a desired behavior in an attempt to increase the frequency of that behavior.

Premack Principle—Use of high-probability activities to reinforce low-probability activities.

present level of performance (PLP)—Skills and abilities of a child at a given time.

process information—Form or quality of a movement; the description of how a child performs the skill. This is also one of the assessment components of the 3Ps system.

product—Quantitative values produced by the student's performance of a skill, such as how many, how fast, or how far. This is also one of the assessment components of the 3Ps system.

prompting—Procedure for increasing appropriate behavior in which cues are given to students prior to any output to ensure they know what you want them to do and to avoid misbehavior.

referral—Process in which an educational professional or parent indicates that a child does not demonstrate developmentally appropriate or age-appropriate skill behaviors and should receive additional testing for disabilities.

reinforcer—Something provided as a consequence of a behavior; to increase desired behavior, it must be perceived as valuable to the student.

related services—Services provided to students with disabilities as needed to allow them to benefit from their educational experiences (e.g., occupational therapy, speech therapy, physical therapy).

reliable assessment—Test that yields consistent results repeatedly.

rubric—Form of assessment used to measure the attainment of skills, knowledge, or performance against a consistent set of criteria.

same-age peer tutoring—Approach in which students in the same grade tutor each other; can be done in unidirectional and bidirectional models.

screening—Professional observation of student actions to determine whether these actions differ considerably from typical behavior; used to determine whether a child has a unique need and is entitled to special education services.

self-contained physical education class—PE class comprised predominantly of children with disabilities.

self-determination theory—Theory that posits that people have three basic psychological needs: competence (need to feel capable and have control over the outcome of a situation), connected-ness (need for relationships with others), and autonomy (need for control over their life, or independence).

shaping—Procedure for increasing appropriate behavior that reinforces sequential steps that lead to the terminal behavior.

short-term objectives—Goals to be met within 6 months of the IEP meeting (also called benchmarks).

special education—Specially designed instruction that meets the unique needs of children with disabilities and is provided at no cost to parents.

speech therapist—Multidisciplinary team member who addresses the treatment of speech and communication disorders.

system of least prompts—Support that allows individuals with disabilities to perform skills as independently as possible; the least intensive prompt is a verbal cue, a more intensive prompt is a model or demonstration, and the most intensive prompt is physical assistance.

task analysis assessment—Test in which a skill is divided into its component tasks and the level of assistance required for each is given a numerical value.

time-out—Behavior modification that involves temporarily removing a child from an environment in which unacceptable behavior occurred.

token economy—Behavior modification in which tokens are provided as positive reinforcers for appropriate behavior; the tokens are later exchanged for a meaningful object or privilege.

transition services—Opportunities for students with disabilities to practice skills that prepare them for the transition from school to the community and assist them in becoming independent, active, and healthy individuals.

unidirectional peer tutoring—Model in which the trained peer tutor teaches the entire time and the student with a disability is the tutee; most effective with students who have more severe disabilities (such as severe autism, intellectual disability, visual impairment, or cerebral palsy).

Universal Design for Learning (UDL)—Strategy for eliminating barriers to student learning by designing physical, social, and learning environments that support diverse learners through powerful possibilities for teaching and learning.

valid assessment—Test that measures a specific skill (e.g., to assess throwing maturity, the assessment task must yield a throw).

References and Resources

Part I

Block, M.E. (2016). *A teacher's guide to adapted physical education* (4th ed.). Baltimore, MD: Paul H. Brookes.

Davis, R.W., Kotecki, J.E., Harvey, M.W., & Oliver, A. (2007). Responsibilities and training needs of paraeducators in physical education. *Adapted Physical Activity Quarterly, 24*, 70-83.

Falvey, M.A., Givner, C.C., & Kimm, C. (1995). What is an inclusive school? In R.A. Villa and J.S. Thousand (Eds.), *Creating an inclusive school* (pp. 34-58). Alexandria, VA: Association for Supervision and Curriculum Development.

Haibach, P., Wagner, M., & Lieberman, L.J. (2014). Determinants of gross motor skill performance in children with visual impairments. *Research in Developmental Disabilities, 35*, 2577-2584.

Hodge, S., Lieberman, L.J., & Murata, N. (2012). *Essentials of teaching physical education: Culture, diversity, and inclusion.* Scottsdale, AZ: Holcom Hathaway.

Lieberman, L.J., Houston-Wilson, C., & Kozub, F. (2002). Perceived barriers to including students with visual impairments and blindness into physical education. *Adapted Physical Activity Quarterly, 19*(3), 364-377.

Murphy, N.A., & Carbone, P.S. (2008). Promoting the participation of children with disabilities in sport, recreation and physical activities. *Pediatrics, 121*(5), 1057-1061.

National Center for Education Statistics. (2016). Children and youth with disabilities. https://nces.ed.gov/programs/coe/indicator_cgg.asp

Chapter 1

Block, M.E. (2016). *A teacher's guide to adapted physical education* (4th ed.). Baltimore, MD: Paul H. Brookes.

Block, M.E., & Obrusnikova, I. (2007). Inclusion in physical education: A review of the literature from 1995-2005. *Adapted Physical Activity Quarterly, 24*, 123-124.

Boer, A., Pijl, S., Minnaert, A., & Post, W. (2014). Evaluating the effectiveness of an intervention program to influence attitudes toward peers with disabilities. *Journal of Autism & Developmental Disorders, 44*, 572-583.

Bredahl, A. (2013). Sitting and watching the others being active: The experiences and difficulties in physical education when having a disability. *Adapted Physical Activity Quarterly, 30*, 40-58.

Bryan, R.R., McCubbin, J.A., & van der Mars, H. (2013). The ambiguous role of the paraeducator in the general

physical education environment. *Adapted Physical Activity Quarterly, 29*, 164-183.

Choi, S., French, R., & Silliman-French, L. (2013). Knowledge sharing strategies among adapted physical educators. *Palaestra, 27*, 25-29.

Coates, J. (2012). Teaching inclusively: Are secondary physical education student teachers sufficiently prepared to teach in inclusive environments? *Physical Education and Sport Pedagogy, 17*, 349-365.

Coates, J., & Vickerman, P. (2008). Let the children have their say: Children with special educational needs and their experiences of physical education—a review. *Support for Learning, 23*(4), 168-175.

Coates, J., & Vickerman, P. (2010). Empowering children with special educational needs to speak up: Experiences of inclusive physical education. *Disability and Rehabilitation, 32*, 1517-1526.

de Schipper, T., Lieberman, L.J., & Moody, B. (2017). Kids like me, we go lightly on the head: Experiences of children with a visual impairment on the physical self-concept. *British Journal of Visual Impairment, 35*, 55-68.

Elliott, S. (2008). The effect of teachers' attitude toward inclusion on the practice and success levels of children with and without disabilities in physical education. *International Journal of Special Education, 23*, 48-55.

Fitzgerald, H., & Stride, A. (2012). Stories about PE from young people with disabilities. *International Journal of Disability Development and Education, 59*, 283-293.

Foley, J., Tindall, D.W., Lieberman, L.J., & Kim, S. (2007). How to develop disability awareness using the sport education model. *Journal of Physical Education, Recreation & Dance, 78*, 32-36.

Goodwin, D. (2001). The meaning of help in PE: Perceptions of students with physical disabilities. *Adapted Physical Activity Quarterly, 18*, 289-303.

Goodwin, D., & Watkinson, J. (2000). Inclusive physical education from the perspective of students with physical disabilities. *Adapted Physical Activity Quarterly, 17*, 144-160.

Grenier, M.A. (2011). Co-teaching in physical education: A strategy for inclusive practice. *Adapted Physical Activity Quarterly, 28*, 95-112.

Haegele, J.A., & Sutherland, S. (2015). Perspectives of students with disabilities toward physical education: A qualitative inquiry review. *Quest, 67*(3), 255-273.

Halle, J.W., Gabler-Halle, D., & Bembren, D.A. (1989). Effects of a peer-mediated aerobic conditioning program on fitness measures with children who have moderate and severe disabilities. *Journal of the Association for Persons with Severe Handicaps, 14*, 33-47.

Hardin, B. (2005). Physical education teachers' reflections on preparation for inclusion. *The Physical Educator, 62*, 44-57.

Houston-Wilson, C., Lieberman, L.J., Horton, M., & Kasser, S. (1997). Peer tutoring: A plan for instructing students of all abilities. *Journal of Physical Education, Recreation & Dance, 6*, 39-44.

Individuals with Disabilities Education Improvement Act of 2004 (IDEIA), Public Law No. 108-446 (2004). Retrieved from http://idea.ed.gov/

James, A., Kellman, M., & Lieberman, L.J. (2011). Perspectives on inclusion from students with disabilities and responsive strategies for teaching. *Journal of Physical Education, Recreation & Dance, 82*, 33-38, 54.

Kalyvas, V., & Reid, G. (2003). Sport adaptation, participation and enjoyment of students with and without disabilities. *Adapted Physical Activity Quarterly, 20*, 182-199.

Klavina, A., & Block, M.E. (2008). The effect of peer tutoring on interaction behaviors in inclusive physical education. *Adapted Physical Activity Quarterly, 25*, 132-158.

Lieberman, L.J., Arndt, K.L., & Daggett, S. (2007). Promoting leadership in physical education and recreation. *Journal of Physical Education, Recreation & Dance, 78*, 46-50.

Lieberman, L.J., Dunn, J.M., van der Mars, H., & McCubbin, J.A. (2000). Peer tutors' effects on activity levels of deaf students in inclusive elementary physical education. *Adapted Physical Activity Quarterly, 17*(1), 20-39.

Lytle, R.K., & Hutchinson, G.E. (2004). Adapted physical educators: The multiple roles of consultants. *Adapted Physical Activity Quarterly, 21*, 34-49.

Martin, J., & Smith, K. (2002). Friendship quality in youth disability sport: Perceptions of a best friend. *Adapted Physical Activity Quarterly, 19*, 472-482.

Morley, D., Bailey, R., Tan, J., & Cooke, B. (2005). Inclusive physical education: Teachers' views of including pupils with special education needs and/or disabilities in physical education. *European Physical Education Review, 11*, 84-107.

Obrusnikova, I., & Kelly, L. (2009). Caseloads and job demographics of adapted physical educators in the United States. *Perceptual and Motor Skills, 109*, 737-746.

Obrusnikova, I., Valkova, H., & Block, M. (2003). Impact of inclusion in general physical education on students without disabilities. *Adapted Physical Activity Quarterly, 20*, 230-245.

Place, K., & Hodge, S. (2001). Social inclusion of students with physical disabilities in general physical education: A behavioral analysis. *Adapted Physical Activity Quarterly, 18*, 389-404.

Seymour, H., Reid, G., & Bloom, G.A. (2009). Friendship in inclusive physical education. *Adapted Physical Activity Quarterly, 26*, 201-219.

Silliman-French, L., Candler, C., French, R., & Hamilton, M.L. (2007). I have students with physical and motor problems: How can an APE, OT or PT help? *Strategies, 21*, 15-19.

Suomi, J., Collier, D., & Brown, L. (2003). Factors affecting social experiences of students in elementary physical education classes. *Adapted Physical Activity Quarterly, 22*, 186-202.

Tindall, D., Foley, J., & Lieberman, L.J. (2016). Incorporating sport education roles for students with visual impairments and blindness as part of a sport camp experience. *Palaestra, 30*, 31-36.

Verderber, J.M.S., Rizzo, T.L., & Sherrill, C. (2003). Assessing student intention to participate in inclusive physical education. *Adapted Physical Activity Quarterly, 20*, 26-45.

Ward, P., & Ayvazo, S. (2006). Classwide peer tutoring in physical education: Assessing its effects with kindergartners with autism. *Adapted Physical Activity Quarterly, 3*, 233-244.

Winnick, J.P. (2017). Introduction to adapted physical education and sport. In J.P. Winnick & D.L. Porretta (Eds.), *Adapted physical education and sport* (6th ed., pp. 3-21). Champaign, IL: Human Kinetics.

Wiskochil, B., Lieberman, L.J., Houston-Wilson, C., & Petersen, S. (2007). The effects of trained peer tutors on academic learning time—physical education on four children who are visually impaired or blind. *Journal of Visual Impairment and Blindness, 101*, 339-350.

Wright, P.W.D., & Wright, P.D. (2010). Physical education for students with disabilities. Retrieved from www.wrightslaw.com/info/pe.index.htm

Chapter 2

Block, M.E. (2016). *A teacher's guide to adapted physical education* (4th ed.). Baltimore, MD: Paul H. Brookes.

Bruininks, R.H., & Bruininks, R.D. (2005). *Bruininks-Oseretsky test of motor proficiency* (2nd ed.). Circle Pines, MN: American Guidance Services.

Carson, L.M., Bulger, S.M., & Townsend, J.S. (2007). Enhancing responsible decision making in physical activity. In W.E. Davis & G.E. Broadhead (Eds.), *Ecological task analysis and movement* (pp. 141-147). Champaign, IL: Human Kinetics.

Columna, L., Davis, T., Lieberman, L.J., & Lytle, R. (2010). Determining the most appropriate physical education placement for students with disabilities. *Journal of Physical Education, Recreation & Dance, 81*, 30-37.

Folio, M.R., & Fewell, R.R. (2000). *Peabody developmental motor scales* (2nd ed.) Austin, TX: PRO-ED.

Frankenburg, W.K., & Dodds, J.B. (1990). *The Denver II Developmental Screening Test*. Denver: University of Colorado Medical Center. Retrieved from www.DenverII.com

Garrahy, D. (2015). Role of adapted physical education specialists. In F.E. Obiakor & J.P. Bakken (Eds.), *Interdisciplinary connections to special education: Key related professionals involved (Advances in special education, vol. 30B)* (pp. 107-118). Bingley, United Kingdom: Emerald Group Publishing Limited.

Good, T.L. (2014). What do we know about how teachers influence student performance on standardized tests: And why do we know so little about other student outcomes? *Teachers College Record, 116*, 1-41.

Haegele, J.A., & Lieberman, L.J. (2016). The current status of physical education at schools for the blind in the US. *Journal of Visual Impairment and Blindness, 110*, 323-334.

Horvat, M., Block, M.E., & Kelly, L.E. (2007). *Developmental and adapted physical activity assessment*. Champaign, IL: Human Kinetics.

Houston-Wilson, C. (1993). *SUNY Brockport aquatics skills checklist*. Brockport, NY: Author.

Houston-Wilson, C. (1995). Alternate assessment procedures. In J. Seaman (Ed.), *Physical best and individuals with disabilities: A handbook for inclusion in fitness programs* (pp. 91-109). Reston, VA: American Alliance for Health, Physical Education, Recreation and Dance.

Kasser, S.L., & Lytle, R.K. (2013). *Inclusive physical activity: Promoting health for a lifetime*. Champaign, IL: Human Kinetics.

Kowalski, E., Houston-Wilson, C., & Daggett, S. (in press). *The basic skills assessment*. Little Falls, NY: NYS-AHPERD.

Kowalski, E., & Lieberman, L. (Eds.). (2011). *Assessment for everyone: Modifying NASPE assessments to include all children*. Reston, VA: National Association for Sport & Physical Education.

Lieberman, L.J., Cavanaugh, L., Haegele, J.A., Aiello, R., & Wilson, W. (2017). The modified physical education class: An option for the least restrictive environment. *Journal of Physical Education, Recreation & Dance, 88*.

Lund, J., & Veal, M.L. (2013). *Assessment driven instruction in physical education*. Champaign, IL: Human Kinetics.

Melograno, V.J. (2006). *Professional and student portfolios for physical education* (2nd ed.). Champaign, IL: Human Kinetics.

Mitchell, S., & Oslin, J. (2007). Ecological task analysis in games teaching: Tactical games model. In W.E. Davis & G.E. Broadhead (Eds.), *Ecological task analysis and movement* (pp. 161-177). Champaign, IL: Human Kinetics.

Mitchell, S.A., & Walton-Fisette, J.L. (2016). *Essentials of teaching physical education: Curriculum, instruction, and assessment*. Champaign, IL: Human Kinetics.

SHAPE America. (2014). *National standards & grade-level outcomes for K-12 physical education*. Champaign, IL: Human Kinetics.

Ulrich, D.A. (2017). *The test of gross motor development* (3rd ed.). Austin, TX: PRO-ED.

Wessel, J.A., & Zittel, L.L. (1995). *Smart start: Preschool movement curriculum designed for children of all abilities*. Austin, TX: PRO-ED.

Wessel, J.A., & Zittel, L.L. (1998). *I CAN primary skills K-3*. Austin, TX: PRO-ED.

Winnick, J.P., & Short, F.X. (2014). *Brockport physical fitness test manual: A health-related assessment for youngsters with disabilities* (2nd ed.). Champaign, IL: Human Kinetics.

Zittel, L. (1994). Gross motor assessment of preschool children with special needs: Instrument selection considerations. *Adapted Physical Activity Quarterly, 11*, 245-260.

Chapter 3

Block, M.E. (2016). *A teacher's guide to adapted physical education* (4th ed.). Baltimore, MD: Paul H. Brookes.

Columna, L., Davis, T., Lieberman, L.J., & Lytle, R. (2010). Determining the most appropriate physical education placement for students with disabilities. *Journal of Physical Education, Recreation & Dance, 81*, 30-37.

de Schipper, T., Lieberman, L.J., & Moody, B. (2017). Kids like me, we go lightly on the head: Experiences of children with a visual impairment on the physical self-concept. *British Journal of Visual Impairment, 35*(1), 55-68.

Dunn, J.M., & Leitschuh, C.A. (2014). *Special physical education* (8th ed.). Dubuque, IA: Kendall Hunt Publishing.

Gartner, A., & Kerzner-Lipsky, D. (2011). Beyond special education: Toward a quality education for all students. *Harvard Educational Review, 57*, 367-396.

Haegele, J.A., & Sutherland, S. (2015). Perspectives of students with disabilities toward physical education: A qualitative inquiry review. *Quest, 67*(3), 255-273.

Hersman, B.L., & Hodge, S.R. (2010). High school physical educators' beliefs about teaching differently abled students in an urban public school district. *Education and Urban Society, 42*(6), 730-757.

Hodge, S.R., & Akuffo, P.B. (2007). Adapted physical education teachers' concerns in teaching students with disabilities in an urban public school district. *Exceptional Child, 54*(4), 399-416.

Hodge, S.R., Ammah, J.O.A., Casebolt, K.M., LaMaster, K., Hersman, B., Samalot-Rivera, A., & Sato, T. (2009). A diversity of voices: Physical education teachers' beliefs about inclusion and teaching students with disabilities. *International Journal of Disability, Development and Education, 56*(4), 401-419.

Individuals with Disabilities Education Improvement Act of 2004 (IDEIA), Public Law No. 108-446 (2004). Retrieved from http://idea.ed.gov/

Lieberman, L.J., Brian, A., & Grenier, M. (in press). Validation of the Lieberman/Brian Inclusion Rating Scale for Physical Education. *European Physical Education Review*.

Lieberman, L.J., Cavanaugh, L., Haegele, J.A., Aiello, R., & Wilson, W. (2017). The modified physical education class: An option for the least restrictive environment. *Journal of Physical Education, Recreation & Dance, 88*.

Lieberman, L.J., Houston-Wilson, C., & Kozub, F. (2002). Perceived barriers to including students with visual impairments and blindness into physical education. *Adapted Physical Activity Quarterly, 19*(3), 364-377.

Obrusnikova, I. (2008). Physical educators' beliefs about teaching children with disabilities. *Perceptual and Motor Skills, 106*(2), 637-644.

Özer, D., Nalbant, S., Ağlamış, E., Baran, F., Samut, P.K., Aktop, A., & Hutzler, Y. (2013). Physical education teachers' attitudes towards children with intellectual disability: The impact of time in service, gender, and previous acquaintance. *Journal of Intellectual Disability Research, 57*(11), 1001-1013.

Perkins, K., Columna, L., Lieberman, L.J., & Bailey, J. (2013). Parental perceptions toward physical activity for their children with visual impairments and blindness. *Journal of Visual Impairments and Blindness, 107*, 131-142.

Roth, K., Zittel, L., Pyfer, J., & Auxter, D. (2016). *Principles and methods of adapted physical education and recreation* (12th ed.). Burlington, MA: Jones and Bartlett Learning.

SHAPE America. (2014). *National standards & grade-level outcomes for K-12 physical education*. Champaign, IL: Human Kinetics.

Winnick, J.P., & Porretta, D.L. (Eds.). (2017). *Adapted physical education and sport* (6th ed.). Champaign, IL: Human Kinetics.

Chapter 4

Block, M.E. (2016). *A teacher's guide to adapted physical education* (4th ed.). Baltimore, MD: Paul H. Brookes.

Bruininks, R.H., & Bruininks, R.D. (2005). *Bruininks-Oseretsky test of motor proficiency* (2nd ed.). Circle Pines, MN: American Guidance Services.

Dunn, J.M., & Leitschuh, C.A. (2017). *Special physical education* (10th ed.). Dubuque, IA: Kendall/Hunt.

Fronske, H.A., & Heath, E.M. (2015). *Teaching cues for sport skills for secondary school students* (6th ed.). New York, NY: Pearson.

Houston-Wilson, C., & Lieberman, L.J. (1999). Becoming involved in the individualized education program: A guide for regular physical educators. *Journal of Physical Education, Recreation & Dance, 70*(3), 60-64.

Individuals with Disabilities Education Improvement Act of 2004 (IDEIA), Public Law No. 108-446 (2004). Retrieved from http://idea.ed.gov/

Kowalski, E., Lieberman, L., & Daggett, S. (2006). Getting involved in the IEP process. *Journal of Physical Education, Recreation & Dance, 77*(7), 35-39.

Kowalski, E., Lieberman, L.J., Pucci, G., & Mulawka, K. (2005). Implementing IEP and 504 goals and objectives into general physical education. *Journal of Physical Education, Recreation & Dance, 76*(7), 33-37.

Kowalski, E., McCall, R., Aiello, R., & Lieberman, L.J. (2009). Utilizing IEP goal banks effectively. *Journal of Physical Education, Recreation & Dance, 80*, 44-48, 52.

Lieberman, L.J., Robinson, B., & Rollheiser, H. (2006). Youth with visual impairments: Experiences within general physical education. *RE:View, 38*(1), 35-48.

Samalot, A., & Lieberman, L.J. (2017). My inclusion in the IEP process makes my job most enjoyable. *Palaestra*, September.

Ulrich, D.A. (2017). *Test of gross motor development* (3rd ed.). Austin, TX: PRO-ED.

Winnick, J.P., & Short, F.X. (2014). *Brockport physical fitness test manual: A health-related assessment for youngsters with disabilities* (2nd ed.). Champaign, IL: Human Kinetics.

Chapter 5

Alstot, A.E., & Alstot, C.D. (2015). Behavior management: Examining the functions of behavior. *Journal of Physical Education, Recreation & Dance, 2*, 22-28.

Block, M.E., Henderson, H., & Lavay, B. (2016). Positive behavior support of children with challenging behaviors. In M.E. Block, *A teacher's guide to adapted physical education* (4th ed.; pp. 305-332). Baltimore, MD: Paul H. Brookes.

Collier, D. (2017). Instructional strategies for adapted physical education. In J.P. Winnick & D.L. Porretta (Eds.), *Adapted physical education and sport* (6th ed., pp. 121-149). Champaign, IL: Human Kinetics.

Cothran, D.J., Kulinna, P.H., & Garrahy, D.A. (2009). "This is kind of giving a secret away...": Students' perspectives on effective class management. *Teaching and Teacher Education, 19*, 435-444.

Lavay, B.W., French, R., & Henderson, H.L. (2016). *Positive behavior management in physical activity settings* (3rd ed.). Champaign, IL: Human Kinetics.

Lavay, B., Guthrie, S., & Henderson, H. (2014). The behavior management training and teaching practices of nationally Certified Adapted Physical Education (CAPE) teachers. *Palaestra, 28*, 24-31.

Lavay, B., Henderson, H., French, R., & Guthrie, S. (2012). Behavioral management instructional strategies and content of college/university physical education teacher education programs. *Physical Education & Sport Pedagogy, 17*, 195-210.

Loovis, E.M. (2017). Behavior management. In J.P. Winnick & D.L. Porretta (Eds.), *Adapted physical education and sport* (6th ed., pp. 101-119). Champaign, IL: Human Kinetics.

Wheeler, J.J., & Richey, D.D. (2005). *Behavior management principles and practices of positive behavior support*. Upper Saddle River, NJ: Prentice Hall.

Chapter 6

Bevans, K., Sanchez, L., Fitzpatrick, B., & Forrest, C.B. (2010). Individual and instructional determinants of student engagement in physical education. *Journal of Teaching Physical Education, 29*, 399-416.

Block, M.E., Hutzler, Y., Barak, S., & Klavina, A. (2013). Creation and validation of the self-efficacy instrument for physical education teacher education majors toward inclusion. *Adapted Physical Activity Quarterly, 29*, 184-205.

Bowes, M., & Tinning, R. (2015). Productive pedagogies and teachers' professional learning in physical education. *Asia-Pacific Journal of Health, Sport and Physical Education, 6*, 93-109.

Bredahl, A.M. (2013). Sitting and watching the others being active: The experienced difficulties in physical education when having a disability. *Adapted Physical Activity Quarterly, 30*(1), 40-58.

Brian, A., & Haegele, J.A. (2014). Including students with visual impairments: Softball. *Journal of Physical Education, Recreation & Dance, 85*(3), 39-45.

Coates, J., & Vickerman, P. (2008). Let the children have their say: Children with special educational needs and their experiences of physical education—a review. *Support for Learning, 23*(4), 168-175.

Davis, R. (2011). *Teaching disability sport*. Champaign, IL: Human Kinetics.

Deci, E.L., & Ryan, R.M. (1983). The basis of self-determination: Intrinsic motivation and integrated internalizations. *Academic Psychology Bulletin, 5*, 21-29.

de Schipper, T., Lieberman, L.J., & Moody, B. (2017). Kids like me, we go lightly on the head: Experiences of children with a visual impairment on the physical self-concept. *British Journal of Visual Impairment, 35*(1), 55-68.

Getchell, N., & Gagen, L. (2006). Adapting activities for all children: Considering constraints can make planning simple and effective. *Palaestra, 22*(1), 20-27, 43, 48.

Gregory, G.H., & Chapman, C. (2007). *Differential instructional strategies*. Thousand Oaks, CA: Corwin Press.

Grenier, M., Dyson, B., & Yeaton, P. (2005). Cooperative learning that includes students with disabilities: An effective teaching strategy, cooperative learning promotes student interaction, benefiting students with and without disabilities. *Journal of Physical Education, Recreation & Dance, 76,* 29-36.

Grenier, M., & Kearns, C. (2012). The benefits of implementing disability sport into physical education: A model for success. *Journal of Physical Education, Recreation & Dance, 83*(4), 24-27.

Grenier, M., & Lieberman, L.J. (2018). *Physical education for children with severe disabilities.* Champaign, IL: Human Kinetics.

Grenier, M., Rogers, R., & Iarrusso, K. (2008). Including students with Down syndrome in adventure programming. *Journal of Physical Education, Recreation & Dance, 79,* 30-35.

Grenier, M., Wright, S., Collins, K., & Kearns, C. (2014). "I thought it was going to be lame": Perceptions of a disability sport unit in general physical education. *Adapted Physical Activity Quarterly, 31*(1), 49-66.

Haegele, J.A., & Sutherland, S. (2015). Perspectives of students with disabilities toward physical education: A qualitative inquiry review. *Quest, 67*(3), 255-273.

Hall, T., Meyer, A., & Rose, D.H. (2012). *Universal design for learning in the classroom: Practical application.* New York, NY: Guilford Press.

Healy, S., Msetfi, R., & Gallagher, S. (2013). "Happy and a bit nervous": The experiences of children with autism in physical education. *British Journal of Learning Disabilities, 41,* 222-228.

Hodge, S., Lieberman, L., & Murata, N. (2012). *Essentials of teaching adapted physical education.* Scottsdale, AZ: Holcomb Hathaway.

Kowalski, E., Lieberman, L.J., Pucci, G., & Mulawka, C. (2005). Implementing IEP or 504 goals and objectives into general physical education. *Journal of Physical Education, Recreation & Dance, 76*(7), 33-37.

Kowalski, E., McCall, R., Aiello, R., & Lieberman, L.J. (2009). Utilizing IEP goal banks effectively. *Journal of Physical Education, Recreation & Dance, 80,* 44-48, 52.

Lalvani, P., & Broderick, A.A. (2013). Institutionalized ableism and the misguided "Disability Awareness Day": Transformative pedagogies for teacher education. *Equity and Excellence in Education, 46,* 468-483.

Leo, J., & Goodwin, D. (2016). Simulating others' realities: Insiders reflect on disability simulations. *Adapted Physical Activity Quarterly, 33,* 156-176.

Lieberman, L.J. (2016). Infusing the Paralympics into the physical education curriculum. *Journal of Physical Education, Recreation & Dance, 87,* 3-4.

Lieberman, L.J., & Block, M.E. (2016). Inclusive settings in adapted physical education: A world wide reality? In C. Ennis (Ed.), *Handbook of physical education* (pp. 262-276). New York, NY: Routledge/Taylor & Francis.

Lieberman, L.J., Cavanaugh, L., Haegele, J.A., Aiello, R., & Wilson, W. (2017). The modified physical education class: An option for the least restrictive environment. *Journal of Physical Education, Recreation & Dance, 88.*

Lieberman, L.J., & Cowart, J. (2011). *Games for people with sensory impairments* (2nd ed.). Louisville, KY: American Printing House for the Blind.

Lieberman, L.J., Haibach, P., & Wagner, M. (2014). Let's play together: Sports equipment for children with and without visual impairments. *Palaestra, 28,* 13-15.

Lieberman, L.J., Lytle, R., & Clarcq, J. (2008). Getting it right from the start: Employing the Universal Design for Learning approach to your curriculum. *Journal of Physical Education, Recreation & Dance, 79,* 32-39.

Lieberman, L.J., Ponchillia, P., & Ponchillia, S. (2013). *Physical education and sport for individuals who are visually impaired or deafblind: Foundations of instruction.* New York, NY: American Federation of the Blind Press.

Menear, K.S., & Davis, T. (2007). Modifying physical activities to include individuals with disabilities: A systematic approach. *Journal of Physical Education, Recreation & Dance, 78,* 37-41.

Meyer, A., & Rose, D.H. (2000). Universal design for individual differences. *Educational Leadership, 58*(3), 39-43.

Moola, F., Fusco, C., & Kirsh, J.A. (2011). "What I wish you knew": Social barriers toward physical activity in youth with congenital heart disease (CHD). *Adapted Physical Activity Quarterly, 28*(1), 56-77.

Odem, S.L., Brantlinger, E., Gersten, R.H., Thompson, B., & Harris, K.R. (2005). Research in special education: Scientific methods and evidence-based practices. *Exceptional Children, 71,* 137-148.

Perkins, K., Columna, L., Lieberman, L.J., & Bailey, J. (2013). Parental perceptions toward physical activity for their children with visual impairments and blindness. *Journal of Visual Impairments and Blindness, 107,* 131-142.

Perez, K. (2014). *The new inclusion: Differentiated strategies to engage all students.* New York, NY: Teachers College Press.

Petersen, J.C., & Piletic, C.K. (2006). Facility accessibility: Opening the doors to all. *Journal of Physical Education, Recreation & Dance, 77,* 38-44.

Rapp, W. (2014). *Universal design for learning in action.* Baltimore, MD: Paul H. Brookes.

Rapp, W., & Arndt, K. (2012). *Teaching everyone: An introduction to inclusive education.* Baltimore, MD: Paul H. Brookes.

Rose, D.H., & Meyer, A. (2002). *Teaching every student in the digital age: Universal Design for Learning.* Alexandria, VA: Association for Supervision and Curriculum Development.

Samalot, A., & Aiello, R. (2018). Recreation opportunities beyond school. In M. Grenier & L.J. Lieberman, *Physical education for children with moderate to severe disabilities.* Champaign, IL: Human Kinetics.

Samalot, A., & Lieberman, L.J. (2016). Community programs. In R. Aiello (Ed.), *Sports, fitness and motor activities for children with disabilities: A practical approach to increased physical activity beyond the school day* (pp. 41-52). Lanham, MD: Rowman and Litterfield.

Sherlock-Shangraw, R. (2013). Creating inclusive youth sports environments with the Universal Design for Learning. *Journal of Physical Education, Recreation & Dance, 84,* 40-46.

Spencer-Cavaliere, N., & Watkinson, E.J. (2010). Inclusion understood from the perspectives of children with disability. *Adapted Physical Activity Quarterly, 27,* 275-293.

Spooner, F., Baker, J., Harris, A., Ahlgrim-Delzell, L., & Browder, D. (2007). Effects of training in Universal Design for Learning on lesson plan development. *Remedial and Special Education, 28*, 108-116.

Tepfer, A., & Lieberman, L.J. (2012). Using cross curricular ideas to infuse Paralympic sport. *Journal of Physical Education, Recreation & Dance, 83*(4), 20-23, 27.

Thousand, J.S., Villa, R.A., & Nevin, A.I. (2007). *Differentiating instruction: Collaborative planning and teaching for universally designed learning.* Thousand Oaks, CA: Corwin Press.

Waugh, L., Bowers, T., & French, R. (2007). Use of picture cards in integrated physical education. *Strategies, 20*, 18-20.

White, G., Casebolt, K., & Hull, S. (2004). Low-organized games: An approach to inclusion. *Strategies, 18*, 27-29.

Wolfensberger, W. (1972). *Normalization.* Toronto: National Institute on Mental Retardation.

Chapter 7

Aiello, R., & Lieberman, L.J. (2018). Paraeducators in physical education. In M. Grenier & L.J. Lieberman (Eds.), *Physical education for children with moderate to severe disabilities.* Champaign, IL: Human Kinetics.

Batista, P.J., & Pittman, A. (2005). Peer-grading passes the Supreme Court test. *Journal of Physical Education, Recreation & Dance, 76*(2), 10-12.

Broer, S., Doyle, M., & Giangreco, M. (2005). Perspectives for students with intellectual disabilities about their experiences with paraeducator support. *Exceptional Children, 71*, 415-430.

Bryan, R., McCubbin, J.A., & van der Mars, H. (2013). The ambiguous role of the paraeducator in the general physical education environment. *Adapted Physical Activity Quarterly, 29*, 164-183.

Butler, S.A., & Hodge, S.R. (2001). Enhancing student trust through peer assessment in physical education. *Physical Educator, 58*, 30-42.

Byra, M., & Marks, M. (1993). The effect of two pairing techniques on specific feedback and comfort levels of learners in the reciprocal style of teaching. *Journal of Teaching in Physical Education, 12*, 286-300.

Causton-Theoharis, J., & Mamgren, K. (2005). Building bridges: Strategies to help paraprofessionals promote peer interaction. *Teaching Exceptional Children*, July/August, 20.

Cervantes, C.M., Lieberman, L.J., Magnesio, B., & Wood, J. (2013). Peer tutoring: Meeting the demands of inclusion in today's general physical education settings. *Journal of Physical Education, Recreation & Dance, 84*, 43-48.

Copeland, S.R., McCall, J., Williams, C.R., Guth, C., Carter, E.W., Fowler, S.E., et al. (2002, September/October). High school peer buddies: A win-win situation. *The Council for Exceptional Children*, 16-21.

d'Arripe-Longueville, F., Gernigon, C., Huet, M., Cadopi, M., & Winnykamen, F. (2002). Peer tutoring in a physical education setting: Influence of tutor skill level on novice learners' motivation and performance. *Journal of Teaching in Physical Education, 22*(1), 105-123.

Davis, R.W., Kotecki, J.E., Harvey, M.W., & Oliver, A. (2007). Responsibilities and training needs of paraeducators in physical education. *Adapted Physical Activity Quarterly, 24*, 70-83.

DePaepe, J.L. (1985). The influence of three least restrictive environments on the content, motor-ALT, and performance of moderately mentally retarded students. *Journal of Teaching in Physical Education, 5*, 34-41.

Dunn, J.M., Morehouse, J.W., & Fredericks, H.D. (1986). *Physical education for the severely handicapped: A systematic approach to data based gymnasium.* Austin, TX: PRO-ED.

Folsom-Meek, S.L., & Aiello, R. (2007). Instruction strategies. In L.J. Lieberman (Ed.), *Paraeducators in physical education: A training guide to roles and responsibilities* (pp. 47-59). Champaign, IL: Human Kinetics.

Friend, M.D. (2014). *Special education: Contemporary perspectives for school professionals.* Boston, MA: Allyn & Bacon.

Giangreco, M.F., Edelman, S., Luiselli, T.E., & MacFarland, S. (1997). Helping or hovering? Effects of instructional assistant proximity on students with disabilities. *Exceptional Children, 64*, 7-18.

Haegele, J.A., & Kozub, F.M. (2010). A continuum of paraeducator support for utilization in adapted physical education. *Teaching Exceptional Children Plus, 6*(5), Article 2.

Hauge, J.M., & Babkie, A.M. (2006). 20 ways to develop collaborative special educator–paraprofessional teams: One para's view. *Intervention in School and Clinic, 42*, 51-53.

Hodge, S., Lieberman, L.J., & Murata, N. (2012). *Essentials of teaching physical education: Culture, diversity, and inclusion.* Scottsdale, AZ: Holcomb Hathaway.

Horvat, M., Block, M.E., & Kelly, L.E. (2007). *Developmental and adapted physical activity assessment.* Champaign, IL: Human Kinetics.

Houston-Wilson, C., Dunn, J.M., van der Mars, H., & McCubbin, J.A. (1997). The effect of peer tutors on motor performance in integrated physical education classes. *Adapted Physical Activity Quarterly, 14*(4), 298-313.

Hughes, C., Fowler, S.E., Copeland, S.R., Agran, M., Wehmeyer, M.L., & Church-Pupke, P.P. (2004). Supporting high school students to engage in recreational activities with peers. *Behavior Modification, 28*, 3-27.

Johnson, M., & Ward, P. (2001). Effects of classwide peer tutoring on correct performance of striking skills in 3rd grade physical education. *Journal of Teaching in Physical Education, 20*, 247-263.

Kasser, S., & Lytle, R. (2013). *Inclusive physical activity: Promoting health for a lifetime.* Champaign, IL: Human Kinetics.

Klavina, A., & Block, M.E. (2008). The effect of peer tutoring on interaction behaviors in inclusive physical education. *Adapted Physical Activity Quarterly, 25*(2), 132-158.

Klavina, A., & Lieberman, L.J. (2017). Peer tutoring. In M. Grenier & L.J. Lieberman (Eds.), *Physical education for children with moderate to severe disabilities.* Champaign, IL: Human Kinetics.

Kowalski, E.M., & Lieberman, L.J. (2011). *Assessment for everyone.* Reston, VA: NASPE.

Lee, S.H., & Haegele, J.A. (2016). Tips for effectively utilizing paraprofessionals in physical education. *Journal of Physical Education, Recreation & Dance, 87*(1), 46-48.

Lieberman, L.J. (Ed.) (2007). *A paraprofessional training guide for physical education.* Champaign, IL: Human Kinetics.

Lieberman, L.J., & Conroy, P. (2013). Paraeducator training for physical education for children with visual impairments. *Journal of Visual Impairments and Blindness, 107*, 17-28.

Lieberman, L.J., Dunn, J.M., van der Mars, H., & McCubbin, J.A. (2000). Peer tutors' effects on activity levels of deaf students in inclusive elementary physical education. *Adapted Physical Activity Quarterly, 17*(1), 20-39.

Lieberman, L.J., & Houston-Wilson, C. (2011). Marginalization and adapted physical education: Strategies for increasing the status and value of adapted physical education in schools. *Journal of Physical Education, Recreation & Dance, 82*, 25-28.

Lytle, R., Lieberman, L.J., & Aiello, R. (2007). Motivating paraeducators to be actively involved in physical education programs. *Journal of Physical Education, Recreation & Dance, 78*, 26-30, 50.

Mach, M. (2000). Using assistants for physical education. *Strategies, 14*(2), 8.

Mauerer, K. (2004). *The use of paraprofessionals in general physical education.* Unpublished master's degree thesis, SUNY Brockport.

Piletic, C., Davis, R., & Aschemeier, A. (2005). Paraeducators in physical education. *Journal of Physical Education, Recreation & Dance, 76*(5), 47-55.

Trautman, M.L. (2004). Preparing and managing paraprofessionals. *Intervention in School and Clinic, 39*, 131-139.

Ward, P., & Ayvazo, S. (2006). Classwide peer tutoring in physical education: Assessing its effects with kindergartners with autism. *Adapted Physical Activity Quarterly, 3*, 233-244.

Ward, P., & Lee, M. (2005). Peer-assisted learning in physical education: A review of theory and research. *Journal of Teaching in Physical Education, 24*, 205-225.

Wiskochil, B., Lieberman, L.J., Houston-Wilson, C., & Petersen, S. (2007). The effects of trained peer tutors on academic learning time-physical education on four children who are visually impaired or blind. *Journal of Visual Impairment and Blindness, 101*, 339-350.

Chapter 8

Aiello, R. (2016). *Sports, fitness and motor activities for children with disabilities: A practical approach to increased physical activity beyond the school day.* Blue Ridge, PA: Rowman and Littlefield.

Flexer, R.W., Baer, R.M., Luft, P., & Simmons, T.J. (2013). *Transition planning for secondary students with disabilities* (4th ed.). Upper Saddle River, NJ: Pearson.

Foley, K.R., Dyke, P., Girdler, S., Bourke, J., & Leonard, H. (2012). Young adults with intellectual disability transitioning from school to post-school: A literature review framed within the ICF. *Disability & Rehabilitation, 34*(20), 1747-1764.

Hodge, S.R., Lieberman, L., & Murratta, N. (2012). *Essentials of teaching adapted physical education: Diversity, culture and inclusion.* Scottsdale, AZ: Holcomb Publishers.

Individuals with Disabilities Education Improvement Act of 2004 (IDEIA), Public Law No. 108-446 (2004). Retrieved from http://idea.ed.gov/

Lieberman, L.J., & Linsenbigler, K. (2017). Teaching recreation activities to children who are visually impaired or deafblind. *Palaestra, 31*, 40-46.

National Organization on Disability. (2010). *Survey of Americans with disabilities.* Washington, DC: Author. Retrieved from www.2010disabilitysurveys.org/indexold.html

Newman, L., Wagner, M., Knokey, A.-M., Marder, C., Nagle, K., Shaver, D., et al. (2011). *The post-high school outcomes of young adults with disabilities up to 8 years after high school: A report from the National Longitudinal Transition Study-2 (NLTS2) (NCSER 2011-3005).* Menlo Park, CA: SRI International.

Rehabilitation Act of 1973, Public Law No. 93-112, 87 Stat. 355 (1973).

Samalot-Rivera, A., & Porretta, D.L. (2012). The influence of social skills instruction on sport and game related behaviors of students with emotional or behavioral disorders. *Physical Education and Sport Pedagogy, 17*, 1-16.

U.S. Department of Education Office for Civil Rights. (2013). *Dear colleague letter: Extracurricular athletics for students with disabilities.* Retrieved from www2.ed.gov/about/offices/list/ocr/letters/colleague-201301-504.pdf

U.S. Government Accountability Office. (2010). *Students with disabilities: More information and guidance could improve opportunities in physical education and athletics.* Report to Congressional Requesters. Retrieved from www.gao.gov/assets/310/305770.pdf

Equipment Companies

Flaghouse: www.Flaghouse.com

Gopher: www.Gophersport.com

Sportime: www.store.schoolspecialty.com

US Games: www.USgames.com

Training Videos

Training video for paraeducators: www.uwlax.edu/CDHAPA/Adapted-Physical-Education-instructional-videos/

Training video for paraeducators and physical education teachers working with children with visual impairments: www.youtube.com/watch?v=77fyMsRWrYs

Index

Note: The italicized *f* and *t* following page numbers refer to figures and tables, respectively.

About the Authors

Lauren J. Lieberman, PhD, is a distinguished service professor at the College at Brockport, State University of New York. She has taught higher education since 1995 and previously taught in the Deafblind Program at Perkins School for the Blind. She teaches undergraduate and graduate courses in adapted physical education. She is on the editorial board of the *Journal of Physical Education, Recreation and Dance (JOPERD)*.

Lieberman has written 20 books on adapted physical education and more than 118 peer-reviewed articles. She started Camp Abilities, an overnight educational sports camp for children with visual impairments. This camp is now replicated in 18 states and eight countries.

Lieberman is past chair of the Adapted Physical Activity Council (APAC). She is currently on the board of the division of recreation and sport for the Association for the Education and Rehabilitation of the Blind and Visually Impaired (AER), and she serves on the board of the United States Association of Blind Athletes (USABA). She acts as a consultant for the American Printing House for the Blind and the New York Deaf-Blind Collaborative. In her leisure time, she enjoys playing Ultimate Frisbee, biking, running, kayaking, hiking, and playing the guitar.

Cathy Houston-Wilson, PhD, is a professor at the College at Brockport, State University of New York. She also serves as chairperson for the department of kinesiology, sport studies, and physical education. Cathy has taught in higher education since 1993, teaching classes in adapted physical education and pedagogy. She is a frequent presenter on adapted physical education (APE) at conferences and workshops and provides in-service training on APE to school districts across New York State. Houston-Wilson has taught APE in a residential facility as well as in public schools. She is past president of the adapted physical education section of New York State AHPERD, and she is past president and a current board member of Phi Epsilon Kappa. In addition, she is actively involved in a variety of community-based activities, including Lifetime Assistance, an agency dedicated to serving individuals with developmental disabilities; SportsNet, an agency dedicated to providing sport opportunities for individuals with disabilities; Brockport Community Rowing Club, a club of which she is president and a founding member; and Camp Koinonia, a faith-based camp for families. In her leisure time, she enjoys accompanying her youngest daughter to Irish dance competitions, practicing yoga, and coaching a highly competitive girls soccer team.

You'll find other outstanding
physical education resources at

www.HumanKinetics.com

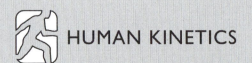
HUMAN KINETICS

In the U.S. call	1.800.747.4457
Canada	1.800.465.7301
Europe	+44 (0) 113 255 5665
International	1.217.351.5076